The last subject in the world I would expect to find interesting is economics—money—but I found Michael Schut's book written with such wit and clarity and insight that it both enriched my understanding and delighted my spirit. I hope it has the success it deserves.

—Frederick Buechner, author of *Secrets in the Dark: A Life in Sermons* and *The Yellow Leaves: A Miscellany*

Jesus said, "You cannot love both God and money." But you can't do entirely without money. It's how you use it and for what purposes that matters. Michael Schut has given deep thought to using money wisely in pursuit of a truly Christian life. *Money and Faith: The Search for Enough* combines his own thinking with wonderful essays from writers as different as humorist Dave Barry and theologian Walter Brueggemann. The quality of the prose is uniformly excellent and the book points away from the idolatry of materialism toward lives of love and service. This book deserves a place in every church discussion series and a wide reading by all Americans.

—John de Graaf, co-author, *Affluenza: The All-Consuming Epidemic* and editor of *Take Back Your Time*

The essays in this book are incredible, but what is really exciting is the study circle guide, for it is the small group that brings about social change. Yes, this kind of deliberation is essential for a democracy, but even more than that, it is in the small group that you learn to care for the Other. It is in the small group, where you have intimate, authentic conversations and connect with others, that you experience caring and being cared for. It is *caring* that leads us to commit to the common good, so without caring we're lost.

—Cecile Andrews, author of *Slow is Beautiful* and *The Circle of Simplicity*

We are a 'moneyed' people. Money is how we relate to most everyone and everything. Yet over and over again our getting, having, and spending is in the pursuit of small things, not great things. Or, rather, the small things are mistaken for the great things. Moreover, few treatments of money ever get beyond the small things. Few treatments give both money and meaning, money and faith, money and the great things, their due. Michael Schut's text does and we are in his debt. It's a good debt to carry.

—Larry Rasmussen, Reinhold Niebuhr Professor Emeritus of Social Ethics, Union Theological Seminary, New York City; author of *Earth Community, Earth Ethics*

Money & Faith

The Search for Enough

Introduction by Michael Schut

with Jean-Bertrand Aristide
Peter Barnes
Dave Barry
Leonardo Boff
David Boyle
Lester Brown
Walter Brueggemann
William Greider
Maria Harris
Lewis Hyde
Rich Lang
Andy Loving
Sallie McFague
Bill McKibben
Wayne Muller
Ched Myers
Ted Nace
K. Killian Noe
Henri Nouwen
Sarah Tarver-Wahlquist
Lynne Twist
Susan Wilkes and Jim Klobuchar

Study Guide by Michael Schut

edited and compiled by Michael Schut

Dedicated to my parents
Wayne and Joyce Schut
All who know them, know their authenticity, their compassion,
their love and their desire to live out their faith.
With gratitude and love.

In memory of my grandparents
Henry and Wilma Van Roekel
Henry and Hazel Schut

Morehouse Education Resources,
   a division of Church Publishing Incorporated
Editorial Offices: 600 Grant Street, Suite 400
Denver, CO 80203
www.morehouseeducation.com

Cover Design: Linda Brooks
Graphic Designer: Sue MacStravic

Printed in the United States of America.

The scripture quotations used within are from *The Holy Bible, New International Version.* © 1973, 1978, 1984 by International Bible Society. Used by permission of Zondervan Bible Publishers.

ISBN 978-0-8192-2327-2

$\mathcal{G}$ratitudes

Any book, even those written by only one person, is the culmination of the efforts and wisdom of many people. This is even more the case, then, for an anthology such as this, combining the wisdom of the included authors with the input and wisdom from many members of my community. This book is all the richer and fuller for it, and I am grateful.

The Valparaiso Institute's "Practicing Our Faith" grants program provided the initial funding for this project. Thank you to Dorothy Bass, Susan Briehl, Doretta Kurzinski, and especially Program Director Don Richter, for believing in me and this project, for your support, ideas, availability and patience.

My dear friends Fred Wardenburg and Francie Rutherford and the Loyal Bigelow and Jedediah Dewey Foundation offered generous financial support as well. When Fred first heard me describe the book, he said "That needs to be done and we want to help make it possible." While this book was in process, Fred passed away. I miss him; I hope he would be pleased at having supported this project. Thank you, Fred.

My publisher Living the Good News, part of Church Publishing Inc., has always been good to work with. I am blessed that they recognized the possibilities in my first two edited anthologies and study guides, and that their interest has continued. Special thanks to Liz Riggleman, James Creasey, designer Sue MacStravic, project manager Dirk deVries and editor Kathy Coffey.

New Creation Community, my faith community, sees supporting the gifts and calls of its members as one of its missions in the world. So the church both offered financial support and served as my fiscal sponsor. Thank you for your steadfastness and kindness: especially to Bart Preecs and David Coffey.

To the feisty and thoughtful group of people who came together to go through *Money and Faith's* study guide: I couldn't get you on the cover, but you all helped me a great deal. Naomi Checkowitz, Kathy Keefe, Rich Lang, Brad Liljequist, LeAnne Moss, Bart Preecs, David Shull and Martha Tanner. Thank you for spending ten Monday evenings together!

I am especially indebted to LeAnne Moss who believed in me and this project from its inception and supported me throughout.

As I pause and reflect now, I am perhaps most touched by the goodness and generosity of the community of friends and family that stood by me emotionally and financially during this book's launch, gestation and completion. You warm my heart. With many, many thanks:

Geoff and Naoko Barnes, Tanya and Aaron Barnett, LeeAnne and Ken Beres, Sally Bingham, Wendy Blight and Tara Barber, Eric and Melissa Carlberg, Paul Chiocco and Doug McCrary, John Cockayne, Lesli Corthell, Jeanine Diller and Larry Murphy, Pete Dorman and Cassandra Newell, David and Amy Fujimoto, Darel Grothaus, Maureen Horgan and Albert Foster, Peter Ilgenfritz and David Shull, Katie Larkin, Gerhard and Eunice Letzing, Brian Lloyd, Brad Liljequist,

Arlys and Fred McLaughlin, Chris and Tiffany Megargee, John and Cherie Miles, LeAnne Moss, Marlene and Leo Muller, Jim and Ruth Mulligan, Randall Mullins and Sharon Pavelda, Killian and Bernie Noe, Wendell and Betty Obetz, David and Molly Perry, Bart Preecs and Jane Long, Carla and Eric Pryne, Kara-Lee Ruotolo, Paul, Lynn and Carter Schafer, Katrina Schut, Martha Schut, Wayne and Joyce Schut, Ed and Darlene Scott, Joel Sisolak, Judy Stampler, Theron Shaw, Martha Tanner, Ruby Takushi and Mark Chinen, Sean and Julie Walsh, Faith Wilder.

Of those, a number deserve special recognition. LeAnne Moss, Brad Liljequist, Lesli Corthell and Marlene Muller organized and hosted a house party to raise funds. Cynthia Moe-Lobeda, an author and scholar in the eco-justice field, spoke at that house party.

Cecile Andrews, John de Graaf, Joe Hastings, Rozie Hughes, Rich Lang, Cynthia Moe-Lobeda, Ched Myers, all leaders in their own fields, offered feedback on the book. Jack Jezreel and his staff at JustFaith Ministries generously reviewed and commented on the book's direction, as did Mike Little and Jan Sullivan from Ministry of Money. And Paul Schafer helped me with research.

I was especially fortunate to spend a two-week writing retreat at Mesa Refuge. Located next to Point Reyes National Seashore in California, Mesa Refuge supports writers working at the nexus of ecology and economics. Thank you to all who make that program possible. While there, I met with both Jonathan Rowe and Peter Barnes who generously offered their suggestions on *Money and Faith*.

I also organized my own writing retreat at the exquisite cabin of my dear friends, Jim and Ruth Mulligan. Thank you.

As I began work on *Money and Faith* I had the opportunity to participate in a three week course titled "The Future of Money" at Schumacher College in England. A wonderful community developed there; I learned a great deal from them and my teachers Bernard Lietaer, Lynne Twist, Ann Pettifor and David Boyle.

Prior to launching this book project, I worked for 11 years as a staff member at Earth Ministry (*www.earthministry.org*) in Seattle. While there I edited two books: *Simpler Living, Compassionate Life: A Christian Perspective* and *Food and Faith: Justice, Joy and Daily Bread*. I am grateful to the organization for the opportunity to work on those books, and trust that *Money and Faith* will also further their good work. Thank you to LeeAnne Beres and the staff for promoting this book.

Finally, I owe many thanks to John Hoerster, Scott Warner, and the law firm Garvey, Schubert and Barer. This book took shape in office space provided at no cost to me. Scott provided expert *pro bono* legal services.

Table of Contents

Study Guide by Michael Schut

 *Foreword*

by Bill McKibben

Occasionally I teach a course at Middlebury College, a place absolutely over-flowing with bright, inquisitive, earnest, ethical young people. No matter the sub-ject of the course, I usually ask them at some point in the semester to do a small exercise. In the course of the evening, they are to sit down with a piece of paper and figure out, as best they can, how much money they will need to lead the kind of life they want to live.

It's always an interesting exercise, for them and for me. The numbers vary widely, from about $30,000 a year on up. (Remember, these are kids at an elite col-lege, who could almost all step straight on to Wall Street if they so desired.) They don't think of everything (19-year-olds underestimate the role of insurance in their future finances) and they're often quite unsure. But they all seem glad to have done it.

It's an exercise I wish someone had given me at some point—actually, again and again. Because while we're carefully schooled in how to make money, we're left entirely untutored on equally important questions, most importantly: how much is enough? As a result, the default assumption of our entire society has become 'more is better.' You aim for a good—read, high-paying—job, then move up whatever lad-der you're on, adjust your lifestyle to whatever you can afford (and often, thanks to credit cards, a little more) and assume that that is natural and obvious.

But it isn't, of course. You could just as rationally pare expenses as increase income. You could just as rationally choose to value time over money. You could just as rationally heed the witness of the Gospels and their insistence that we must choose in the end. All these strategies, practical and moral, appear in the pages that follow. This book serves as a kind of Berlitz for a new language of money, one that considers it as a far more complicated, treacherous and interesting tongue than the pidgin version we've learned in a consumer society.

This book couldn't come at a better moment. In the last few years the econo-mists, long the priests of our consumptive religion, have begun to realize that they know less than they thought. For several generations, neo-classicists have held that we can tell what makes people happy by what they buy—"utility" is the term of art. Hence, more buying means more happiness for individuals. And more aggregate buying—higher GDP—means more happiness for societies, nations, civilizations.

That seems to be true up to a point—a not very high point, about $10,000 per year, the figure where a person's basic needs can be secured. Most of the world sits below that line, of course, and hence needs more. But most of us sit well above it, and the evidence is that at the upper reaches more adds little if anything to our satisfaction. Indeed, just the opposite, it tends to insulate us from the natural world (in our giant suburban houses) and from each other. If you have a credit card, you're likely to have no practical need of your neighbors, a new experience for a primate.

But the witness of all religious traditions, back through the Buddha at least, and most certainly including the Christ, is that we're most fully alive not when we're at the center of our own little universe, but when we're engaged with others, serving others. When our insulation is stripped away, we're in contact with the world around us.

I've always been haunted by the story of the rich young ruler, told by Jesus to give away all that he had and come follow him. The young man couldn't—the hold of his possessions was too strong. But he "went away sorrowful." This book is about how to go away joyful—to meet the challenge posed by wealth to our faith and humanity, and to meet it with good cheer and good grace. It's hard to think of a more necessary volume.

Introduction

The great obstacle is simply this: the conviction that
we cannot change because we are dependent upon
what is wrong. But that is the addict's excuse, and
we know that it will not do.

—*Wendell Berry*

We must confess that the central problem of our
lives is that we are torn apart by the conflict
between our attraction to the good news of
God's abundance and the power of our belief
in scarcity.

—*Walter Brueggemann*

Welcome

by Michael Schut

Welcome to an exciting, challenging, freeing and community-building exploration of money and faith. This book invites you into a conversation between your
own life and perspectives, those of the authors included in this anthology, and
those friends with whom you may gather to discuss the book's content.

Money and Faith is designed for individuals and for small groups. The study guide
(see page 227) is ideal for exploring this book with others. You have your own reasons for picking up this book. Here are a few of the reasons I felt motivated to bring
Money and Faith together in the first place.

Personal, Prophetic, Pastoral and Purposeful

I want this book to be all of these things—yet these goals sometimes felt at odds
with each other. But we need them all.

In our personal lives, and the ways in which we relate to money, feel about
money and dream about money, we need to experience the nurturing companion-
ship of a wise, compassionate pastor or spiritual guide.

In some of our society's more powerful assumptions—such as "more (money) is
better," "time is money" and "economic growth is an unquestioned societal good"—
we need to experience the power, strength, anger and call to repent (to turn
around) reminiscent of an Old Testament prophet.

Facing great inequities and ecological degradation, we need purposeful guidance
to lead to actions, decisions and policies that will help create a world with enough
for all.

Good pastors and priests are all these things. They are personal—they get to
know us and honor our journey. They are prophetic—not afraid to clearly speak the
truth. Even when that truth pierces our assumptions or fundamentally challenges
our lives, they invite us to see in a new way. And they are purposeful—helping us
answer, in light of our own stories and today's realities, "How shall we then live?"

As you journey through Money and Faith, I trust you will receive and learn from
the pastor, the prophet and the purposeful guide. These are its primary themes:

The Spirituality of Money

This book uses money as both a window and a mirror into life's sacred journey.
My hope is that we all find greater peace, trust and freedom in our own personal
relationship with money.

Abundance

In spite of experiences of scarcity in my own life, and ever-present images of scarcity, I do believe that God's intention is a world where there is enough for all. Not only is that the intention, but also a real possibility. Our work, and the work of this book, is to help create a world where that possibility becomes reality.

A More Satisfying Way to Live

In spite of North America's economic wealth, we're not a happier people! In the wealthier countries, "more" no longer automatically means "better." This book explores that claim and points in more satisfying directions.

Giving Voice to the Voiceless

Even a cursory reading of the Gospels reveals Jesus as one who continually acted on behalf of the voiceless. Today that means writing, speaking and advocating on behalf of those our economic system refuses to hear: among them the over one billion people who live on less than $1 a day and the endangered animals, plants and ecosystems.

Earthly Economics

During my time working at Earth Ministry, as my colleagues and I sought to connect faith with care and justice for all God's creation, I continually met the perception that living more lightly on Earth would be nice and all, but our fundamental priority must be to "grow the economy."

The structure of our economy often clashes with creation's well-being. So, we need to explore and create ways to alter economics to support Earth's flourishing. We need to explore how our society's relationship with and pursuit of money affect the health of our communities and the well-being of our Earth-home.

Fundamentally, the economy ought to serve the well-being of communities, rather than communities serving the well-being of the economy.

The Jubilee and Inequity

Over half of the world's people survive on less than $2 per day. Debt-service payments from Third World countries—over $375 billion per year in 2004—are "more than all Third World spending on health and education and 20 times what developing countries receive annually in foreign aid."[1] The Biblical Jubilee addresses such inequity.

What Can We Do?

I like to think of this book as a journey. Part of that journey includes exploring ways we can respond to the themes highlighted above, and discovering practical ways that individuals, governments and corporations are using money creatively to rebuild communities, create authentic wealth and protect creation.

---

1. John Perkins, *Confessions of an Economic Hitman* (San Francisco: Berrett-Koehler Publishers), xviii.

Overview

by Michael Schut

Money and Faith: The Search for Enough is both an anthology of essays and a community-building study guide, similar in format to my two previous books *Simpler Living, Compassionate Life* and *Food and Faith*.

Money and Faith begins with an invitation to explore experiences of scarcity and abundance and an opportunity to view our lives through the window of our own relationship with money. Section Two, "Demystifying Money" somewhat playfully explores money itself—what it is, how it's created. "What Is Compassion's Call?" (Section Three) begins with that question and reflects on redistributive justice.

The first three sections focus on the personal: how do you see the world? what role does money play in your life? how does your faith inform all of this? In Sections Four through Seven the book's focus shifts from the personal to the prophetic, from our personal relationship with money to asking how faith calls us to relate to that money-making system we call the economy.

(Now, at the first mention of "economy" or "economics," some of us freeze as if caught in the headlights of an oncoming truck. So before you decide it's probably best to quietly lose this book under the couch and go do your laundry, this economic exploration will be done in an approachable way. We won't be getting into economic minutia. At its simplest, after all, economics concerns itself with who gets what and with how we manage and share the gifts of Earth.)

The title of Section Four—"Is More (Money/Growth) Better?"—describes the section's themes. Section Five, "Corporations Are People Too?" takes a refreshing look at a particularly powerful player in the money-generating system. The writers in Section Six, "Whose Voices Are Rarely Heard?" invite personal, theological and economic voices from the global South into the discussion. Finally, "What Is the Jubilee?" (Section Seven) introduces the biblical tradition of Jubilee.

Money and Faith next asks, "How shall we then live?" "Practicing Abundance" (Section Eight) considers Sabbath and tithing while Section Nine, "Moving toward Jubilee" explores investments and retirement, areas where many wonder, "what does enough mean?"

Because this book draws attention to significant concerns (sustainability and inequity, for example) Section Ten, "Moving toward Jubilee on a Grand Scale," draws attention to significant solutions to those concerns. *Money and Faith's* Epilogue seeks to reveal our interconnectedness and nurture a spirituality that allows us to rest in God's grace.

Inclusive language: Finally, wherever possible, *Money and Faith* uses inclusive language. Because many essays were written by others and first published elsewhere, doing so is not always possible. Grammatical styles will also vary.

by Michael Schut

Michael Schut is the editor/author of the award-winning *Simpler Living, Compassionate Life: A Christian Perspective.* He also edited *Food and Faith: Justice, Joy and Daily Bread.* Currently the Associate Program Officer: Economic and Environmental Affairs for the National Episcopal Church, he served for 11 years on Earth Ministry's (*www.earthministry.org*) staff. Michael has an M.S. in Environmental Studies from the University of Oregon and a B.S. in Biology from Wheaton College. Originally from Vermont and Minnesota, he now lives in Seattle, where he backpacks, hikes, climbs, bikes and hangs out with his nephew Carter.

Michael has spoken and taught around the country. Contact him via *www.michaelschut.org*

An Opening Story: Spring Lake Ranch

A gravel road south of Rutland, Vermont, meets Route 103. Turn west and ascend steeply at first, then gradually, through sugar maple hardwood forests, by stone-fenced pastures, a few scattered cattle and a weathered barn. About a mile up the hill, the forest canopy opens and you're there: Spring Lake Ranch.

The rust-red Main House with the dining hall, living room, game room and bedrooms upstairs for residents. The treasured maple sugaring house. Expansive gardens. Resident and staff housing. The lawn, featuring a volleyball net and outdoor pig and black bear roasting spit. Just a little further up the road stands the house where I lived for my first eight years. Beyond that lies the repair shop, the wood shop, the volleyball gym my dad helped build. Continue on past the cow pasture and a small A-frame roughhewn chapel overlooking generous meadows. The road ends about one mile later at the cold, clear, spring-fed Spring Lake.

Since 1932 Spring Lake Ranch's mission has been to serve the seriously mentally ill, based on the belief that healing best takes place in a setting that is supportive and respectful and does not treat people with mental illness as "patients" or "cases."

The Ranch offered counseling and drug therapy but it also understood the therapeutic value of fresh air and physical labor. My father served on staff there for ten years. Among other things, he led work crews: gardening, cider-pressing, wood-cutting, maple sugaring, shoveling snow, ice-cutting, haying.

This was not make-work. The community burned the wood over the cold winters, ate the garden produce, drank the cider, and sold the maple syrup at the Route 103 roadside stand. The ice, cut from Spring Lake with a large cross-saw, later cooled our summer drinks. In their lives outside the Ranch, I imagine many residents struggled with self-worth. Their undeniable limitations, combined with social stigmas and an inability to survive in a competitive economy, often leave the mentally ill with little sense of belonging or inherent worth. But at the Ranch, their strength, labor and contributions were integral to the community's well-being.

For a kid, the Ranch was an idyllic place to grow up. The Wells family and their kids lived right next door. We played outside in every season. We learned to swim in Spring Lake. We walked the mile down the ranch hill to Route 103 to catch the school bus. I helped a bit in the gardens. I collected sap from the tapped maple trees. And when the sap was boiled down to its delicious concentrate, I would fill a battered tin cup and drink the maple syrup straight out of a vat in the sugaring house!

Looking back on my eight years in Vermont, I realize that one of the Ranch's biggest blessings for me was simply growing up among those living with mental illness. The best thing about that is the absence of a memory: I do not remember internally segregating the well from the less-well. And though I may have done so had I lived there longer, my parents and the Spring Lake community did not teach the prejudices our society so often holds against the mentally ill. The Ranch community was surely my first experience of being in relationship with someone ostensibly "other." But the "other" was not ignored, ostracized or abused, but seen, accepted and valued.

Leaving the Ranch

My parents were both raised on farms in the Midwest: Dad in Minnesota, Mom in Iowa. Once a year my parents packed my two sisters and me into our Ford Torino station wagon to visit the extended family. Shortly after my eighth birthday, we moved back, settling in Minnesota.

Working at Spring Lake Ranch was far from lucrative, but what it lacked in monetary rewards it made up for in abundant community wealth and sublime natural beauty. Need a babysitter? See if the Wells family next door can watch the kids for a bit. Tired of cooking? Walk down to the main house and enjoy a meal with the Ranch staff and residents. Need a break? Open the door and walk in the woods or swim in the lake. Need some exercise? Join the morning volleyball game. Need a reminder of the struggles many face? Work with or visit your neighbors, many of whom wrestle mightily with mental illness.

So, even though my family made little money, I do not remember worrying about it. Now, maybe most eight-year-olds don't fret over money. But it does seem significant to me that, not too long after leaving Vermont for Minnesota, I first recall worrying that we might not have quite enough.

When my parents did decide to move, they sought to start a community in southeastern Minnesota modeled after Spring Lake Ranch. Not wanting mentally ill people as neighbors, a group of the county's farmers organized against the project.

The county denied the necessary licenses and the project fell through.

When we left Vermont not only did we do so without financial reserves, but we left a community that offered all of us an extraordinary abundance. It's not hard to see why, in losing that community and in the "Minnesota Spring Lake" project falling through, my family and I began to feel a sense of scarcity and worry.

A Pop and Some Levis

My first specific memory about money is one of my mom and me shopping at Apache Mall (in Rochester, Minnesota, where we settled). I am ten and school is about to begin. I need a new pair of Levis. But I do not ask for them. I feel bad about spending money; mom and dad are stressed about it. I don't want to stress them further. Magically, as best I can figure, mom knows I need some new pants, so we do buy a pair (brown, I think). But I am not comfortable with the whole transaction.

My second memory centers around Mountain Dew, which my good friend Kayne loves. So what does he do? He buys some for himself. Spends a whole quarter, maybe even 35 cents! Any change in my pocket stayed right there. I had already decided to not spend money on myself. There wasn't enough. I had to save. I was awfully disciplined.

The Faith Component

Mixed up in all these experiences was my faith. I read that I could not serve both God and mammon. I sensed Jesus addressed money more than any other issue, and I interpreted a majority of his teachings as coming down pretty hard on wealth and the wealthy. Somewhere along the way I decided that if I wanted to follow God's will for my life, I certainly would not make much money...and wondered if it would even be acceptable to do so.

I knew rationally that in comparison with most anyone on the planet I enjoyed great material abundance. I knew I already had more than my fair share of "stuff." And I felt inspired to work toward a more equitable distribution of the world's wealth. Yet I more often than not felt this internally palpable scarcity. I obviously lived with dissonance and discomfort, compounded by my tendency to judge my feelings of scarcity, thinking it must be possible to "seek first God's kingdom" and trust that, just like the lilies and the sparrows, my needs would be met. It must be possible, but I was not good at doing so.

It's safe to say my relationship with money was not peaceful. Eventually I decided to try to ignore the whole topic. Of course trying to ignore the importance of money in our society is a bit like a fish downplaying the importance of water.

The Telling of Stories

I believe that in telling and listening to our stories, we discover signs of God's passing and presence—faint tracks, haunting harmonies, flickering images, unspeakable longings. Author Frederick Buechner (pronounced Beekner) contends that each of our journeys through this life is sacred. In his autobiographical work, *The*

Sacred Journey, he proposes to listen to his "life as a whole...for whatever of mean-ing, of holiness, of God, there may be in it to hear."[1] He likens the telling of his story to opening a scrapbook where we, the readers, flip through the pages and scan the images for signs of our own sacred journey. Through the telling of his story, Buechner hopes that all of us might be inspired to open the scrapbooks of our own lives.

It seems that when we open to those pages connected with our experiences of abundance or scarcity, we often end up telling stories pregnant with some of our most poignant sorrows or deepest joys. They are experiences of what the Celts call "thin places," where the barrier between our everyday perceptions of the world and the holiness of life become membrane-thin.

When we begin to plumb, poke, or peek into our relationship with money, that exploration often leads to thin places: to questions of trust, security, values, and to experiences of abundance and joy, as well as scarcity and fear. When we get in touch with those sorts of experiences we need not travel far to discover moments of holiness, moments that deeply inform our sense of who God is and whether or not we feel we will be provided for in this life.

Abundance and Scarcity

So this is a book about money. Most fundamentally, though, this is a book about how we experience the world and our lives within it. That is, aside from how much money or stuff we each have, do we experience our relationship with it as enough, as an abundance, as scarce, as fraught with worry?

On a larger scale, in light of the reality that over three billion of us live on less than $2 per day, climate change is under way, and species are going extinct at a rate not seen since the disappearance of the dinosaurs, do we believe it's possible to create a world where all creation has enough and we experience the world as a place of abundance? This question connects to money, but does so on a global scale, and shifts our gaze from the personal to the societal. It deals with how we divide up the abundance. So this is also a book about economics and equity.

I have slight misgivings about the word "abundance." Some misuse the word to support a lifestyle of excess with an apparent lack of concern for the consequences of such excess. Or, some associate material abundance as a sign of God's favor—and the lack thereof as proof of God's disfavor. Words like "sufficiency" or "enough" come to mind as possible alternatives.

But the word "abundance" connotes a kind of joy, an overflowing, which I believe is central to God's desire for all of us. Jesus himself said, "I came so that they might have life and have it more abundantly" (John 10:10b, *New American Bible*). Any contact with even relatively intact places on God's Earth confirms God's abundant creativity and desire for life to thrive.

In no way do I mean to downplay the fact that most of us are familiar with feel-ings and experiences characterized by scarcity, when we do not feel a sense of suffi-ciency or "enoughness," much less abundance. These feelings occur in relationship to money, of course, but also in relationship to time, support, friendship and love. But the world God intends is a world where there is enough for all, enough for each soul's well-being, enough for all to eat and drink, enough for all God's creatures to have a home. This is God's vision of God's kin-dom and what we are called to make real in the world. I believe that world is possible.

God's Economy

For that world to become a reality we need an economy to help us get there. The one most of the world follows today is simply not doing the job. Later chapters in this book address why that is so. But for now it's important to note that it is possible to at least imagine an economy that would help create a world where there is enough for all. Imagining is the first step toward realization.

To even attempt to imagine, though, we first need to not immediately plug our ears, turn, and run the other direction when we see the word *economy* or *economics*. After all, at its most essential, economics is not primarily esoteric language and mathematical modeling, but concerns itself with who gets what.

Read almost any Christian theological reflection on economics and you come across the Greek word *oikos*, translated "household." Economics, in Greek *oikonomia*, is the management of the household. Theologians stress that the heart of a Christian economic paradigm is "to imagine the whole Earth as God's household."[2] Good economic practice, then, commits itself to the well-being of God's entire household, all of God's creation. Douglas Meeks, in his book *God the Economist*, summarizes characteristics of God's economy:

> *God's interest is transforming the world into a household in which all of God's creatures can find abundant life* [italics added]....God's economy is meant for this world. Therefore it entails a conflict with all those who would build households excluding the poor and oppressed, the uneducated, those less than adequate at bargaining, and those without political power. God's economy also entails a conflict with those who would exclude nature from home as if it were mere stuff to be manipulated for our ends.[3]

So to claim God has an economy, as the phrase "God's economy" does, is not primarily to argue about its form—whether it is capitalist or socialist, say. But it *does* argue about its characteristics.

First, God's economy imagines and intends an *abundant* life. Second, God's economic household includes room for *all* creation, challenging any economic system that excludes concern and care for the entirety of life. Third, God's economy pays special attention to the poor and powerless, and argues with those whose households exclude them. Finally, God's economy is "meant for this world," is meant to be embodied here and now, challenging those who believe that abundance is a promise meant only for the sweet hereafter.

To return to the image of household, theologian Sallie McFague writes that in God's economy "housemates must abide by three main rules: take only your share, clean up after yourselves, and keep the house in good repair for future occupants."[4]

Depends on the Way That You See

Musician-poet Bruce Cockburn's song "Child of the Wind" goes like this:

> Little round planet/In a big universe
> Sometimes it looks blessed/Sometimes it looks cursed
> Depends on what you look at, obviously,
> But even more it depends on the way that you see.[5]

As I look back on my growing up, I know there were other ways of seeing. Many experiences spoke of abundance. I did get those Levis, I studied trombone and piano and took tennis lessons. Mom and Dad raised a ton of vegetables. We enjoyed camping trips to national parks across the country and had a great community of friends.

As Cockburn says, whether the world looks blessed or cursed (or seems abundant or scarce) "depends on the way that you see." No matter how each of us sees, however, our culture trains us, every day, to look through scarcity's prism. The incessant drive to consume is itself dependent upon seeing through scarcity's lens: you are not rich, sexy, good-looking, thin, young, competent...enough; but buy this or don this image, and you will be. Beyond the personal, many political debates turn into bickering about the most efficient way of allocating "scarce" resources.

However, the biblical vision stands firmly in the belief that another world is possible as articulated in the following passage by Mary Jo Leddy:

> The personal or political decision to declare that *there is not enough* is the beginning of social cruelty, war and violence on a petty or vast scale. On the other hand, the choice to affirm that *there is enough* for all is the beginning of social community, peace and justice. The option to assume that there is enough frees the imagination to think of new political and economic possibilities.[6]

That assumption, there is enough for all, undergirds this book. May our imaginations be freed to create new possibilities.

1. Frederick Buechner, *The Sacred Journey* (New York: HarperCollins, 1982), 6.

2. Sallie McFague, *Life Abundant: Rethinking Theology and Economy for a Planet in Peril* (Minneapolis, Minnesota: Fortress Press, 2001), 36.

3. Douglas Meeks, *God the Economist: The Doctrine of God and Political Economy* (Minneapolis, Minnesota: Augsburg Fortress Press, 1989), 24.

4. McFague, *Life Abundant*, 122.

5. Bruce Cockburn, *Nothing but a Burning Light* (New York: Sony Music Entertainment, 1991).

6. Mary Jo Leddy, *Radical Gratitude* (Maryknoll, New York: Orbis Books, 2002), 57.

Abundance and Scarcity
—How Do *You* See?

All of creation is a symphony of joy and jubilation.

—*Hildegaard of Bingen (12th Century)*

God's interest is transforming the world into a household in which all of God's creatures can find abundant life.

—*Douglas Meeks*

Introduction—I

I am a gardener. The most important task I have as a gardener is to build healthy soil. Healthy soil is full of life, retains water, holds nutrients, helps minimize pests and plant disease and is the foundation for a delicious harvest. Unhealthy soil is bereft of life, sloughs off water and nutrients and does much less to protect plants from pests and disease.

Abundance and scarcity are two markedly different soils, producing very different harvests.

To paraphrase Mary Jo Leddy, living out of a framework of scarcity—there is not enough—nurtures seeds of fear, war, hoarding and injustice. Living out of a framework of abundance—there is enough—nurtures seeds of generosity, trust, peace and community.

My essay "Enough for All" serves as a kind of extended introduction to the next three pieces. The first is an exercise more than an essay: writing your money autobiography. Brueggemann and Twist then reflect on the themes of scarcity and abundance, themes which are foundational to our experience of life in general, and our experience of money specifically.

Writing Your Money Autobiography

by Michael Schut and Ministry of Money

In this book's introduction (see page 15), I suggested that each of our lives is a sacred journey. We can look through any number of windows to guide or frame the process of reflecting on that journey. We could take our relationship with our parents through which we would learn not only about that specific relationship, but about ourselves and our views on life. Or we could reflect on life through the lens of a significant event, time period or belief system.

Writing a "money autobiography" often provides a revealing window through which we can access a great deal of insight into who we are and what we value.

Whether you are reading through this book on your own or as part of a study/support group, I strongly encourage you to give yourself the time to prepare your money autobiography. As described below, the idea is to write a three-page (or longer if you wish) autobiography dealing with the subject of your life as it relates to money. Doing so will undoubtedly enrich and deepen your engagement with the authors and ideas presented throughout this anthology. A money autobiography can invite light and a gentle breeze into the web of insecurity, passion, fear, pride, joy, and hope all tangled up in our relationship with money. Writing such a piece often provides greater understanding, healing and freedom in that relationship.

Below please find guidelines for writing. Try not to be concerned about whether you feel your words are eloquent or well organized. You don't need to be a "good writer," just be honest and open in relating how your relationship with money came to be, and how it continues to change and manifest in your life. Obviously, the reflection questions are a guide; work with those most meaningful to you. Some of you may find it helpful to integrate other creative avenues, such as poetry or drawing/painting in the process of writing and creating your money autobiography.

Guidelines for Writing Your Money Autobiography

Writing a money autobiography is a challenging and crucial step in understanding our behavior and the powerful feelings evoked by money. Even for those of us who find it difficult to write, reflection on money and our life's journey yields insights and deepened awareness.

Conversion is hearing and knowing God's love and call in our lives, becoming conscious of what has been previously unheard or unaccepted. Jesus repeatedly spoke about money and challenged the disciples, the scribes, and the crowds to become conscious of money and their relationship to it. We, too, need to examine our thoughts, feelings and behaviors which relate to money. As we discern the ways we earn, inherit, invest, spend, give or waste money, often without conscious choice or a deliberate faith stance, we will be enabled to respond more fully to God.

A money autobiography can be useful not only in personal growth, but also in the growth of the church. Whatever blocks our response to God as individuals also cripples the Body of Christ, the church. The Spirit cannot set us free to be communities of liberation if we are in bondage to an ancient idol. As we grieve over our entanglement with materialism, status and power and as we open ourselves to compassion, new vision and hope will flow through the church to the world.

We encourage you to set aside some quiet time, take up your pen, and discover for yourself the gifts of healing, insight and freedom which often come when we acknowledge feelings, attitudes and experiences evoked by money.

How to Prepare a Money Autobiography

Elizabeth O'Connor, in *Letters to Scattered Pilgrims* (Harper & Row), has given guidelines for writing a money autobiography. It is important to focus on feelings and relationships as well as reflecting on factual accounts. *Use some or all of the following questions as appropriate and helpful.* Write a three-page autobiography which deals only with the subject of your life as it is related to money.

Include the role of money in your childhood. What is your happiest memory in connection with money? What is your unhappiest memory? What attitude did your mother and/or father have about money? What was your attitude toward money as a child? Did you feel poor or rich? Did you worry about money?

What was your attitude about money as a teenager? What are your memories of this period?

How do you feel about your present financial status? What is your present financial status? What is your income? What are your other assets? What will your income be at age 65, 75, 80? Will you inherit money? Do you think about that?

Are you generous or stingy with your money? Do you spend money on yourself? If so, do you do it easily?

Do you gamble with your money? Do you worry about money?

When you eat with friends and there is a group check, are you the one to pick it up? Do you make sure that you pay your share and that it includes tax and tip?

Do you tend to be more on the giving end of things, or on the receiving end?

If you lacked money, how would you feel about others helping you pay your rent, or treating when you went out and were not in a position to reciprocate?

Do you tithe? If so, how do you really feel about it? Do you tithe because this is how you want your money used, or do you tithe because you want to belong and are willing to pay this cost of belonging?

Have you made a will? If not, why not? Did you include anyone in your will besides your family? The biblical faith says that we have a common life together—a common wealth. How do you feel about a private will?

Additional Questions to Consider

How do you deal with the fact that two-thirds of the world's people are poor? If you have personal relationships with people who are poor and/or work for social justice, how has that affected your attitude toward money?

In what ways is your relationship to money a training ground for your spiritual journey, or an expression of your deepest values?

Used by permission of Ministry of Money, an organization (*www.ministryofmoney.org*) providing "opportunities for women and men to explore their relationship to money from a faith perspective."

The Liturgy of Abundance, the Myth of Scarcity

by Walter Brueggemann

Dr. Walter Brueggemann is the William Marcellus McPheeters Professor of Old Testament at Columbia Theological Seminary in Decatur, Georgia. Particularly known for his studies and writings on Old Testament theology, he is ordained in the United Church of Christ and has published more than 58 books and hundreds of articles. His titles include *The Prophetic Imagination*, *The Message of the Psalms*, *The Land* and *Hopeful Imagination*.

The majority of the world's resources pour into the United States. And as we Americans grow more and more wealthy, money is becoming a kind of narcotic for us. We hardly notice our own prosperity or the poverty of so many others. The great contradiction is that we have more and more money and less and less generosity—less and less public money for the needy, less charity for the neighbor.

Robert Wuthnow, sociologist of religion at Princeton University, has studied stewardship in the church and discovered that preachers do a good job of promoting stewardship. They study it, think about it, explain it well. But folks don't get it. Though many of us are well-intentioned, we have invested our lives in consumerism. We have a love affair with "more"—and we will never have enough. Consumerism is not simply a marketing strategy. It has become a demonic spiritual force among us, and the theological question facing us is whether the gospel has the power to help us understand it.

The Bible starts out with a liturgy of abundance. Genesis 1 is a song of praise for God's generosity. It tells how well the world is ordered. It keeps saying, "It is good, it is good, it is good, it is very good." It declares that God blesses—that is, endows with vitality—the plants and the animals and the fish and the birds and humankind. And it pictures the creator as saying, "Be fruitful and multiply." In an orgy of fruitfulness, everything in its kind is to multiply the overflowing goodness that pours from God's creator spirit. And as you know, the creation ends in Sabbath. God is so overrun with fruitfulness that God says, "I've got to take a break from all this. I've got to get out of the office."

And Israel celebrates God's abundance. Psalm 104...surveys creation and names it all: the heavens and the earth, the waters and springs and streams and trees and birds and goats and wine and oil and bread and people and lions. This goes on for 23 verses....The psalm ends by picturing God as a great respirator. It says, "If you give your breath the world will live; if you ever stop breathing, the world will die." But the psalm makes clear that we don't need to worry. God is utterly, utterly reliable. The fruitfulness of the world is guaranteed.

Psalm 150 is an exuberant expression of amazement at God's goodness. It just says, "Praise Yahweh, praise Yahweh with lute, praise Yahweh with trumpet, praise, praise, praise." Together, these three scriptures proclaim that God's force of life is loose in the world. Genesis 1 affirms generosity and denies scarcity. Psalm 104 celebrates the buoyancy of creation and rejects anxiety. Psalm 150 enacts abandoning oneself to God and letting go of the need to have anything under control.

Later in Genesis God blesses Abraham, Sarah and their family. God tells them to be a blessing, to bless the people of all nations. Blessing is the force of well-being active in the world, and faith is the awareness that creation is the gift that keeps on giving. That awareness dominates Genesis until its 47th chapter. In that chapter Pharaoh gets organized to administer, control and monopolize the food supply. Pharaoh introduces the principle of scarcity into the world economy. For the first time in the Bible, someone says, "There's not enough. Let's get everything."

...Because Pharaoh is afraid that there aren't enough good things to go around, he must try to have them all. Because he is fearful, he is ruthless. Pharaoh hires Joseph to manage the monopoly. When the crops fail and the peasants run out of food, they come to Joseph. And on behalf of Pharaoh, Joseph says, "What's your collateral?" They give up their land for food, and then, the next year, they give up their cattle. By the third year of famine they have no collateral but themselves. And that's how the children of Israel become slaves—through an economic transaction.

The text shows that the power of the future is not in the hands of those who believe in scarcity and monopolize the world's resources; it is in the hands of those who trust God's abundance.

By the end of Genesis 47 Pharaoh has all the land except that belonging to the priests, which he never touches because he needs somebody to bless him. The notion of scarcity has been introduced into biblical faith. The Book of Exodus records the contest between the liturgy of generosity and the myth of scarcity—a contest that still tears us apart today.

The promises of the creation story continue to operate in the lives of the children of Israel. Even in captivity, the people multiply....

By the end of Exodus, Pharaoh has been as mean, brutal and ugly as he knows how to be—and as the myth of scarcity tends to be. Finally, he becomes so exasperated by his inability to control the people of Israel that he calls Moses and Aaron to come to him. Pharaoh tells them, "Take your people and leave. Take your flocks and herds and just get out of here!" And then the great king of Egypt, who presides over a monopoly of the region's resources, asks Moses and Aaron to bless him. The powers of scarcity admit to this little community of abundance, "It is clear that you are the wave of the future, lay your powerful hands upon us and give us energy." The text shows that the power of the future is not in the hands of those who believe in scarcity and monopolize the world's resources; it is in the hands of those who trust God's abundance.

When the children of Israel are in the wilderness, beyond the reach of Egypt, they still look back and think, "Should we really go? All the world's glory is in Egypt and with Pharaoh." But when they finally turn around and look into the wilderness, where there are no monopolies, they see the glory of Yahweh.

In answer to the people's fears and complaints, something extraordinary happens. God's love comes trickling down in the form of bread. They say, "Manhue?"—Hebrew for "What is it?"—and the word 'manna' is born. They had never before received bread as a free gift that they couldn't control, predict, plan for or own. The meaning of this strange narrative is that the gifts of life are indeed given by a generous God. It's a wonder, it's a miracle, it's an embarrassment, it's irrational, but God's abundance transcends the market economy.

Three things happened to this bread in Exodus 16. First, everybody had enough. But because Israel had learned to believe in scarcity in Egypt, people started to hoard the bread. When they tried to bank it, invest it, it turned sour and rotted, because you cannot store up God's generosity. Finally, Moses said, "You know what we ought to do? We ought to do what God did in Genesis 1. We ought to have a Sabbath." Sabbath means that there's enough bread, that we don't have to hustle every day of our lives. There's no record that Pharaoh ever took a day off. People who think their lives consist of struggling to get more and more can never slow down because they won't ever have enough.

When the people of Israel cross the Jordan River into the Promised Land the manna stops coming. Now they will have to grow their own food. Very soon Israel suffers defeat in battle and Joshua conducts an investigation to find out who or what undermined the war effort. He finally traces their defeat to a man called A'chan, who stole some of the spoils of battle and withheld them from the community. Possessing land, property and wealth makes people covetous, the Bible warns.

We who are now the richest nation are today's main coveters. We never feel that we have enough; we have to have more and more, and this insatiable desire destroys us. Whether we are liberal or conservative Christians, we must confess that the central problem of our lives is that we are torn apart by the conflict between our attraction to the good news of God's abundance and the power of our belief in scarcity—a belief that makes us greedy, mean and unneighborly. We spend our lives trying to sort out that ambiguity.

The conflict between the narratives of abundance and scarcity is the defining problem confronting us.... The gospel story of abundance asserts that we originated in the magnificent, inexplicable love of a God who loved the world into generous being. The baptismal service declares that each of us has been miraculously loved into existence by God. And the story of abundance says that our lives will end in God, and that this well-being cannot be taken from us. In the words of St. Paul, "neither life nor death nor angels nor principalities nor things"—nothing can separate us from God.

What we know about our beginnings and our endings, then, creates a different kind of present tense for us. We can live according to an ethic whereby we are not driven, controlled, anxious, frantic or greedy, precisely because we are sufficiently at home and at peace to care about others as we have been cared for.

But if you are like me, while you read the Bible you keep looking over at the screen to see how the market is doing. If you are like me, you read the Bible on a good day, but you watch Nike ads every day. And the Nike story says that our beginnings are in our achievements, and that we must create ourselves. My wife and I have some young friends who have a four-year-old son. Recently, the mother told us that she was about to make a crucial decision. She had to get her son into the right kindergarten because if she didn't, then he wouldn't get into the right prep school. And that would mean not being able to get into Davidson College. And, if he didn't go to school there, he wouldn't be connected to the bankers in Charlotte and be able to get the kind of job where he would make a lot of money. Our friends' story is a kind of parable of our notion that we must position ourselves because we must achieve, and build our own lives.

According to the Nike story, whoever has the most shoes when he dies wins. The Nike story says there are no gifts to be given because there's no giver. We end up only with whatever we manage to get for ourselves. This story ends in despair. It gives us a present tense of anxiety, fear, greed and brutality. It produces child and wife abuse, indifference to the poor, the buildup of armaments, divisions between people and environmental racism. It tells us not to care about anyone but ourselves—and it is the prevailing creed of American society.

Wouldn't it be wonderful if liberal and conservative church people…came to a common realization that the real issue confronting us is whether the news of God's abundance can be trusted in the face of the story of scarcity? What we know in the secret recesses of our hearts is that the story of scarcity is a tale of death. And the people of God counter this tale by witnessing to the manna. There is a more excellent bread than crass materialism. It is the bread of life and you don't have to bake it. We must decide where our trust is placed.

The great question now facing the church is whether our faith allows us to live in a new way. If we choose the story of death, we will lose the land—to excessive chemical fertilization, or by pumping out the water table for irrigation, perhaps. Or maybe we'll only lose it at night, as going out after dark becomes more and more dangerous.

Joshua 24 puts the choice before us. Joshua begins by reciting the story of God's generosity, and he concludes by saying, "I don't know about you, but I and my house will choose the Lord." This is not a church growth text. Joshua warns the people that this choice will bring them a bunch of trouble. If they want to be in on the story of abundance, they must put away their foreign gods—I would identify them as the gods of scarcity.

Jesus said it more succinctly. You cannot serve God and mammon. You cannot serve God and do what you please with your money or your sex or your land. And then he says, "Don't be anxious, because everything you need will be given to you." But you must decide. Christians have a long history of trying to squeeze Jesus out of public life and reduce him to a private little Savior. But to do this is to ignore what the Bible really says. Jesus talks a great deal about the kingdom of God—and what he means by that is a public life reorganized toward neighborliness.

As a little child, Jesus must often have heard his mother, Mary, singing. And as we know, she sang a revolutionary song, the Magnificat—the anthem of Luke's Gospel. She sang about neighborliness; about how God brings down the mighty from their thrones and lifts up the lowly; about how God fills the hungry with good things and sends the rich away empty. Mary did not make up this dangerous song. She took it from another mother, Hannah, who sang it much earlier to little Samuel, who became one of Israel's great revolutionaries. Hannah,

> **Wouldn't it be wonderful if liberal and conservative church people...came to a common realization that the real issue confronting us is whether the news of God's abundance can be trusted in the face of the story of scarcity?**

Mary and their little boys imagined a great social transformation. Jesus enacted his mother's song well. Everywhere he went he broke the vicious cycles of poverty, bondage, fear and death: he healed, transformed, empowered and brought new life. Jesus' example gives us the mandate to transform our public life.

Telling parables was one of Jesus' revolutionary activities, for parables are subversive re-imaginings of reality. The ideology devoted to encouraging consumption wants to shrivel our imagination so that we cannot conceive of living in any way that would be less profitable for the dominant corporate structure. But Jesus tells us that we can change the world. The Christian community performs a vital service by keeping the parables alive. These stories haunt us and push us in directions we never thought we would go.

Performing what the Bible calls "wonders and signs" was another way in which Jesus enacted his mother's song. These signs—or miracles—may seem odd to us, but in fact they are the typical gifts we receive when the world gets reorganized and placed under the sovereignty of God. Everywhere Jesus goes the world is rearranged: the blind receive their sight, the lame walk, the lepers are cleansed, the deaf hear, the dead are raised and the poor are freed from debt. The forgiveness of debts is listed last because it's the hardest thing to do—harder even than raising the dead to life. Jesus left ordinary people dazzled, amazed and grateful; he left powerful people angry and upset, because every time he performed a wonder, they lost a little of their clout. The wonders of the new age of the coming of God's kingdom may scandalize and upset us. They dazzle us, but they also make us nervous. The people of God need pastoral help in processing this ambivalent sense of both deeply yearning for God's new creation and deeply fearing it.

The feeding of the multitudes, recorded in Mark's Gospel, is an example of the new world coming into being through God. When the disciples, charged with feeding the hungry crowd, found a child with five loaves and two fishes, Jesus *took, blessed, broke* and *gave* the bread. These are the four decisive verbs of our sacramental existence. Jesus conducted a Eucharist, a gratitude. He demonstrated that the world is filled with abundance and freighted with generosity. If the bread is broken and shared, there is enough for all. Jesus is engaged in the sacramental, subversive reordering of public reality.

The profane is the opposite of the sacramental. "Profane" means flat, empty, one-dimensional, exhausted. The market ideology wants us to believe that the world is profane—life consists of buying and selling, weighing, measuring and trading, and then finally sinking into death and nothingness. But Jesus presents an entirely different kind of economy, one infused with the mystery of abundance and a cruciform kind of generosity. Five thousand are fed and twelve baskets of food are left.... Jesus transforms the economy by blessing it and breaking it beyond self-interest. From broken Friday bread comes Sunday abundance. In this and in the following account of a miraculous feeding in Mark, people do not grasp, hoard, resent or act selfishly; they watch as the juices of heaven multiply the bread of earth....

When people forget that Jesus is the bread of the world, they start eating junk food—the food of the Pharaoh and of Herod, the bread of moralism and of power. Too often the church forgets the true bread and is tempted by the junk food. Our faith is not just about spiritual matters, it is about the transformation of the world. The closer we stay to Jesus, the more we will bring a new economy of abundance to the world. The disciples often don't get what Jesus is about because they keep trying to fit him into the old patterns—and to do so is to make him innocuous, irrelevant and boring. But Paul gets it.

In 2 Corinthians 8, Paul directs a stewardship campaign for the early church and presents Jesus as the new economist. Though Jesus was rich, Paul says, "Yet for your sakes he became poor, that by his poverty you might become rich." We say it takes money to make money; Paul says it takes poverty to produce abundance. Jesus gave himself to enrich others, and we should do the same. Our abundance and the poverty of others need to be brought into a new balance. Paul ends his stewardship letter by quoting Exodus 16: "And the one who had much did not have too much, and the one who had little did not have too little." The citation is from the story of manna that transformed the wilderness into abundance.

It is, of course, easier to talk about these things than to live them. Many people both inside and outside of the church haven't a clue that Jesus is talking about the economy. We haven't taught them that he is. But we must begin to do so now, no matter how economically compromised we may feel. Our world absolutely requires this news. It has nothing to do with being Republicans or Democrats, liberals or conservatives, socialists or capitalists. It is much more elemental: the creation is infused with the Creator's generosity, and we can find practices, procedures and institutions that allow that generosity to work. Like the rich young ruler in Mark

10, we all have many possessions. Sharing our abundance may, as Jesus says, be impossible for mortals, but nothing is impossible for God. None of us knows what risks God's spirit may empower us to take. Our faith, ministry and hope…are that the Creator will empower us to trust his generosity, so that bread may abound.

Scarcity: The Great Lie
by Lynne Twist

Lynne Twist is a fund-raiser, activist, author and teacher, as well as founder of the Soul of Money Institute and The Pachamama Alliance. One of the founding executives of The Hunger Project, she has devoted her life to service in support of sustainability, human rights and spiritual authenticity.

Lynne Twist has worked and interacted with both the resource-rich and the very resource-poor. But no matter their background or life circumstances, she finds that almost all share a mind-set of scarcity. In this essay, Lynne writes about the three myths under-girding "the great lie" of scarcity: There's Not Enough; More is Better; and That's Just the Way It Is. Imagine the freedom and possibility, whether in your own life or within our economic system, if we operated more and more frequently out of a mindset of sufficiency for all, rather than one of scarcity.

∞

There is a natural law of abundance which pervades the entire universe, but it will not flow through a doorway of belief in lack and limitation.

—Paul Zaiter

I have been engaged for all these years in the lives and circumstances of people, many of whom live in crushing conditions where the lack of food, water, shelter, freedom, or opportunity drives every move and every conversation. Others, by every measure, have bounty way beyond their needs—more money, more food, more cars, more clothes, more education, more services, more freedom, more opportunity, more of everything. Yet, surprisingly, in that world of over abundance, too, the conversation is dominated by what they don't have and what they want to get. No matter who we are or what our circumstances, we swim in conversations about what there isn't enough of.

I see it in myself. For me, and for many of us, our first waking thought of the day is "I didn't get enough sleep." The next one is "I don't have enough time." Whether true or not, that thought of *not enough* occurs to us automatically before we even think to question or examine it. We spend most of the hours and the days of our lives hearing, explaining, complaining, or worrying about what we don't have enough of. We don't have enough time. We don't have enough rest. We don't have enough exercise. We don't have enough work. We don't have enough profits. We don't have enough power. We don't have enough wilderness. We don't have enough weekends. Of course we don't have enough money—ever.

In the mindset of scarcity, our relationship with money is an expression of fear; a fear that drives us in an endless and unfulfilling chase for more...

We're not thin enough, we're not smart enough, we're not pretty enough or fit enough or educated or successful enough, or rich enough—ever. Before we even sit up in bed, before our feet touch the floor, we're already inadequate, already behind, already losing, already lacking something. And by the time we go to bed at night, our minds race with a litany of what we didn't get, or didn't get done, that day. We go to sleep burdened by those thoughts and wake up to that reverie of lack.

This mantra of *not enough* carries the day and becomes a kind of default setting for our thinking about everything, from the cash in our pocket to the people we love or the value of our own lives. What begins as a simple expression of the hurried life, or even the challenged life, grows into the great justification for an unfulfilled life. It becomes the reason we can't have what we want or be who we want to be. It becomes the reason we can't accomplish the goals we set for ourselves, the reason our dreams can't come true, or the reason other people disappoint us, the reason we compromise our integrity, give up on ourselves or write off others.

It's the same in the inner city or the suburbs, in New York or Topeka or Beverly Hills or Calcutta. Whether we live in resource-poor circumstances or resource-rich ones, even if we're loaded with more money or goods or everything you could possibly dream of wanting or needing, we live with scarcity as an underlying assumption. It is an unquestioned, sometimes even unspoken, defining condition of life. It is not even that we necessarily experience a lack of something, but that scarcity as a chronic sense of inadequacy about life becomes the very place from which we think and act and live in the world. It shapes our deepest sense of ourselves, and becomes the lens through which we experience life. Through that lens our expectations, our behavior, and their consequences become a self-fulfilling prophecy of inadequacy, lack and dissatisfaction.

This internal condition of scarcity, this mind-set of scarcity, lives at the very heart of our jealousies, our greed, our prejudice and our arguments with life, and it is deeply embedded in our relationship with money. In the mind-set of scarcity, our relationship with money is an expression of fear; a fear that drives us in an endless and unfulfilling chase for more, or into compromises that promise a way out of the chase or discomfort around money. In the chase or in the compromises we break from our wholeness and natural integrity. We abandon our soul and grow more and more distanced from our core values and highest commitments. We find ourselves trapped in a cycle of disconnection and dissatisfaction. We start to believe the profit-driven commercial and cultural messages that suggest money *can* buy happiness, and we begin to look outside of ourselves to be fulfilled. Intuitively, we know it isn't so, but the money culture shouts down the wiser inner voice, and we feel compelled to seek even the most transient relief and comforts that money can buy.

Some would suggest that scarcity is the true, natural and inevitable basis for our relationship with money and resources. There is, after all, only so much of everything. More than two hundred years ago, around the time of the American Revolution, the Scottish philosopher and economist Adam Smith suggested that "the natural effort of every individual to better his own condition" was more powerful than any obstacle in its way, and he went on to articulate the founding principles of a modern (for the time) "free market" economy in which "the invisible hand" of self-interest was accepted as the dominant and most natural guiding force.

But how natural and accurate was that premise? The world of that day—that is, the world of the white, European, traditionally educated theorist Adam Smith— was one in which most white people dismissed indigenous people and people of color as "primitive" and "savage," rather than valued them as resourceful and wise in ways "civilized" societies would only begin to appreciate generations later. The dominant white classes of that day accepted, and practiced, racial, religious and sex discrimination as a moral and economic assumption. In those days, self-interest and nationalism were not yet informed by an awareness of the global interconnectedness that today we recognize affects us, our wealth and our security profoundly, and necessarily expands the boundaries of self-interest to include the well-being of all people, everywhere. The fundamental economic principles and structures of that bygone era were based on flawed assumptions and wrong thinking—about nature, about human potential and about money itself.

Contemporary European author, Bernard Lietaer, former senior officer of the Belgian Central Bank and one of the chief architects of the Euro currency, in his book, *Of Human Wealth*, says that greed and fear of scarcity are programmed; they do not exist in nature, not even in human nature. They are built into the money system in which we swim, and we've been swimming in it so long that these shadows have become almost completely transparent to us. We have learned to consider them normal and legitimate behavior. He concludes that Adam Smith's system of economics could more accurately be described as the allocation of scarce resources through the process of individual greed. The whole process of Smith's "modern" economics actually has its roots in primitive fears of scarcity, greed, and the implementation tool—the process by which this became real—was money.

When we step out of the shadow of this distorted and outdated system and the mind-set it generates, what we discover is this: Scarcity is a lie. Independent of any actual amount of resources, it is an unexamined and false system of assumptions, opinions and beliefs from which we view the world as a place where we are in constant danger of having our needs unmet.

It would be logical to assume that people with excess wealth do not live with the fear of scarcity at the center of their lives, but I have seen that scarcity is as oppressive in those lives as it is for people who are living at the margins and barely making ends meet. It is so illogical that people who have tremendous excess would be thinking they don't have enough, that as I encountered this time and again, I began to question the source of their concerns. Nothing in their actual circumstances justified it. I began to wonder if this anxiety over having enough was based on a set of assumptions, rather than circumstances. The more I examined these ideas and the more I interacted with individuals in a broad range of circumstances and a broad range of cultures and ethics, the more I saw that the fundamental assumption of scarcity was all-pervasive. The myths and the language of scarcity were the dominant voice in nearly every culture, often overriding logic and evidence, and the mind-set of scarcity created distorted, even irrational, attitudes and behaviors, especially around money. What I have found is that no matter where we are in the political, economic, or financial resource spectrum, the myths and mind-set of scarcity create an underlying fear that we, and the people we love or care about, won't have enough of what's needed to have a satisfying, happy, productive, or even survivable life.

This mind-set of scarcity is not something we intentionally created or have any conscious intention to bring into our life. It was here before us and it will likely persist beyond us, perpetuated in the myths and language of our money culture. We do, however, have a choice about whether or not to buy into it and whether or not to let it rule our lives.

The Toxic Myths of Scarcity

Myths and superstitions have power over us only to the extent that we believe them, but when we believe, we live completely under their spell and in that fiction. Scarcity is a lie, but it has been passed down as truth and with a powerful mythology that insists on itself, demands compliance, and discourages doubt or questioning.

In my work with people across the spectrum of money and resources, I found that it is possible to unpack this set of beliefs and assumptions, this kind of overarching way of seeing life, and get some distance from it, free ourselves from its grip and see for ourselves—each of us in our own life—whether or not it's a valid way to live life. When we unpack the mind-set of scarcity, we find three central myths that have come to define our relationship with money and that block our access to more honest and fulfilling interactions with it.

Toxic Myth #1: There's Not Enough

The first prevailing myth of scarcity is that *there's not enough*. There's not enough to go around. Everyone can't make it. Somebody's going to be left out. There are way too many people. There's not enough food. There's not enough water. There's not enough air. There's not enough time. There's not enough money.

There's not enough becomes the reason we do work that brings us down or the reason we do things to each other that we're not proud of. *There's not enough* generates a fear that drives us to make sure that we're not the person, or our loved ones aren't the people, who get crushed, marginalized or left out.

Once we define our world as deficient, the total of our life energy, everything we think, everything we say, and everything we do—particularly with money— becomes an expression of an effort to overcome this sense of lack and the fear of losing to others or being left out. It becomes noble and responsible to make sure we take care of our own, whoever we deem that to be. If there's not enough for everyone, then taking care of yourself and your own, even at others' expense, seems unfortunate, but unavoidable and somehow valid. It's like the child's game of musical chairs. With one seat short of the number of people playing, your focus is on not losing and not being the one who ends up at the end of the scramble without a seat. We don't want to be the poor suckers without, so we compete to get more than the other guy, determined to stay ahead of some impending doom.

The deficiency and fear reflect in the way we conduct our lives, and the systems and institutions we create to control access to any resource we perceive as valuable or limited. As members of the global community, our fear-based responses lead us at times—in the demand for foreign oil, for instance—to put our own material desires above the health, safety and well-being of other people and other nations. In our own communities, we respond to the fear that *there's not enough* by creating systems that favor us or exclude others from access to basic resources such as clean water, good schools, adequate health care or safe housing. And in our own families, *there's not enough* drives us to buy more than we need or even want of some things, to value, favor, or curry favor with people on the basis of their value to us in relation to money, rather than qualities of character.

Toxic Myth #2: More Is Better

The second toxic myth is that *more is better*. More of anything is better than what we have. It's the logical response if you fear there's not enough, but *more is better* drives a competitive culture of accumulation, acquisition and greed that only heightens fears and quickens the pace of the race. And none of it makes life more valuable. In truth, the rush for more distances us from experiencing the deeper value of what we acquire or already have. When we eat too fast or too much, we cannot savor any single bite of food. When we are focused constantly on the next thing—the next dress, the next car, the next job, the next vacation, the next home improvement—we hardly experience the gifts of that which we have now. In our relationship with money, *more is better* distracts us from living more mindfully and richly with what we have.

Our drive to enlarge our *net* worth turns us away from discovering and deepening our *self*-worth.

More is better is a chase with no end and a race without winners. It's like a hamster wheel that we hop onto, get going, and then forget how to stop. Eventually, the chase for more becomes an addictive exercise, and as with any addiction, it's almost impossible to stop the process when you're in its grip. But no matter how far you go, or how fast, or how many other people you pass up, you can't win. In the mind-set of scarcity, even too much is not enough.

It doesn't make sense to someone who makes forty thousand dollars a year that someone who makes five million dollars a year would be arguing over their golden parachute package and need at least fifteen million dollars more. Some of the people with fortunes enough to last three lifetimes spend their days and nights worrying about losing money on the stock market, about being ripped off or conned or not having enough for their retirement. Any genuine fulfillment in their life of financial privilege can be completely eclipsed by these money fears and stresses. How could people who have millions of dollars think they need more? They think they need more because that's the prevailing myth. We all think that, so they think that, too. Even those who have plenty cannot quit the chase. The chase of *more is better*—no matter what our money circumstances—demands our attention, saps our energy and erodes our opportunities for fulfillment. When we buy into the promise that *more is better*, we can never arrive. Wherever we are, it is not enough because more is always better. People who follow that credo, consciously or unconsciously—which is all of us to some degree—are doomed to a life that is never fulfilled; we lose the capacity to reach a destination. So even those who have plenty, in this scarcity culture, cannot quit the chase.

More is better misguides us in a deeper way. It leads us to define ourselves by financial success and external achievements. We judge others based on what they have and how much they have, and miss the immeasurable inner gifts they bring to life. All the great spiritual teachings tell us to look inside to find the wholeness we crave, but the scarcity chase allows no time or psychic space for that kind of introspection. In the pursuit of more we overlook the fullness and completeness that are already within us waiting to be discovered. Our drive to enlarge our *net* worth turns us away from discovering and deepening our *self*-worth.

The belief that we need to possess, and possess more than the other person or company or nation, is the driving force for much of the violence and war, corruption and exploitation on earth. In the condition of scarcity, we believe we must have more—more oil, more land, more military might, more market share, more profits, more stock, more possessions, more power, more money. In the campaign to gain, we often pursue our goals at all costs, even at the risk of destroying whole cultures and peoples.

Do other countries need American fast food or theme parks or cigarettes, or have American companies shrewdly expanded their markets internationally to increase their profits, disregarding the impact they have on local cultures, agriculture, economy and public health, at times even in the face of widespread protests against their presence?

Do we need or even really want all the clothing, cars, groceries and gadgets we bring home from our shopping trips, or are we acting on impulse, responding to the call of the consumer culture and the steady, calculated seduction by fashion, food and consumer product advertising? Does a five-year-old *need* more than a few thoughtfully chosen birthday presents to feel celebrated? Whose interests are we really serving when we give children far more than they need or even appreciate at one time?

The unquestioned, unchecked drive for more fuels an unsustainable economy, culture and way of being that has failed us by blocking our access to the deeper, more meaningful aspects of our lives and ourselves.

Toxic Myth #3: That's Just the Way It Is

The third toxic myth is that *that's just the way it is*, and there's no way out. There's not enough to go around, more is definitely better, and the people who have more are always people who are other than us. It's not fair, but we'd better play the game because *that's just the way it is* and it's a hopeless, helpless, unequal, unfair world where you can never get out of this trap.

That's just the way it is is just another myth, but it's probably the one with the most grip, because you can always make a case for it. When something has always been a certain way, and tradition, assumptions, or habits make it resistant to change, then it seems logical, just commonsensical, that the way it is is the way it will stay. This is when and where the blindness, the numbness, the trance, and, underneath it all, the resignation of scarcity sets in. Resignation makes us feel hopeless, helpless and cynical. Resignation also keeps us in line, even at the end of the line, where a lack of money becomes an excuse for holding back from commitment and contributing what we do have—time, energy and creativity—to making a difference. Resignation keeps us from questioning how much we'll compromise ourselves or exploit others for the money available to us in a job or career, a personal relationship or a business opportunity.

That's just the way it is justifies the greed, prejudice and inaction that scarcity fosters in our relationship with money and the rest of the human race. For generations, it protected the early American slave trade from which the privileged majority built farms, towns, business empires and family fortunes, many of which survive today. For more generations it protected and emboldened institutionalized racism, sex discrimination and social and economic discrimination against other ethnic and religious minorities. It has throughout history, and still today, enabled dishonest business and political leaders to exploit others for their own financial gain.

Globally, the myth of *that's just the way it is* makes it so that those with the most money wield the most power and feel encouraged and entitled to do so. For instance, the United States, with 4 percent of the world's population, generates 25 percent of the pollution that contributes to global warming. According to *Geo 2000*, a 1999 United Nations environmental report, the excessive consumption by the affluent minority of the earth's population and the continued poverty of the majority are the two major causes of environmental degradation. Meanwhile, developing nations adopting Western economic models are replicating patterns that, even in political democracies, place inordinate power in the hands of the wealthy few, design social institutions and systems that favor them, and fail to adequately address the inherent inequities and consequences that undermine health, education and safety for all.

We say we feel bad about these and other inequities in the world, but the problems seem so deeply rooted as to be insurmountable and we resign ourselves to *that's just the way it is*, declaring ourselves helpless to change things. In that resignation, we abandon our own human potential and the possibility of contributing to a thriving, equitable, healthy world.

That's just the way it is presents one of the toughest pieces of transforming our relationship with money, because if you can't let go of the chase and shake off the helplessness and cynicism it eventually generates, then you're stuck. If you're not willing to question that, then it is hard to dislodge the thinking that got you stuck. We have to be willing to let go of *that's just the way it is*, even if just for a moment, to consider the possibility that there isn't *a way it is* or *way it isn't*. There is the way we choose to act and what we choose to make of circumstances.

Demystifying Money—
What Is the Stuff Anyway?

The ancient Chinese…[used] seashells as money. The
advantage of this system was that seashells were small,
durable, clean and easy to carry. The drawback was that
they were, in a word, seashells. This meant that anybody with access to the sea could get them. By the time
the ancient Chinese had figured this out, much of the
country was the legal property of gulls.

—*Dave Barry*

Money is one of the most common subjects in
the entire Bible. Jesus spoke about it frequently.
Opinions differ as to the number of parables in the
Bible. In one count of 43 parables, 23 (or 62%)
refer to money and possessions. One of every
seven verses in the Synoptic Gospels, and one
out of 10 in the four Gospels deals with money
and/or possessions. In the Bible there are 500
references to prayer, slightly fewer than 500
dealing with faith, but more than 2000 verses
deal with money and possessions.

—*Eugène Grimm*

Introduction—II

When I started this book, I knew very little about money. I suspect that is the case for many of us. Which is curious, as money is so present a reality in all of our lives. Not a day goes by without dealing with money: how much do we have, how much do we make, how much do we need, how much does something cost? Most all of us worry at least a bit about money. To an extent, we all plan our lives in relationship to the stuff.

For something with such a significant presence, we rarely speak openly about money. It is a conversational taboo, both in the church and the larger culture. It carries a certain mystique. It promises power. It provides opportunity. It sets us free and holds us hostage. With it we meet our most basic needs and coddle our every want.

Money often has the status of an idol: something which cannot deliver that which it promises.

For all that, money is simply high-grade paper, printed just so. It has a history. It functions the way it does as a result of choices our ancestors have made over centuries. Making different choices is certainly conceivable. Other cultures today live with their money very differently than we live with ours.

We may well experience money and how it works in our society as "that's just the way it is." But, as Lynne Twist reminded us, that is one of our more powerful myths.

I've actually found it somewhat freeing to learn some relatively simple things about money. The stuff carries a little less mystique; I've laughed about it, smiled at myself, gained some distance, some objectivity. So here are some of those things I learned or re-learned:

- Money is created, not by our government, but by bankers issuing credit.
- Money's value is based on belief in its value, not anything of intrinsic worth.
- The Federal Reserve Bank is not a government institution; it is private, run for the profit of its owners.
- Our national money, of course, bears interest. Other monetary systems were actually organized around a negative interest (demurrage). For example, ancient Egypt's bags of corn served as a kind of money—one that truly lost value over time (imagine what rats and rot could do to an Egyptian bank). As a result, Egyptians circulated, rather than saved, cash.
- Money is not value neutral. The kind of money we use shapes our behaviors and attitudes. The previous is but one example.
- Money originated, as Boyle points out in his essay, as a way to keep peace.

This section seeks to demystify money, gain some distance and provide new perspectives. In the following essays, humorist Barry pokes serious fun at the stuff. Boyle describes the origins of money; Hyde poignantly reminds us of the reality and values of a "gift economy."

How Money Works
Or: Everybody Clap for Tinker Bell!

by Dave Barry

Humorist Dave Barry is, well, a very funny guy. A Pulitzer-Prize winner, Barry wrote a nationally syndicated column for *The Miami Herald* from 1983-2005. Barry, along with a number of other writers formed the band The Rock-Bottom Remainders for the American Booksellers Association Convention in 1992. Band members have included writers Barbara Kingsolver, Stephen King, Amy Tan, Roy Blount Jr. and Matt Groening. According to Barry, members "are not musically skilled, but they are extremely loud." Mr. Barry is the author of over 30 books.

I actually briefly toyed with the idea of titling this book "Money is Hilarious" or something along those lines. Because it really is, especially when you get a little distance from the everyday concerns connected to cash, de-personalize and de-mystify it a bit. But the title didn't quite capture the book's overall ethos. However, the following essay by Dave Barry is the perfect antidote to money's weightier matters. Find out why money is valuable, just what backs up its value (hint: it ain't gold), and how large swaths of ancient China became the legal property of gulls.

∞

WHY IS MONEY VALUABLE? Why are people willing to work so hard for it, lie for it, cheat for it, go to prison for it, fight for it, kill for it, give up their children for it...*even marry Donald Trump for it?*

I mean, look at the dollar bill. What is it, really? It's a piece of paper! What's more, it's a piece of paper that appears to have been designed by a disturbed individual. On one side, you have a portrait of George Washington, who, granted, was the Father of Our Country and a great leader and everything, but who looks, in this particular picture...

...like a man having his prostate examined by Roto-Rooter.

And then on the *other* side of the dollar you have:

What is *that* about? Why is there a picture of a pyramid, instead of a structure traditionally associated with the fundamental values of the United States of America, such as a WalMart? And why is the pyramid being hovered over by an eyeball the size of a UPS truck?

Whatever the explanation, the design of the dollar would not seem to inspire confidence in its value. And yet if you drop a few dollars from an overpass onto a busy freeway at rush hour, people will run into traffic and literally risk their lives in an effort to grab them. Try it!

What does this tell us? It tells us that people are stupid. But it also tells us that money is more than just pieces of paper. But what makes it valuable? To answer that question, we need to consider:

The History of Money

In prehistoric times, there was no such thing as money. When people needed to buy something, they had to charge it. And then when the bills came, nobody could understand them, because there was also no such thing as reading. This led to a lot of misunderstandings and hitting with rocks.

The first form of money that we are aware of by looking it up on the Internet was animals. From the start there were problems with this type of money, particularly the smaller denominations, such as squirrels, which were always biting the payee and scampering away.

By 9000 B.C., the most commonly accepted form of animal money was cattle. When you bought something, you would give the other person a cow, and the other person would give your change in calves. This was better than squirrels, but still not an efficient system. The cash registers were disgusting.

By 3000 B.C., the Mesopotamians[1] had invented two concepts that revolutionized economic activity: (1) writing and (2) banking. This meant that, for the first time, it was possible for a Mesopotamian to walk into a bank and hand the teller a stone tablet stating:

> GIVE ME ALL YOUR COWS
> AND NOBODY GETS HURT

These robbers were captured quickly, because they had to make their getaways at very slow speeds. Still, it was clear that a better medium of exchange was needed.

The ancient Chinese tried to solve the problem by using seashells as money. The advantage of this system was that seashells were small, durable, clean, and easy to carry. The drawback was that they were, in a word, seashells. This meant that anybody with access to the sea could get them. By the time the ancient Chinese had figured this out, much of their country was the legal property of gulls.

And so the quest continued for a better form of money. Various cultures experimented with a number of commodities, including tea, grains, leather, tobacco, and Pokemon cards. Then, finally, humanity hit upon a medium of exchange that had no disadvantages—a medium that was durable, portable, beautiful, and universally recognized to have lasting value. That medium, of course, was beer.

No, seriously, it was precious metals, especially gold and silver, which—in addition to being rare and beautiful—could be easily shaped into little disks that fit into vending machines.

Before long, many cultures were using some form of gold for money. It came in a wide variety of shapes and designs, as we see in these photographs of ancient coins unearthed by archeologists:

SOURCE: The British Museum of Really Old Things

The problem was that gold is too heavy to be constantly lugged around. So, to make it easier for everybody, governments began to issue pieces of paper to represent gold. The deal was, whenever you wanted, you could redeem the paper for gold. The government was just *holding your gold for you.* But it was YOUR gold! You could get it anytime! That was the sacred promise that the government made to the people. That's why the people trusted paper money. And that's why, to this very day, if you—an ordinary citizen—go to Fort Knox and ask to exchange your U.S. dollars for gold, you will be used as a human chew toy by large federal dogs.

Because the government changed the deal. We don't have the gold standard anymore. Nobody does. Over the years, all the governments in the world, having discovered that gold is, like, *rare,* decided that it would be more convenient to back their money with something that is easier to come by, namely: nothing. So even though the U.S. government still allegedly holds tons of gold in "reserve," you can no longer exchange your dollars for it. You can't even *see* it, because visitors are not allowed. For all you know, Fort Knox is filled with Cheez Whiz.

Which brings us back to the original question: If our money really is just pieces of paper, backed by nothing, why is it valuable? The answer is: *Because we all believe it's valuable.*

Really, that's pretty much it. Remember the part in *Peter Pan* where we clap to prove that we believe in fairies, and we save Tinker Bell? That's our monetary system! It's the Tinker Bell System! We see everybody else running around after these pieces of paper, and we figure, *Hey, these pieces of paper must be valuable.* That's why if you exchanged your house for, say, a pile of acorns, everybody would think you're insane; whereas if you exchange your house for a pile of dollars, everybody thinks you're rational, because you get...pieces of paper! The special kind, with the big hovering eyeball!

And you laughed at the ancient Chinese, with the seashells.

So what does all this mean? Does it mean that our monetary system is a giant house of cards that would collapse like, well, a giant house of cards if the public stopped believing in the pieces of paper? Could all of our "wealth"—our savings, our investments, our pension plans, etc.—suddenly become worthless, meaning that the only truly "wealthy" people would be the survivalist wing nuts who trade all their money for guns and beef jerky?

Yes. But that probably won't happen. Because, fortunately, the public prefers not to think about economics. Most people are unable to understand their own telephone bills, let alone the U.S. monetary system. And as long as we don't question the big eyeball, Tinker Bell is safe.

OK, now you know what money actually is. (Don't tell anybody!) The next question is: How come some people have so *much* money, while others have so little? Why does the money distribution seem so unfair? Why, for example, are professional athletes paid tens of millions of dollars a year for playing silly games with balls, while productive, hardworking people with infinitely more value to society, such as humor writers, must struggle to make barely half that? And above all, how can *you*, personally, get more money?

We'll address these questions in future chapters[2] which will be chock-full of sure-fire, can't-miss, no-nonsense, common-sense, easy-to-apply, on-the-money hyphenated phrases. You'll be on your way to riches in no time! All you have to do is really believe in yourself! Come on, show that you really believe! Clap your hands!

Also, just in case, you should get some jerky....

1. Official cheer: WE don't! WE don't! We don't Meso ROUND!
2. Although not necessarily in *this* book.

What Is Money? And Where Has It Come From?

by David Boyle

David Boyle is an associate of the New Economics Foundation in London. He is the author of numerous books including *The Tyranny of Numbers*, *The Sum of Our Discontent*, *Funny Money* and *The Money Changers*. Boyle first became interested in money as an environmental journalist. The excerpt below is from *The Little Money Book*, a very accessible, quick and delightful read.

"Money is human happiness in the abstract; and so, the man who is no longer capable of enjoying such happiness in the concrete sets his whole heart on money."

—Arthur Schopenhauer

For something we all use so much of, and think about as much as we do, money is extraordinarily elusive. Nobody quite agrees what it is or even, sometimes, what it's for.

At the end of the spectrum, it can be shells from the beach which are used as money in parts of Polynesia. It can be 12-foot-round blocks of stone, used as money in the Caroline Islands—unlikely to be stolen out of your purse but less than useful as small change. Or, if you're on Wall Street, money can be screeds and screeds of digital information, unrelated to any product in the real world.

It isn't that one is real and the other isn't. Both are profoundly real and relate to the different functions that money plays. According to the economists, there are three of these: as a store of value (like the stones), as a standard of value (which everyone can understand) and as a medium of exchange (like the shells—they need have no value in themselves, but help you exchange at an exact price).

Money can be anything—like cigarettes—which helps you account for what you need to buy. It can be something valuable, like coins. It can be something scarce like gold, with intrinsic value. It can be something sophisticated and elastic like shares or copper futures. It can be something that can be accidentally deleted by your bank just because someone sits on the keyboard (this happens surprisingly often). And sometimes it can be a bit of all of these, like the gold that the Spanish conquistadors found in Latin America, extracted from the Incas and shipped back to Europe. Almost anything can be used as money.

The trouble for us is that money is a bit of all of these things. It is coins and it is debt. It is credit card plastic and it is infinite bytes and bytes and bytes in cyberspace—the place where banks actually keep our deposits.

Except that for some of us, money is a good deal more elastic than it is for others. While the poorest people in the world make do with the equivalent of a few cents a day, the "masters of the universe" in Wall Street and the City of London—as Tom Wolfe called them in *The Bonfire of the Vanities*—have a money system that is almost infinitely elastic. When the rogue financier Robert Maxwell fell off his yacht in the Bay of Biscay in 1991, he had stretched his money so much that he owed twice as much as Zimbabwe. That is the heart of all the great injustices of the money system. For some people money is stretchy, insubstantial and infinite, for others it is horribly concrete. Some people make and remake the rules; some people die by them.

But where does it come from in the first place?

There is a popular misconception that the wealth of the world is underpinned by great bars of gold in the vaults of the Federal Reserve, Fort Knox and the Bank of England. Not any more it isn't.

There is still gold in the vaults, and it is still shifted from cage to cage—each one assigned to a different world government—rather than shipped round the world. But that's an historic anomaly and a simple way of storing some of the nation's reserves. Central banks actually spent most of the 1990s trying to sell off their gold reserves surreptitiously without lowering the world gold price. (They failed.)

Actually, the UK pound hasn't been backed by gold since 1931, at the height of the Great Depression, and the final link between money and gold was broken in 1971 when Richard Nixon finally ended the pretense that the U.S. dollar had gold backing.

Of course there are coins, but these are made of cupro-nickel and are no longer worth anything like the 10¢ or 25¢ stamped on the front. The total value of notes and coins in circulation is only a tiny percentage of the country's money.

Where does all the rest come from? Well, astonishingly, nobody agrees—but most people seem to accept that it is lent into existence by the commercial banks. When you stash money in the bank, they must keep around 8% of that loan on deposit—in case there's a run on the bank—but all the rest is lent out again, many times over. In other words, most of our mortgages and bank loans are created, as if by magic, by a stroke of the pen.

And one day it will have to be paid back, plus interest to the bank, when it can be used as the 8% backing for yet more loans. And so it goes on. It's a magical money-making system that is, surprisingly, seldom commented on, limited these days by only two things: the regulations of the Bank for International Settlements in Basle, and fear of having to pay it back if the loan fails—and a good 10% usually do fail.

That's the strange truth behind modern money. We don't mine it, we don't find it on a beach, it bears no relation to anything real, but still some people have vast amounts of it and some people have none at all. And we hardly ever talk about it.

Excerpted from *The Little Money Book* by David Boyle, courtesy of The Disinformation Company Ltd.

Origins of Money: It's not What We Think

by David Boyle

"The worst thing is not giving presents. We give what we have. That is the way we live together."

—Kalahari Bushman,
quoted in William Bloom's *Money, Heart and Mind*

There are so many myths about money, and the myths lie behind so much of what we are told about economics, that it would take more than a book to outline them all—but the first, and the most insidious, is about its origin.

We are constantly told by economists and politicians that money began as a way of facilitating trade. We are told that it developed because barter was inefficient and that for this reason, the drive toward individual wealth and competition that seems at the heart of economics is also at the heart of all of us. Or that money is just an expression of our inner drive to compete with each other in business.

This is simply not true; neither greed nor inefficiencies "drove" the growth of money. Of course barter had its inefficiencies. You have to want what the other person's got, and life doesn't always work like that. The barter schemes that allow some societies to get by without enough cash—like Russia during the 1990s—are fiendishly complicated and devilishly inconvenient. But that wasn't why money began.

Most anthropologists agree that money started as a form of ritual gift—something you gave the next door tribe when you met, or gave the father of the woman you were going to marry, or gave to God at the temple. The word "pay" comes from the Latin *pacare*, which means to pacify, appease, or make peace with. Money began as a way to make peace.

Take, for example, the meeting between Solomon and the Queen of Sheba around 950 B.C.:

> "Extravagant ostentation, the attempt to outdo each other in the splendor of the exchanges, and above all, the obligations of reciprocity were just as typical in this celebrated encounter, though at a fittingly princely level, as with the more mundane types of barter in other parts of the world," says Glyn Davies, author of *The History of Money*.

In fact, the ornamental metallic objects known as "manillas" in West Africa were used as money as recently as 1949. Some ceremonies in the Pacific still use special whale's teeth or edible rats as ritual gifts of money. The origins of money are still there to see, if you are sharp enough, but they have always been regarded with a peculiar horror by modern economists, and officials have even tried to stamp the whole idea out. Canadian authorities outlawed Native American "potlatch" ceremonies—the mixture between social, ceremonial, ritual and barter that were the heart of their societies—between 1884 and 1951.

What does this mean? It means that economics wasn't originally about savage people competing over scarce resources, using money to do each other down. It was about mutual recognition and facilitating human relationships. It's important to remember this now that money's secondary function is to replace human relationships with monetary ones. When things are sold rather than given, when old people live in nursing homes rather than with their children, relationships get driven out by money.

"This is to say that people do not work and create the economy because they want to support the economy," says the writer William Bloom. "They create and relate—and this, in turn, creates the economy." So don't be taken in by economics. We created the economy around us, and if we want to change it, we can do just that.

Excerpted from *The Little Money Book* by David Boyle, courtesy of The Disinformation Company Ltd.

$\mathcal{S}$ome Food We Could Not Eat

by Lewis Hyde

Lewis Hyde is a MacArthur Fellow and the author of the much-praised 1998 book *Trickster Makes This World: Mischief, Myth and Art*, an exploration of human creativity. Hyde taught creative writing at Harvard University for six years. His poetry and essays have appeared in numerous journals, including the *American Poetry Review*, the *Nation*, the *Kenyon Review* and the *Paris Review*. He has received grants from the National Endowment for the Humanities, the National Endowment for the Arts and the Massachusetts Council on the Arts.

In the previous essay David Boyle pointed out that "money started as a form of ritual gift." The following chapter from Lewis Hyde's beautifully articulated book *The Gift* depicts a number of indigenous cultures and folk tales, all characterized by the one essential of the gift economy: "the gift must always move." In describing the

Maori of New Zealand, the Old Testament Israelites, and Pacific Northwest tribal cultures, Hyde writes "abundance is in fact a consequence of treating wealth as a gift."

Hyde's piece describes other kinds of money (food, durable goods, and so on), as well as another way of employing and interacting with money, one that operates out of a sense of abundance. It is fundamentally founded on the reality that all we have is a gift, that the "Earth is the Lord's" (Psalm 24:1).

The Motion

When the Puritans first landed in Massachusetts, they discovered a thing so curious about the Indians' feelings for property that they felt called upon to give it a name. In 1764, when Thomas Hutchinson wrote his history of the colony, the term was already an old saying: "An Indian gift," he told his readers, "is a proverbial expression signifying a present for which an equivalent return is expected." We still use this, of course, and in an even broader sense, calling that friend an Indian giver who is so uncivilized as to ask us to return a gift he has given.

Imagine a scene. An Englishman comes into an Indian lodge, and his hosts, wishing to make their guest feel welcome, ask him to share a pipe of tobacco. Carved from a soft red stone, the pipe itself is a peace offering that has traditionally circulated among the local tribes, staying in each lodge for a time but always given away again sooner or later. And so the Indians, as is only polite among their people, give the pipe to their guest when he leaves. The Englishman is tickled pink. What a nice thing to send back to the British Museum! He takes it home and sets it on the mantelpiece. A time passes and the leaders of a neighboring tribe come to visit the colonist's home. To his surprise he finds his guests have some expectation in regard to his pipe, and his translator finally explains to him that if he wishes to show his goodwill he should offer them a smoke and give them the pipe. In consternation the Englishman invents a phrase to describe these people with such a limited sense of private property. The opposite of "Indian giver" would be something like "white man keeper" (or maybe "capitalist"), that is, a person whose instinct is to remove property from circulation, to put it in a warehouse or museum (or, more to the point for capitalism, to lay it aside to be used for production).

The Indian giver (or the original one, at any rate) understood a cardinal property of the gift: whatever we have been given is supposed to be given away again, not kept. Or, if it is kept, something of similar value should move on in its stead, the way a billiard ball may stop when it sends another scurrying across the felt, its momentum transferred. You may keep your Christmas present, but it ceases to be a gift in the true sense unless you have given something else away. As it is passed along, the gift may be given back to the original donor, but this is not essential. In fact, it is better if the gift is not returned but is given instead to some new, third party. The only essential is this: *the gift must always move.* There are other forms of property that stand still, that mark a boundary or resist momentum, but the gift keeps going.

Tribal peoples usually distinguish between gifts and capital. Commonly they have a law that repeats the sensibility implicit in the idea of an Indian gift. "One man's gift," they say, "must not be another man's capital." Wendy James, a British social anthropologist, tells us that among the Uduk in northeast Africa, "any wealth transferred from one subclan to another, whether animals, grain or money, is in the nature of a gift, and should be consumed, and not invested for growth. If such transferred wealth is added to the subclan's capital [cattle in this case] and kept for growth and investment, the subclan is regarded as being in an immoral relation of debt to the donors of the original gift." If a pair of goats received as a gift from another subclan is kept to breed or to buy cattle, "there will be general complaint that the so-and-so's are getting rich at someone else's expense, behaving immorally by hoarding and investing gifts, and therefore being in a state of severe debt. It will be expected that they will soon suffer storm damage...."

> **...a cardinal property of the gift [is] whatever we have been given is supposed to be given away again, not kept. Or, if it is kept, something of similar value should move on in its stead...**

The goats in this example move from one clan to another just as the stone pipe moved from person to person in my imaginary scene. And what happens then? If the object is a gift, it keeps moving, which in this case means that the man who received the goats throws a big party and everyone gets fed. The goats needn't be given back, but they surely can't be set aside to produce milk or more goats. And a new note has been added: the feeling that if a gift is not treated as such, if one form of property is converted into another, something horrible will happen. In folk tales the person who tries to hold on to a gift usually dies; in this anecdote the risk is "storm damage." (What happens in fact to most tribal groups is worse than storm damage. Where someone manages to commercialize a tribe's gift relationships the social fabric of the group is invariably destroyed.)

...Many of the most famous of the gift systems we know about center on food and treat durable goods as if they were food. The potlatch of the American Indians along the North Pacific coast was originally a "big feed." At its simplest a potlatch was a feast lasting several days given by a member of a tribe who wanted his rank in the group to be publicly recognized. Marcel Mauss translates the verb "potlatch" as "to nourish" or "to consume." Used as a noun, a "potlatch" is a "feeder" or "place to be satiated." Potlatches included durable goods, but the point of the festival was to have these perish as if they were food. Houses were burned; ceremonial objects were broken and thrown into the sea. One of the potlatch tribes, the Haida, called their feasting "killing wealth."

To say that the gift is used up, consumed and eaten sometimes means that it is truly destroyed as in these last examples, but more simply and accurately it means that the gift perishes *for the person who gives it away*. In gift exchange the transaction itself consumes the object. Now, it is true that something often comes back when a gift is given, but if this were made an explicit condition of the exchange, it wouldn't be a gift....This, then, is how I use "consume" to speak of a gift—a gift is consumed when it moves from one hand to another with no assurance of anything in return. There is little difference, therefore, between its consumption and its movement. A market exchange has an equilibrium or stasis: you pay to balance the scale. But when you give a gift there is momentum, and the weight shifts from body to body.

I must add one more word on what it is to consume, because the Western industrial world is famous for its "consumer goods" and they are not at all what I mean. Again, the difference is in the form of the exchange, a thing we can feel most concretely in the form of the goods themselves. I remember the time I went to my first rare book fair and saw how the first editions of Thoreau and Whitman and Crane had been carefully packaged in heat-shrunk plastic with the price tags on the inside. Somehow the simple addition of airtight plastic bags had transformed the books from vehicles of liveliness into commodities, like bread made with chemicals to keep it from perishing. In commodity exchange it's as if the buyer and the seller were both in plastic bags; there's none of the contact of a gift exchange. There is neither motion nor emotion because the whole point is to keep the balance, to make sure the exchange itself doesn't consume anything or involve one person with another. Consumer goods are consumed by their owners, not by their exchange.

The desire to consume is a kind of lust. We long to have the world flow through us like air or food. We are thirsty and hungry for something that can only be carried inside bodies. But consumer goods merely bait this lust, they do not satisfy it. The consumer of commodities is invited to a meal without passion, a consumption that leads to neither satiation nor fire. He is a stranger seduced into feeding on the drippings of someone else's capital without benefit of its inner nourishment, and he is hungry at the end of the meal, depressed and weary as we all feel when lust has dragged us from the house and led us to nothing.

Gift exchange has many fruits, as we shall see, and to the degree that the fruits of the gift can satisfy our needs there will always be pressure for property to be treated as a gift. This pressure, in a sense, is what keeps the gift in motion. When the Uduk warn that a storm will ruin the crops if someone tries to stop the gift from moving, it is really their desire for the gift that will bring the storm. A restless hunger springs up when the gift is not being eaten. The brothers Grimm found a folk tale they called "The Ungrateful Son":

> Once a man and his wife were sitting outside the front door with a
> roast chicken before them which they were going to eat between

them. Then the man saw his old father coming along and quickly took the chicken and hid it, for he begrudged him any of it. The old man came, had a drink, and went away.

Now the son was about to put the roast chicken back on the table, but when he reached for it, it had turned into a big toad that jumped in his face and stayed there and didn't go away again.

And if anybody tried to take it away, it would give them a poisonous look, as if about to jump in their faces, so that no one dared touch it. And the ungrateful son had to feed the toad every day, otherwise it would eat part of his face. And thus he went ceaselessly hither and yon about in the world.

This toad is the hunger that appears when the gift stops moving, whenever one man's gift becomes another man's capital. To the degree that we desire the fruits of the gift, teeth appear when it is hidden away. When property is hoarded, thieves and beggars begin to be born to rich men's wives. A story like this says that there is a force seeking to keep the gift in motion. Some property must perish—its preservation is beyond us. We have no choice. Or rather, our choice is whether to keep the gift moving or to be eaten with it. We choose between the toad's dumb-lust and that other, more graceful perishing in which our hunger disappears as our gifts are consumed....

The Maori have a word, *hau*, which translates as "spirit," particularly the spirit of the gift and the spirit of the forest which gives food. In these tribes, when hunters return from the forest with birds they have killed, they give a portion of the kill to the priests, who, in turn, cook the birds at a sacred fire. The priests eat a few of them and then prepare a sort of talisman, the *mauri*, which is the physical embodiment of the forest *hau*. This *mauri* is a gift the priests give back to the forest, where, as a Maori sage once explained to an Englishman, it "causes the birds to be abundant...that they may be slain and taken by man."

There are three gifts in this hunting ritual; the forest gives to the hunters, the hunters to the priests, and the priests to the forest. At the end, the gift moves from the third party back to the first. The ceremony that the priests perform is called *whangai hau*, which means "nourishing *hau*," feeding the spirit. To give such a name to the priests' activity says that the addition of the third party keeps the spirit of the gift alive. Put conversely, without the priests there is a danger that the motion of the gift will be lost. It seems to be too much to ask of the hunters to both kill the game and return a gift to the forest. Gift exchange is more likely to turn into barter when it falls into the ego-of-two. With a simple give-and-take, the hunters may begin to think of the forest as a place to turn a profit. But with the priests involved, the gift must leave the hunters' sight before it returns to the woods. The priests take on or incarnate the position of the third thing to avoid the binary relation of the hunters and forest which by itself would not be abundant. The priests, by their presence alone, feed the spirit.

Every gift calls for a return gift, and so, by placing the gift back in the forest, the priests treat the birds as a gift of nature. We now understand this to be ecological. Ecology as a science began at the end of the nineteenth century, an offshoot of the rising interest in evolution. Originally the study of how animals survive in their environments, one of ecology's first lessons was that, beneath all the change in nature, there are steady states characterized by cycles. Every participant in the cycle literally lives off the others with only the ultimate energy source, the sun, being transcendent. Widening the study of ecology to include man means to look at ourselves as a part of nature again, not its lord. When we see that we are actors in natural cycles, we understand that what nature gives to us is influenced by what we give to nature. So the circle is a sign of an ecological insight as much as of gift exchange. We come to feel ourselves as one part of a large self-regulating system.

The return gift, the "nourishing *hau*," is literally feedback, as they say in cybernetics. Without it, that is to say, with the exercise of any greed or arrogance of will, the cycle is broken. We all know that it isn't "really" the *mauri* placed in the forest that "causes" the birds to be abundant, and yet now we see that on a different level it is: the circle of gifts enters the cycles of nature and, in so doing, manages not to interrupt them and not to put man on the outside. The forest's abundance is in fact a consequence of man's treating its wealth as a gift.

The consumer of commodities is invited to a meal without passion, a consumption that leads to neither satiation nor fire. He is a stranger seduced into feeding on the drippings of someone else's capital...he is hungry at the end of the meal, depressed and weary as we all feel when lust has dragged us from the house and led us to nothing.

The Maori hunting ritual enlarges the circle within which the gift moves in two ways. First, it includes nature. Second and more important, it includes the gods. The priests act out a gift relationship with the deities, giving thanks and sacrificing gifts to them in return for what they give the tribe. A story from the Old Testament will show us the same thing in a tradition with which we are more familiar. The structure is identical.

In the Pentateuch the first fruits always belong to the Lord. In Exodus the Lord tells Moses: "Consecrate to me all the first-born; whatever is the first to open the womb among the people of Israel, both of man and of beast, is mine." The Lord gives the tribe its wealth, and the germ of that wealth is then given back to the Lord. Fertility is a gift from God, and in order for it to continue, its first fruits are returned to him as a return gift. In pagan times this had apparently included sacrificing the firstborn son, but the Israelites had early been allowed to substitute an animal for the child, as in the story of Abraham and Isaac. Likewise a lamb was substituted for the firstborn of any unclean animal. The Lord says to Moses:

All that opens the womb is mine, all your male cattle, the firstlings of cow and sheep. The firstling of an ass you shall redeem with a lamb, or if you will not redeem it you shall break its neck. All the firstborn of your sons you shall redeem.

Elsewhere the Lord explains to Aaron what is to be done with the firstborn. Aaron and his sons are responsible for the priesthood, and they minister at the altar. The lambs, calves, and kids are to be sacrificed: "You shall sprinkle their blood upon the altar, and shall burn their fat as an offering by fire, a pleasing odor to the Lord; but their flesh shall be yours...." As in the Maori story, the priests eat a portion of the gift. But its essence is burned and returned to the Lord in smoke.

This gift cycle has three stations and more—the flocks, the tribe, the priests and the Lord. The inclusion of the Lord in the circle—and this is the point I began to make above—changes the ego in which the gift moves in a way unlike any other addition. It is enlarged beyond the tribal ego and beyond nature. Now, as I said when I first introduced the image, we would no longer call it an ego at all. The gift leaves all boundary and circles into mystery.

The passage into mystery always refreshes. If, when we work, we can look once a day upon the face of mystery, then our labor satisfies. We are lightened when our gifts rise from pools we cannot fathom. Then we know they are not a solitary egotism and they are inexhaustible. Anything contained within a boundary must contain as well its own exhaustion. The most perfectly balanced gyroscope slowly winds down. But when the gift passes out of sight and then returns, we are enlivened. Material goods pull us down into their bones unless their fat is singed occasionally. It is when the world flames a bit in our peripheral vision that it brings us jubilation and not depression. We stand before a bonfire or even a burning house and feel the odd release it brings, as if the trees could give the sun return for what enters them through the leaf. When no property can move, then even Moses' Pharaoh is plagued with hungry toads. A sword appears to seek the firstborn son of that man who cannot be moved to move the gift. But Pharaoh himself was dead long before his firstborn was taken, for we are only alive to the degree that we can let ourselves be moved. And when the gift circles into mystery the liveliness stays, for it is "a pleasing odor to the Lord" when the first fruits are effused in eddies and drifted in lacy jags above the flame.

Scarcity and abundance have as much to do with the form of exchange as with how much material wealth is at hand. Scarcity appears when wealth cannot flow.

I described the motion of the gift earlier in this chapter by saying that gifts are always used, consumed, or eaten. Now that we have seen the figure of the circle we can understand what seems at first to be a paradox of gift exchange: when the gift is used, it is not used up. Quite the opposite, in fact: the gift that is not used will be lost, while the one that is passed along remains abundant....What is given away feeds again and again, while what is kept feeds only once and leaves us hungry.

...The Maori hunting tale showed us that not just food in parables but food in nature remains abundant when it is treated as gift, when we participate in the moving circle and do not stand aside as hunter or exploiter. Gifts are a class of property whose value lies only in their use and which literally cease to exist as gifts if they are not constantly consumed. When gifts are sold, they change their nature as much as water changes when it freezes, and no rationalist telling of the constant elemental structure can replace the feeling that is lost....

Scarcity and abundance have as much to do with the form of exchange as with how much material wealth is at hand. Scarcity appears when wealth cannot flow. In [E.M. Forster's novel] *A Passage to India*, Dr. Aziz says, "If money goes, money comes. If money stays, death comes. Did you ever hear that useful Urdu proverb?" and Fielding replies, "My proverbs are: A penny saved is a penny earned; A stitch in time saves nine; Look before you leap; and the British Empire rests on them." He's right. An empire needs its clerks with their ledgers and their clocks saving pennies in time. The problem is that wealth ceases to move freely when all things are counted and priced. It may accumulate in great heaps, but fewer and fewer people can afford to enjoy it. After the war in Bangladesh, thousands of tons of donated rice rotted in warehouses because the market was the only known mode of distribution, and the poor, naturally, couldn't afford to buy. Marshall Sahlins begins a comment on modern scarcity with the paradoxical contention that hunters and gatherers "have affluent economies, their absolute poverty notwithstanding." He writes:

> Modern capitalist societies, however richly endowed, dedicate themselves to the proposition of scarcity. [Both Paul Samuelson and Milton Friedman begin their economies with "The Law of Scarcity"; it's all over by the end of Chapter One.] Inadequacy of economic means is the first principle of the world's wealthiest peoples. The apparent material status of the economy seems to be no clue to its accomplishments; something has to be said for the mode of economic organization.

> The market-industrial system institutes scarcity, in a manner completely unparalleled and to a degree nowhere else approximated. Where production and distribution are arranged through the behavior of prices, and all livelihoods depend on getting and spending, insufficiency of material means becomes the explicit, calculable starting point of all economic activity.

Given material abundance, scarcity must be a function of boundaries. If there is plenty of air in the world but something blocks its passage to the lungs, the lungs

do well to complain of scarcity. The assumptions of market exchange may not necessarily lead to the emergence of boundaries, but they do in practice. When trade is
"clean" and leaves people unconnected, when the merchant is free to sell when
and where he will, when the market moves mostly for profit and the dominant
myth is not "to possess is to give" but "the fittest survive," then wealth will lose its
motion and gather in isolated pools. Under the assumptions of exchange trade,
property is plagued by entropy and wealth can become scarce even as it increases.

...Gifts that remain gifts can support an affluence of satisfaction, even without
numerical abundance. The mythology of the rich in the overproducing nations
that the poor are in on some secret about satisfaction—black "soul," gypsy *duende*,
the noble savage, the simple farmer, the virile game keeper—obscures the harsh-
ness of modern capitalist poverty, but it does have a basis, for people who live in
voluntary poverty or who are not capital-intensive do have more ready access to
erotic forms of exchange that are neither exhausting nor exhaustible and whose use
assures their plenty.

If the commodity moves to turn a profit, where does the gift move? The gift
moves toward the empty place. As it turns in its circle it turns toward him who has
been empty-handed the longest, and if someone appears elsewhere whose need is
greater it leaves its old channel and moves toward him. Our generosity may leave
us empty, but our emptiness then pulls gently at the whole until the thing in
motion returns to replenish us. Social nature abhors a vacuum. Counsels Meister
Eckhart, the mystic: "Let us borrow empty vessels." The gift finds that man attractive who stands with an empty bowl he does not own.[1]

The begging bowl of the Buddha, Thomas Merton has said, "represents the ultimate theological root of the belief, not just in a right to beg, but in openness to the
gifts of all beings as an expression of the interdependence of all beings.... The
whole idea of compassion, which is central to Mahayana Buddhism, is based on an
awareness of the interdependence of all living beings.... Thus when the monk begs
from the layman and receives a gift from the layman, it is not as a selfish person
getting something from somebody else. He is simply opening himself to this interdependence...." The wandering mendicant takes it as his task to carry what is
empty from door to door. There is no profit; he merely stays alive if the gift moves
toward him. He makes its spirit visible to us. His well-being, then, is a sign of its
well-being, as his starvation would be a sign of its withdrawal. Our English word
"beggar" comes from the Beghards, a brotherhood of mendicant friars that grew up
in the thirteenth century in Flanders. There are still some places in the East where
wandering mendicants live from the begging bowl; in Europe they died out at the
close of the Middle Ages.

As the bearer of the empty place, the religious mendicant has an active duty
beyond his supplication. He is the vehicle of that fluidity which is abundance. The
wealth of the group touches his bowl at all sides, as if it were the center of a wheel
where the spokes meet. The gift gathers there, and the mendicant gives it away

again when he meets someone who is empty. In European folk tales the beggar often turns out to be Wotan, the true "owner" of the land, who asks for charity though it is his own wealth he moves within, and who then responds to neediness by filling it with gifts. He is godfather to the poor.

Folk tales commonly open with a beggar motif. In a tale from Bengal, a king has two queens, both of whom are childless. A faquir, a wandering mendicant, comes to the palace gate to ask for alms. One of the queens walks down to give him a handful of rice. When he finds that she is childless, however, he says that he cannot accept the rice but has a gift for her instead, a potion that will remove her barrenness. If she drinks his nostrum with the juice of the pomegranate flower, he tells her, in due time she will bear a son whom she should then call the Pomegranate Boy. All this comes to pass and the tale proceeds.

Such stories declare that the gift does move from plenty to emptiness. It seeks the barren, the arid, the stuck, and the poor. The Lord says, "All that opens the womb is mine," for it is He who filled the empty womb, having earlier stood as a beggar by the sacrificial fire or at the gates of the palace.

1. Folk tales are the only proof I shall be able to offer for these assertions. The point is more spiritual than social: in the spiritual world, new life comes to those who give up.

What Is Compassion's Call?

In truth, all human beings are called to be saints, but
that means called to be fully human, to be perfect—
that is, whole, mature, fulfilled. The saints are simply
those men and women who relish the event of life
as a gift and who realize that the only way to honor
such a gift is to give it away.

—*William Stringfellow*

I came that they might have life and
have it abundantly.

—John 10:10

Introduction—III

Compassion means "to suffer with." The Dalai Lama has said that compassion "seems to be the greatest power." I have often felt that those who embody compassion most closely represent Jesus and his mission on Earth. But our understanding and practice of compassion is often watered down. Practicing compassion essentially becomes the expression of empathy: "I'm so sorry; I've been there." Empathy is compassion's first, necessary step. But if we stop there, it is a sentimentalized distant cousin to "the greatest power."

The second step, which lifts compassion to the greatest power, is justice. Frederick Buechner says: "Compassion is the sometimes fatal capacity for feeling what it's like to live inside another's skin [empathy], knowing there can never really be peace and joy for any until there is peace and joy finally for all [justice]." Felt as empathy, compassion is embodied as justice. It calls us *not only* to feel for the rich and lonely, the poor and hungry, the endangered species and the lack of clean water—it calls us to *do something* about it, to enter into and suffer with.

Henri Nouwen writes here that compassion brings joy, consists of mutual giving and receiving and calls us to "downward mobility." Ched Myers works with the Gospel of Mark's story of the rich young man. Jesus' response to him is one of full-throated compassion: Jesus empathized—he loved the young man—and called him to practice justice, to sell all he had to redistribute his wealth to the poor.

Compassion

by Henri Nouwen

Henri Nouwen was a Catholic priest known for his many books on the Christian faith, spirituality, and Christian action and contemplation. He touched the lives of many students while a professor of Pastoral Theology at Yale Divinity School. He spent his last years sharing his life and living with mentally handicapped people in the L'Arche community of Daybreak in Toronto, Ontario.

One: From Competition to Compassion

If there is one notion that is central to all great religions it is that of "compassion." The sacred scriptures of the Hindus, Buddhists, Moslems, Jews, and Christians all speak about God as the God of compassion. In a world in which competition continues to be the dominant mode of relating among people, be it in politics, sports, or economics, all true believers proclaim compassion, not competition, as God's way.

How is it possible to make compassion the center of our lives? As insecure, anxious, vulnerable, and mortal beings—always involved, somehow and somewhere, in the struggle for survival—competition seems to offer us a great deal of satisfaction. In the Olympics, as well as in the American presidential race, it is clear that winning is what is most desired and most admired.

Still, Jesus says: "Be compassionate as your heavenly Father is compassionate," and throughout the centuries all great spiritual guides echo these words. Compassion—which means, literally, "to suffer with"—is the way to the truth that we are most ourselves, not when we differ from others, but when we are the same. Indeed, the main spiritual question is not, "What difference do you make?" but "What do you have in common?" It is not "excelling" but "serving" that makes us most human. It is not proving ourselves to be better than others but confessing to be just like others that is the way to healing and reconciliation.

Compassion, to be with others when and where they suffer and to willingly enter into a fellowship of the weak, is God's way to justice and peace among people. Is this possible? Yes, it is, but only when we dare to live with the radical faith that we do not have to compete for love, but that love is freely given to us by the One who calls us to compassion.

Two: Being the Beloved

Jesus shows us the way of compassion, not only by what he says, but also by how he lives. Jesus speaks and lives as the Beloved Son of God. One of the most central events of Jesus' life is related by Matthew: "When Jesus had been baptized he at once came up from the water, and suddenly, the heavens opened and he saw the Spirit of God descending like a dove and coming down on him. And suddenly there was a voice from heaven, 'This is my Son, the Beloved: my favor rests on him'" (Matthew 3:16-17).

This event reveals the true identity of Jesus. Jesus is the Beloved of God. This spiritual truth will guide all his thoughts, words, and actions. It is the rock on which his compassionate ministry will be built. This becomes very obvious when we are told that the same Spirit who descended on him when he came up from the water, also led him into the desert to be tempted. There the "Tempter" came to him asking him to prove that he was worth being loved. The "Tempter" said to him: "Do something useful, like turning stones into bread. Do something sensational, like throwing yourself down from a high tower. Do something that brings you power, like paying me homage." These three temptations were three ways to seduce Jesus into becoming a competitor for love. The world of the "Tempter" is precisely that world in which people compete for love through doing useful, sensational, and powerful things and so winning medals that gain them affection and admiration.

Jesus, however, is very clear in his response: "I don't have to prove that I am worthy of love. I am the Beloved of God, the One on whom God's favor rests." It was that victory over the "Tempter" that set Jesus free to choose for the compassionate life.

Three: Downward Mobility

The compassionate life is the life of downward mobility! In a society in which upward mobility is the norm, downward mobility is not only discouraged but even considered unwise, unhealthy, or downright stupid. Who will freely choose a low-paying job when a high paying job is being offered? Who will choose poverty when wealth is within reach? Who will choose a hidden place when there is a place in the limelight? Who will choose to be with one person in great need when many people could be helped during the same time? Who will choose to withdraw to a place of solitude and prayer when there are so many urgent demands made from all sides?

My whole life I have been surrounded by well-meaning encouragement to go "higher up," and the most-used argument was: "You can do so much good there, for so many people."

But these voices calling me to upward mobility are completely absent from the Gospel. Jesus says: "Anyone who loves his life loses it; anyone who hates his life in this world will keep it for the eternal life" (John 12:25). He also says: "Unless you become like little children you will never enter the kingdom of heaven" (Matthew 18:3). Finally he says: "You know that among the gentiles the rulers lord it over them, and great men make their authority felt; among you this is not to happen. No; anyone who wants to become great among you must be your servant, and anyone who wants to be first among you must be your slave, just as the Son of Man came, not to be served, but to serve, and to give his life as a ransom for many" (Matthew 20:25-28).

This is the way of downward mobility, the descending way of Jesus. It is the way toward the poor, the suffering, the marginal, the prisoners, the refugees, the lonely, the hungry, the dying, the tortured, the homeless—toward all who ask for compassion. What do they have to offer? Not success, popularity, or power, but the joy and peace of the children of God.

Four: The Secret Gift of Compassion

Downward mobility, moving toward those who suffer and sharing in their pain, seems close to being masochistic and even morbid. What joy can there be in solidarity with the poor, the sick, and the dying? What joy can there be in compassion?

People like Francis of Assisi, Charles de Foucauld, Mahatma Gandhi, Albert Schweizter, Dorothy Day, and many others were far from masochistic or morbid. They all radiated with joy. This, obviously, is a joy largely unknown to our world. When we go by what the media tell us, joy should come from success, popularity, and power, even though those who have these things are often quite heavy of heart and even depressed.

The joy that compassion brings is one of the best-kept secrets of humanity. It is a secret known to only a very few people, a secret that has to be rediscovered over and over again.

I have had a few glimpses of it. When I came to Daybreak, a community with people who have mental disabilities, I was asked to spend a few hours with Adam, one of the handicapped members of the community. Each morning I had to get him out of bed, give him a bath, shave him, brush his teeth, comb his hair, dress him, walk him to the kitchen, give him his breakfast, and bring him to the place where he spends his day. During the first few weeks, I was mostly afraid, always worrying that I would do something wrong or that he would have an epileptic seizure. But gradually I relaxed and started to enjoy our daily routine. As the weeks passed by, I discovered how I had come to look forward to my two hours with Adam. Whenever I thought of him during the day, I experienced gratitude for having him as my friend. Even though he couldn't speak or even give a sign of recognition, there was real love between us. My time with Adam had become the most precious time of the day. When a visiting friend asked me one day: "Couldn't you spend your time better than working with this handicapped man? Was it for this type of work that you got all your education?" I realized that I couldn't explain to him the joy that Adam brought me. He had to discover that for himself.

Joy is the secret gift of compassion. We keep forgetting it and thoughtlessly look elsewhere. But each time we return to where there is pain, we get a new glimpse of the joy that is not of this world.

Five: Right Where We Are

It would be sad if we were to think about the compassionate life as a life of heroic self-denial. Compassion, as a downward movement toward solidarity instead of an upward movement toward popularity, does not require heroic gestures or a sensational turnaround. In fact, the compassionate life is mostly hidden in the ordinariness of everyday living. Even the lives of those whom we look up to for their examples of compassion show that the descending way toward the poor was, first of all, practiced through small gestures in everyday life.

The question that truly counts is not whether we imitate Mother Teresa, but whether we are open to the many little sufferings of those with whom we share our life. Are we willing to spend time with those who do not stimulate our curiosity? Do we listen to those who do not immediately attract us? Can we be compassionate to those whose suffering remains hidden from the eyes of the world? There is much hidden suffering: the suffering of the teenager who does not feel secure; the suffering of the husband and wife who feel that there is no love left between them; the suffering of the wealthy executive who thinks that people are more interested in his money than in him; the suffering of the gay man or woman who feels isolated from family and friends; the suffering of the countless people who lack caring friends, satisfying work, a peaceful home, a safe neighborhood; the suffering of the millions who feel lonely and wonder if life is worth living.

Once we look downward instead of upward on the ladder of life, we see the pain of people wherever we go, and we hear the call of compassion wherever we are.

True compassion always begins right where we are.

Six: Suffering with Others

Compassion is something other than pity. Pity suggests distance, even a certain condescendence. I often act with pity. I give some money to a beggar on the streets of Toronto or New York City, but I do not look him in his eyes, sit down with him, or talk with him. I am too busy to really pay attention to the man who reaches out to me. My money replaces my personal attention and gives me an excuse to walk on.

Compassion means to become close to the one who suffers. But we can come close to another person only when we are willing to become vulnerable ourselves. A compassionate person says: "I am your brother; I am your sister; I am human, fragile, and mortal, just like you. I am not scandalized by your tears, nor afraid of your pain. I too have wept. I too have felt pain." We can be with the other only when the other ceases to be "other" and becomes like us.

This, perhaps, is the main reason that we sometimes find it easier to show pity than compassion. The suffering person calls us to become aware of our own suffering. How can I respond to someone's loneliness unless I am in touch with my own experience of loneliness? How can I be close to handicapped people when I refuse to acknowledge my own handicaps? How can I be with the poor when I am unwilling to confess my own poverty?

When I reflect on my own life, I realize that the moments of greatest comfort and consolation were moments when someone said: "I cannot take your pain away, I cannot offer you a solution for your problem, but I can promise you that I won't leave you alone and will hold on to you as long and as well as I can." There is much grief and pain in our lives, but what a blessing it is when we do not have to live our grief and pain alone. That is the gift of compassion.

Seven: Together in Silence

Moments of true compassion will remain engraved on our hearts as long as we live. Often these are moments without words: moments of deep silence.

I remember an experience of feeling totally abandoned—my heart in anguish, my mind going crazy with despair, my body shaking wildly. I cried, screamed, and pounded the floors and the walls. Two friends were with me. They didn't say anything. They just were there. When, after several hours, I calmed down a little bit, they were still there. They put their arms around me and held me, rocking me like a little child. Then we simply sat on the floor. My friends gave me something to drink; I couldn't speak. There was silence...safe silence.

Today I think of that experience as a turning point in my life. I don't know how I would have survived without my friends.

I also remember the time that a friend came to me and told me that his wife had left him that day. He sat in front of me, tears streaming from his eyes. I didn't know what to say. There simply was nothing to say. My friend didn't need words. What he needed was simply to be with a friend. I held his hands in mine, and we sat there... silently. For a moment, I wanted to ask him how and why it all had happened, but I knew that this was not the time for questions. It was the time just to be together as friends who have nothing to say, but are not afraid to remain silent together.

Today, when I think of that day, I feel a deep gratitude that my friend had entrusted his grief to me.

These moments of compassion continue to bear fruit.

Eight: Giving and Receiving

One of the most beautiful characteristics of the compassionate life is that there is always a mutuality of giving and receiving. Everyone who has truly entered into the compassionate life will say: "I have received as much as I have given." Those who have worked with the dying in Calcutta, those who have lived among the poor in the "young towns" of Lima or the "favellas" of Sao Paulo, those who have dedicated themselves to AIDS patients or mentally handicapped people—they all will express deep gratitude for the gifts received from those they came to help. There is probably no clearer sign of true compassion than this mutuality of giving and receiving.

One of the most memorable times of my own life was the time I spent living with the Osco Moreno family in Pamplona Alta near Lima, Peru. Pablo and his wife, Sophia, with their three children, Johnny, Maria, and Pablito, offered me their generous hospitality, even though they were very poor. I will never forget their smiles, their affection, their playfulness—all of that in the midst of a life full of worries about how to make it for another day. I went to Peru with a deep desire to help the poor. I returned home with a deep gratitude for what I had received. Later, while teaching at Harvard Divinity School, I often felt a real homesickness for "my family." I missed the children hanging onto my arms and legs, laughing loudly and sharing their cookies and drinks with me. I missed the spontaneity, the intimacy, and the generosity with which the poor of Pamplona Alta surrounded me. They literally showered me with gifts of love. No doubt, they were happy and even proud to have this tall "Gringo Padre" with them, but whatever I gave them, it was nothing compared to what I received.

The rewards of compassion are not things to wait for. They are hidden in compassion itself. I know this for sure.

Nine: The Gift of Self-Confrontation

Sometimes a life of compassion offers a gift you are not so eager to receive: the gift of self-confrontation. The poor in Peru confronted me with my impatience and my deep-seated need for efficiency and control. The handicapped in Daybreak keep confronting me with my fear of rejection, my hunger for affirmation, and my never-decreasing search for affection.

I remember quite vividly one such moment of self-confrontation. During a lecture trip to Texas, I had bought a large cowboy hat for Raymond, one of the handicapped members of the house in which I lived. I looked forward to coming home and giving him my gift.

But when Raymond, whose needs for attention and affirmation were as boundless as my own, saw my gift he started yelling at me: "I don't need your silly gift. I have enough gifts. I have no place for them in my room. My walls are already full. You better keep your gift. I don't need it." His words opened a deep wound in me. He made me realize that I *wanted* to be his friend, but instead of spending time with him and offering him my attention, I had given him an expensive gift. Raymond's angry response to the Texan hat confronted me with my inability to enter into a personal relationship with him and develop a real friendship. The hat, instead of being seen as an expression of friendship, was seen as a substitute for it.

Obviously, all of this didn't happen consciously on my side or on Raymond's side. But when Raymond's outburst brought me to tears I realized that my tears were, most of all, tears about my own inner brokenness.

This self-confrontation too is a gift of the compassionate life. It is a gift very hard to receive, but a gift that can teach us much and help us in our own search for wholeness and holiness.

Ten: God's Heart

What does it mean to live in the world with a truly compassionate heart, a heart that remains open to all people at all times? It is very important to realize that compassion is more than sympathy or empathy. When we are asked to listen to the pains of people and empathize with their suffering, we soon reach our emotional limits. We can listen only for a short time and only to a few people. In our society we are bombarded with so much "news" about human misery that our hearts easily get numbed simply because of overload.

But God's compassionate heart does not have limits. God's heart is greater, infinitely greater, than the human heart. It is that divine heart that God wants to give to us so that we can love all people without burning out or becoming numb.

It is for this compassionate heart that we pray when we say: "A pure heart create for me, O God, put a steadfast spirit within me. Do not cast me away from your presence, nor deprive me of your holy spirit" (Psalm 51).

The Holy Spirit of God is given to us so that we can become participants in God's compassion and so reach out to all people at all times with God's heart.

"You lack only one thing."
The Call of the Rich Man
and the Kingdom of God in Mark

by Ched Myers

Ched Myers is co-founder of a small intentional community in California, the Bartimaeus Cooperative, where he focuses on building capacity for biblical literacy, church renewal and faith-based witness for justice.

Ched's books include: *Binding the Strong Man* (1988), *Who Will Roll Away the Stone* (1994), and *Say to This Mountain* (1996, co-authored), all published by Orbis Books. He writes regularly for *Sojourners* and has published more than 100 articles and essays in periodicals in the U.S., England and Australia.

The Gospel account of the rich young man, as Ched Myers says, "is all too familiar to Christendom, yet has never seemed to be overly troubling." Ched, a teacher and "theological animator," here turns his attention to that account in Mark 10:17-31. He writes that the text actually is not a statement about the rich, but rather "a statement about the nature of the Kingdom" of God. Find the Gospel text reproduced below, followed by Ched's reflections.

As Jesus started on his way, a man ran up to him. He fell on his knees before Jesus. "Good teacher," he said, "what must I do to receive eternal life?"

"Why do you call me good?" Jesus answered. "No one is good except God. You know what the commandments say. 'Do not commit murder. Do not commit adultery. Do not steal. Do not give false witness. Do not cheat. Honor your father and mother.'"

"Teacher," he said, "I have obeyed all those commandments since I was a boy."

Jesus looked at him and loved him. "You are missing one thing," he said. "Go and sell everything you have. Give the money to those who are poor. You will have treasure in heaven. Then come and follow me."

The man's face fell. He went away sad, because he was very rich.

Jesus looked around. He said to his disciples, "How hard it is for rich people to enter God's kingdom!"

The disciples were amazed at his words. But Jesus said again, "Children, how hard it is to enter God's kingdom! Is it hard for a camel to go through the eye of a needle? It is even harder for the rich to enter God's kingdom!"

The disciples were even more amazed. They said to each other, "Then who can be saved?"

Jesus looked at them and said, "With man, that is impossible. But not with God. All things are possible with God."

Peter said to him, "We have left everything to follow you!"

"What I'm about to tell you is true," Jesus replied. "Has anyone left home or family or fields for me and the good news? They will receive 100 times as much in this world. They will have homes and families and fields. But they will also be treated badly by others. In the world to come they will live forever. But many who are first will be last. And the last will be first."

The story of Jesus and the rich man (Mk 10:17-31) lies at the crossroads of Mark's gospel narrative. From there Jesus will turn toward Jerusalem, a destination of confrontation with the Powers that evoked dread and denial among Jesus' disciples then (10:32) as now. But the encounter between Jesus and this affluent gentleman represents a theological crossroad as well.

The man's question—"What must I do to inherit eternal life?"—is a straightforward inquiry about salvation (10:17). But Jesus neither opens his arms in universal enfranchisement, as in the tradition of modern liberal-theology, nor does he demand proper belief, as conservative theology dictates. Instead, Jesus challenges him, equally straightforwardly, to redistribute his assets to the poor. An encounter that began with such theological promise thus concludes with the man's decisive *rejection* of discipleship (10:22). Worse, Jesus seems to shrug it off with a crude class explanation: "How difficult it is for the wealthy to enter the Kingdom of God" (10:24).

This story is all too familiar to Christendom, yet has never seemed to be overly troubling. Perhaps this is because theologians have spent so much intellectual energy undermining its plain meaning. The text has occasioned countless homilies on how those who are blessed with wealth must take care not to let their affluence get in the way of their love for God and the church—despite the fact that such an interpretation is *precisely* what this text rejects out of hand. How might we rescue this story from such domestication? We might begin by changing our focus, as does the text itself, from the rich man's concern about eternal life to Jesus' concern about the "Kingdom of God." Now, however, we have another problem, because how we should understand the gospel notion of the Kingdom of God has been no small debate among New Testament scholars. Indeed, for most North American theologians the Kingdom has represented little more than a nebulous, eschatological metaphor that can be attached to any variety of idealism as easily as ignored altogether.

Mark's use of Kingdom language is relatively sparing and somewhat slippery. Sometimes it is portrayed in *temporal* terms: it is an imminent *kairos* (1:15), a powerful moment of revelation (9:1), a future "blessed hope" (14:25). Other times Mark suggests the Kingdom is more *spatial* in character: a place into which one *enters* (9:47; 10:23f) and/or a "state of being" which one *receives* (10:14f). It is *paradoxical*: for disciples it is a "mystery," and for others it is a "parable" (4:11). Yet the Kingdom of God is nevertheless *concrete*. When pressed for an analogy, Mark's Jesus chooses not some arcane symbol but the reality most familiar to poor folk: the land itself (4:26, 30).

We are, in short, never really told definitively what the Kingdom of God *is* by Mark. He does, however, at one point make it clear what it is *not*. So the audience will not forget—repetition being the key to pedagogy—Jesus offers a lyrical little verse, whose point is sharpened with the razor's edge of absurdist humor:

> How difficult it will be for those with riches
> to enter the Kingdom of God!
> ...Children, how difficult it is
> to enter the Kingdom of God!
> It is easier for a camel to go through a needle's eye
> than for a rich man
> to enter the Kingdom of God! (10:23-25)

Whatever else the Kingdom of God may be, it is plainly where the rich are *not*! Today we North American Christians, who can only be defined as rich relative to the global distribution of wealth and power, would do well to reflect at length on this terrifying triplet. For it remains as dissonant to our ears today as it was to the disciples in the story, provoking the same kind of astonishment (10:23, 26).

The clarity of this text has somehow escaped the church through the ages, which instead has concocted a hundred ingenuous reasons why it cannot mean what it says. Christians have been so anxious that Jesus might be saying something exclusive or critical about the rich that they have missed the fact that this triplet is not a statement about *them* at all. It is a statement about the nature of the *Kingdom*. These reiterations—all in the indicative mood—insist that the Kingdom of God is simply that social condition *in which there are no rich and poor*. By definition, then, the rich cannot enter—not, that is, with their wealth intact.

To understand this, let us take a closer look at the whole episode. From his direct approach to Jesus we can tell that the man is socially powerful; he wants something and is willing to give deference in exchange (10:17). But his grandiose claim to innocence ("I have kept all the commandments," 10:20) flies in the face of Jesus' own rejection of his original compliment ("No one is good but God alone," 10:18). Moreover, the religious concern reflected in his original inquiry is not as genuine as it appeared at first glance. The problem is that his question assumes he can inherit eternal life. The root of this verb (Greek, *kleeronomeoo*) is *kleeros*, a parcel of land. In some Hellenistic literature this term is synonymous with *kteema*, "real property," which appears in Mk 10:22. This gentleman, in other words, appears to be exhibiting characteristics associated with the "false consciousness" of class entitlement. For him, eternal life, like property, must be *inherited*.

> **These reiterations...insist that the Kingdom of God is simply that social condition *in which there are no rich and poor*. By definition, then, the rich cannot enter—not, that is, with their wealth intact.**

Beneficiaries of a socio-economic system often envision religion as a reproduction of their own privilege (hence Marx's contention that "material life determines consciousness"). In the case of this man, we are told "he possessed many properties" (10:22). Indeed in first century Palestine, land (not commodities) was the basis of wealth. The tiny landed class of Jewish Palestine took great care to protect its entitlement from generation to generation. As Jesus later suggests in a parable about the struggle over deeded land, in which insurgent tenants try to kill the *kleeronomos* in order to wrest the *kleeronomis* from the absentee landlord, the politics of inheritance was often a bloody business (Mk 12:7).

This story is more interested in *how* this man became so affluent than in his pious claims. The estates of the rich grew in several ways. Assets were sometimes consolidated through the joining of households in marital or political alliances. Other times expropriated land was distributed through political patronage. But...the primary mechanism was acquiring land through the debt-default of the poor. Small agricultural landholders groaned under the burden of rent, tithes, taxes, tariffs and operating expenses. If they fell behind in payments, they were forced to take out loans secured by their land. When unable to service these loans, the land was lost to the lenders. These lenders were in most cases the large landowners, who in the absence of banking institutions made available their surplus capital. This is how socio-economic inequality had become so widespread in the time of Jesus (criticized in Mk 4:24f). It is almost certainly how this man ended up with "many properties." Mark has given us a concise portrait of this man's ideology of *entitlement*.

This brings us to another overlooked piece of the story: Jesus' "short list" of the Decalogue (10:21). That he leaves out the first four "theological" commandments is unremarkable, since their meaning was not a matter of debate for Jews. The twist lies in the last of the six "ethical" commands—"do not covet what belongs to your neighbor" (Ex 20:17). In Jesus' recitation it has been replaced by an allusion to the Levitical censure, "Do not defraud" (Mk 10:19). This commandment appears in a section of Torah that concerns socio-economic conduct in the Sabbath community: "You shall not defraud your neighbor; you shall not steal; you shall not keep for yourself the wages of a laborer" (Lev 19:13).

With this deft bit of editorial interpretation, Mark's Jesus suddenly snaps into focus the cycle of indebtedness just described. The implication is that the "propertied" create and maintain their surplus through "fraud." They may justify their wealth by ideologies of entitlement, but Jesus unmasks it as the result of illegitimate expropriation of their neighbor's land.

> Jesus is not inviting this man to change his attitude toward his wealth, nor to treat his servants better, nor to reform his personal life. He is asserting the precondition for discipleship: economic justice.

"Jesus looked at the man and loved him" (10:21). Now comes the hard truth that arises from Jesus' genuine compassion, the kind of love that refuses to equivocate. "You lack one thing." The word here (Greek, *husterei*) implies that it is this man who is in debt—to the poor he has defrauded. The rich man, in the logic of the Kingdom is poor (see for example the destitute poverty, *hustereeseoos*, of the widow in 12:44, there also contrasted with the wealthy). "Get up," pleads Jesus—this is the verb Mark uses most often for healing episodes. "Sell what you have, give to the poor, and come follow me." That is, he must de-construct the fraudulent system from which he derives his privilege and restore to the poor what has been taken from them. By redistributing his ill-gotten surplus, he stands to receive "*treasure* in heaven" (Greek, *theesauron*, a term distinct from the other three words used to describe wealth in this episode). We might say that Jesus has just radically revalued the currency!

Jesus is not inviting this man to change his attitude toward his wealth, nor to treat his servants better, nor to reform his personal life. He is asserting the precondition for discipleship: economic justice. Stung, the man whirls and slinks away (10:22). In the epilogue to the story Jesus turns and looks at the disciples, perhaps bemused at their incredulity. He then offers his little ditty about the Kingdom of God, summarily dismissing the worldview that equates wealth and power with divine blessing or human meritocracy.

It is little wonder the disciples can only muster an anguished protest (10:26). Here we have arrived at the reason why the discourse of the Kingdom of God has circulated at such a low rate of exchange within modern Christianity. In capitalism, redistributive justice is high heresy—but Mark's Jesus has clearly equated it with the Kingdom of God. Those who are structurally advantaged within a given socio-economic system, therefore, by definition cannot be a part of it. Conversely, to practice redistributive justice is not to be saved by works but to celebrate the new "economy of grace."

I would contend that Jubilee ideology is the only plausible background to the practice of Jesus. From the outset of Mark's narrative, Jesus is portrayed as practicing and exhorting Jubilee redistribution. For example, the narrative sequence of Mk 2:1—3:6 is an extended exposition concerning Sabbath economics in the discipleship community. It begins with Jesus' unilateral disposition of sin/debt (2:5). When the scribes, who control the debt system, warn Jesus that "only God can forgive sin," they are placing redistributive justice beyond the pale of history while protecting their own adjudicatory privileges (2:7). In contrast, Jesus asserts that "the Human One has authority on earth" to deconstruct the condition of indebtedness (2:10).

The next episode portrays *debt-collectors* at table with the *indebted* (2:13-17). This is strange fellowship indeed—*unless* Levi was practicing Jubilee as the precondition to his discipleship. This leads to an action in which the disciples commandeer food from a grain field (2:23ff). There Jesus again asserts the Human One's authority—specifically in relation to Sabbath economics as the practice of surplus redistribution (2:27). The sequence culminates in Jesus' Deuteronomic ultimatum to the synagogue leadership (3:4, see Dt 30:15ff).

Sabbath economics receives still more articulation in the parable of the sower (the "hundredfold" harvest in 4:8 represents abundance) and the manna-action in the wilderness ("everyone had enough," 6:42). Indebted peasants are liberated and the hungry are fed when we break free of the determinations of the market (6:36f). These themes appear again later in Mark's story in Jesus' criticism of the way in which the central institution of the Judean political economy, the Jerusalem Temple, exploits the poor instead of redistributing the community's wealth (see 11:11-25; 12:3—13:2).

The "inverse economics" (the "last are first") of the Jubilee have been well established in Mark's narrative, then, by the time Jesus invites the rich man to relinquish control over his surplus. He does not "follow," but the disciples remind Jesus that *they have* "left everything and followed" (10:28). Indeed, the word used back in 1:18, 20 when the fishermen "left" their nets (Greek *aphienai*) also means "to release" from sin/debt (as in 2:5, 7, 9). This further knits together the theme of discipleship and economic justice in Mark.

In conclusion to the rich man story, Mark shows that the "hundredfold" harvest promised in the sower parable (4:8) was not a pipedream offered to poor peasants, but the concrete result of wealth redistribution. This surplus is created when the entitlements of *household* (basic productive economic unit), *family* (patrimony and inheritance) and *land* (the basic unit of wealth) are "left"—that is, restructured as community assets (10:29f). "Whosoever" practices this Jubilee/Kingdom way will *receive* (not inherit) the community's abundant sufficiency—an allusion to the divine economy of grace. A note of realism is included: persecution will be the inevitable result of such subversive practice. The matter of eternal life, however, is left for "the age to come" (10:30).

This is the answer to the rich man's question. But he has not stuck around to hear it. He has chosen to retain control over his property, unpersuaded by this alternative vision and thus unwilling to change his economic practice. This illustrates another point of Jesus' sower parable: People *of that class* "hear the word, but the anxieties of this age, the love of riches, and the lust for everything else choke the word, so that it proves unfruitful" (4:19). In Mark, the privileged can enter the Kingdom of God neither through "intellectual assent" (as with the scribe in 12:34) nor "openness" (as with Josephus in 15:43), and they certainly cannot *inherit* it. Reparation—the concrete practice of restoring to the poor what is theirs by rights of community justice—is their only way "in." The moral to the rich man story simply reiterates the essence of Jubilee: "The last will be first" (10:31).

Privately controlled wealth is the backbone of capitalism, and it is predicated upon the exploitation of natural resources and human labor. Profit maximization renders socio-economic stratification, objectification and alienation inevitable. According to the gospel, however, those who are privileged within *this* system cannot enter the Kingdom. This is *not* good news for First World Christians—because we are the "inheritors" of the rich man's legacy. So the unequivocal gospel invitation to repentance is addressed to us. To deconstruct our "inheritance" and redistribute the wealth as reparation to the poor—*that* is what it means for *us* to follow Jesus.

"Who, then, can be saved?" (Mk 10:26). The disciples' incredulity at Jesus' teaching anticipates our own. Does Jesus *really* expect the "haves" (that is, us) to participate in Sabbath wealth redistribution as a condition for discipleship? Can we imagine a world in which there are no rich and poor? To the disciples' skepticism, and to ours, Jesus replies simply: "I know it seems impossible to you, but for God all things are possible" (10:27). In other words, economics is ultimately a theological issue.

From *The Biblical Vision of Sabbath Economics*, published by Tell the Word. Reprinted by permission of Ched Myers.

Is More (Money/Growth) Better?

We are in captivity because we have made a god out of an economic system and have worshiped it as if it were the only reality.

—*Mary Jo Leddy*

The ecological model claims that housemates must abide by three main rules: take only your share, clean up after yourselves, and keep the house in good repair for future occupants.

—*Sallie McFague*

Hell is the state in which we are barred from receiving what we truly need because of the value we give to what we merely want. It is a condition of ultimate deprivation, that is, poverty.

—*Jacob Needleman*

Introduction—IV

Up until now, *Money and Faith*'s journey has primarily focused on the more personal. The book now shifts from the personal to the prophetic—in the sense that prophets often make us uncomfortable, ask us to see in a new way, to consider previously unexamined realities. Too often books, teachers and our own thinking and ways of life stop at the personal level: as if faith bore no impact whatsoever on public life, on the marketplace, on the kind of society we create.

Within that larger arena, the book now asks questions like, beyond our personal relationship with money, how does our faith call us to relate to that money-making system we call the economy?

In her essay, Lynne Twist wrote that "that's just the way it is" is one of the myths undergirding the lie of scarcity. When taking on anything so vast and complicated, it's crucial to remember that myth—to know that there are other options, should we as a society decide that the way things are now doesn't seem to work that well.

In this section, I do not mean to make an enemy out of our enormously productive economy or its evangelists. I live, as almost all who will read this book do, at a banquet of luxury, physical comfort and material wealth unimaginable to even my grandparents' generation. It is, however, past time to question the drumbeat "more is better" and the economic system which marches to no other rhythm.

The Eight-Hundred Pound Gorilla

by Michael Schut

I do not like looking for things. I seem to be genetically predisposed to missing the obvious—especially if it's in the fridge. (No way, the butter dish was *not* right there, right in front, when first I opened the door.) The vignette below describes an "eye-opening" experience when I was able to see something that had been right in front of my face. And the instructions, how I was told to observe, were the only thing that changed between the first and second observations. In a sense I was allowed to remove my blinders.

This essay compares that experience with the way we are taught to see the world economically. It invites us to see economics more clearly, to see what we are taught not to see. Perhaps what we most need to recognize is how today's dominant economic system does not see itself as rooted in and wholly dependent on the larger world, Earth's economy. (Note: if you have not read the Introduction on the previous page, please do so now.)

∞

The set-up was simple: three people in white T-shirts, three people in black T-shirts and two basketballs. Our instructor, Bernard, gave clear instructions: "Count the number of times someone in a white T-shirt touches one of the balls."

He pushed "play" and the video rolled. The six players wove in and out, passing the basketballs to their teammates. The fifteen of us students closely followed every movement of the white team.

The video stopped. "So, what did you get?" Our answers ranged from seventeen to twenty. "Did you notice anything else about the video?" Bernard inquired.

A few students said something about a gorilla. A what? Bernard then asked us to watch the video again with new eyes, with no specific instructions. This time I saw, midway through the video clip, someone in a gorilla suit saunter very leisurely to the center of the picture. The gorilla slowly, deliberately, faced the camera, raised his arms and beat his chest for a good while. He then dropped his arms and shuffled out of view, exiting stage left. Most of us had not seen the gorilla; we had been instructed to see something else.

Economics

When it comes to economics, most of us are instructed to "leave it to the experts." It's too complicated, too mathematical, too important, we are told. In following those instructions, though, what is it that we do not see; what gorilla enters, demands attention, and then slowly walks away, completely ignored because we were looking for something else?

The first thing we miss is that economics is, indeed, "too important" but, in contrast with what we are told, it's too important to leave to the experts. We need one another. We need the expert economist to mold and direct our economy, but we also need pastors and spiritual leaders to question the insatiable greed seemingly enshrined in that economy. We need the economist to set the price of a widget, and we need the ecologist to remind us that the price must include the damage (cost) inflicted on the natural world in the making of the widget.

I first became interested in economics because so much of what I cared about—beauty, diversity, human well-being and potentially even our own long-term viability—was being sacrificed on the altar of economic growth. I wanted to better understand economics in order to see how we might effect change in the direction of greater equity and sustainability.

So, in graduate school I took my first economics course: one called "Resource

Economics." The following quarter I enrolled in a class on the economics of inter-national trade. But I dropped that course after the second class, baffled at what seemed to me to be a total disconnect between the graphs and numbers on the chalkboard and the real world. At least the resource economics course gave a nod to the reality of the larger world, acknowledging that our economic system resides somewhere, namely on Earth.

Which leads nicely to the second and probably most important "gorilla" we are trained not to see: today's global economic system does not see itself as rooted in and wholly dependent on the larger world, Earth's economy. For God's sake, the system acts as if it's disembodied, separate from Earth!

So, having hopefully established the need for non-economists (such as myself) to address economics, and having identified the eight-hundred pound gorilla (the system's assumed separation from the larger world), let's briefly explore that system and compare it with the larger world of Earth's economy.[1] Let's name the current dominant human economy (often called neoclassical economics) the Big Human Economy and visualize it as a line. Earth's Economy can be helpfully imagined as a circle. We'll take that up first.

Earth Economy's Circle

The circle includes three distinct characteristics. First, circles represent on-going cycles where "waste equals food."[2] Earth's Economy is the first and most efficient recycler. All sloughed off life-forms become food for another life-form. Nothing is wasted and there is no "away" (as in "throw it away"). Death brings on new life.

Second, Earth's Economy runs off current solar energy.[3] Besides that, Earth's cir-cle is a closed system, operating solely off of the limited bounty of Earth's "one-time endowment."[4]

Third, Earth's Economy depends on diversity, which in turn depends on local resources. A tree grows *somewhere*, feeding off the nutrients and water of a certain place. An animal lives and belongs somewhere as well. (Even migratory animals are dependent on a relatively few spots along their route.) Earth's Economy creates and nurtures a flourishing of diversity. Healthy ecosystems are characterized by that diversity. Indeed, a local community is deemed healthy to the extent that the com-munity's diversity of relationships is intact.

The Big Human Economy's Line

Neoclassical economics, market capitalism as practiced throughout the world today, is usefully envisioned as a line. At one end, capital, labor and natural resources are input. As those inputs travel the production line, a great variety of goods are created, as is a great deal of waste.

A line does not share much in common with a circle. First, and probably the most significant difference in our case, is that the line of the Big Human Economy does not see waste as food. Rather than waste products returning to the system to provide input for further production, the wastes are released. The economy trusts that Earth's Economy will somehow assimilate all waste, a hope we now know is futile.

Second, rather than draw on *current* energy input, the Big Human Economy is almost exclusively dependent on energy stored over millions of years beneath Earth's surface: coal, oil and natural gas. The phenomenal growth of world economic output corresponds with the release of millennia of stored fossil fuel energy.

Third, the Big Human Economy (BHE) does not depend on diversity. Rather, the more uniform the world, the more efficiently it fits into BHE's line. One result of this preference for uniformity is the destruction of cultural diversity. After all, indigenous cultures living and dependent on, say, a tropical rainforest, will often vigorously defend that rainforest, its source of life. To the BHE, that cultural diversity becomes an obstacle to the efficient harvesting of rainforest. In addition, unlike Earth's Economy, the BHE does not depend on local resources; rather it sees the entire world as its rightful playground, its source of raw materials.

One further characteristic of the line needs highlighting. The line is wholly dependent on and contained within the circle of Earth's Economy. All inputs— capital, labor, natural resources—are gifts of a healthy Earth. Yet the Big Human Economy does not know this. It does not see the "eight-hundred pound gorilla."

With this admittedly brief and relatively simple description, it's possible to further contrast not only the economic differences embodied within these two economies, but the way we feel and are valued within them. What's fascinating is that these two economies take different views of human nature and the place of community.

The Two Economies' Views of Community and Human Nature

I belong to a large HMO. When I call, a helpful customer service representative (eventually) answers. Their first question: "What is your consumer number?" Before answering, I remind them that prior to having a number assigned as my identity, I had a name. "My name is Mike, and my number is…" I reply.

And that's how the Big Human Economy sees you and me: as a consumer. Or, as theologian John Cobb puts it, we are "individuals-in-a-market"[5] where, Sallie McFague writes, human beings are seen as fundamentally greedy. "Neoclassical economics assumes the unquestionable importance of the individual and his or her desires."[6]

Alternatively, within Earth's Economy human beings are seen as "persons-in-community," according to Cobb.[7] McFague suggests that in Earth's Economy we become fundamentally needy, in the sense of being radically dependent, relational beings. "We may be greedy, but more basically we are needy...."[8]

This latter view of human nature is much more akin to a Christian anthropology, which views us as profoundly relational with, and dependent on, first of all, our Creator. Second, it sees us as persons-in-community, which strikes me as similar to our call to be members of one body, namely the Church or the Body of Christ. The "unquestionable importance of the individual" in the Big Human Economy becomes tempered with "love your neighbor as yourself."

Let's move on now to the role of community in the two economies. Simply put, Earth's Economy creates and nurtures diverse communities. It respects and needs such diversity. A healthy community, in Earth's Economy, is strong and stable to the extent that the myriad relationships within that community are intact. As more of those relationships are frayed or lost, the community declines and will eventually crash.

The Big Human Economy takes a look at communities, again comprised of humans and others as well, and sees value to the extent that that community can serve one of three purposes:

- as a resource (labor, natural resources, capital) for production
- as a market for consumption
- as a sink (dump) for waste.

An old-growth forest is valuable as lumber or paper; a town and its people are valuable as consumers of those products; a river is valuable as a site to dump waste from the mill. Or, a Bangladeshi community becomes valuable as low-wage textile laborers; American consumers' apparent insatiability does its part as a valuable market; and, the atmosphere (a community of sorts, I suppose) becomes a handy dump for greenhouse gases emitted in transporting those textiles.

I write in this rather stark manner, creating a sort of caricature of the Big Earth Economy, to help us see it more clearly—see characteristics not necessarily apparent to us, and certainly not advertised by that economy. Rather, our economy trumpets to the world that it provides employment to otherwise destitute Bangladeshis. And that is often true. However, our economy does not also proclaim that the low-wage Bangladeshi workers are valuable as a community only until even lower-wage workers are found in another country.

As I said in this section's introduction, most everyone reading this book benefits greatly from our economy. And it often seems like there is no alternative. But there *are* alternatives, and if we are to create them, we do need to know some of the current system's problems. It is to three of those that we turn our attention now.

Troubles with the Line

First, Externalities

Perhaps saying "externalities" will someday feel like a Freudian slip. Something we're a little embarrassed about, something that requires explaining.

Unlike Earth's Economy, where waste equals food, in the Big Human Economy waste equals…well, waste. We end up calling our waste an "externality" (a negative one). The word itself reveals what we hope for: let's ignore this thing, externalize it, maybe no one will notice. So, to take just one example, in the process of making paper, dioxin is produced. If the paper mill can get away with it, the dioxin is quietly released into the nearby river channel. The paper mill internalizes the profits from their paper, and externalizes the costs of properly disposing of dioxin. Those externalized costs are then paid by others; in this case perhaps in the form of increased cancer rates among those living downstream, and the loss of fish habitat.

The externality garnering most of the attention these days, and justifiably so, is the emission of greenhouse gases, a negative externality of our fossil fuel appetite.

Second, Gross National Product

Most of the world has accepted the Gross National Product (GNP) as *the* measure of economic growth; growth in GNP is a good thing. To imagine a politician seriously questioning that—is to imagine that politician's career as over.

GNP is a measurement of the exchange of goods and services within an economy. GNP recognizes growth when money exchanges hands. So when both parents work, GNP increases not only as a result of their labor but also because they must now pay for child-care. When we pay professionals to care for our parents, GNP grows. When we do so within our own homes, GNP remains oblivious. Divorce increases GNP. Violence, crime, war, ecological degradation: they all pay. As Bill McKibben writes, "Under the current system, as many have pointed out…the most economically productive citizen is a cancer patient who totals his car on his way to meet with his divorce lawyer."[9]

So when policies and priorities focus on increasing GNP, we are not necessarily creating a world that provides more of what we as citizens value. And there are alternatives; measuring economic growth via GNP is not inevitable.

Third, "Free" Services

In 1997 a group of economists published a paper in the prestigious journal *Nature*. Their goal was to assign a monetary value to "ecosystem services," things like pollination, soil creation, and decomposition; things the Big Human Economy counts as free, services that Earth's Economy provides. The group's estimate of the value of these services came to $33 trillion *annually*, far larger than the Big Human Economy's annual output.[10]

Ironically, once these services are damaged—say, topsoil loss exceeds the rate of natural soil replenishment—we then begin paying for those services. In this example we pay for fertilizers, or the planting of wind breaks. Because money changes hands for something that used to be free, GNP goes up. Meanwhile, we're told our economy is growing, and more is better.

Geez, That's Discouraging

The main purpose of this discussion has been to highlight significant problems with the Big Human Economy. The following section in this book, titled "The Purposeful: How Shall We Then Live?" is dedicated to solutions, hopeful stories and ways to get involved. But it seems important to at least provide, in this essay, a couple responses to the three "Troubles with the Line" highlighted above.

First, ecological economists have turned their attention to creating "full cost accounting" or "getting prices right." For instance, the cost of a gallon of gas would internalize the costs associated with its production and use. The externality of pollution and climate change would be paid for at the pump. According to some estimates, then "gasoline would cost $7 or $8 a gallon, and the SUV would never have been invented."[11]

Implementing this sort of accounting would profoundly influence behavior because prices would change profoundly. And prices are bits of information to which markets, and each one of us, all respond. Can you imagine the kind of cars Detroit might come up with in response to $8 a gallon gasoline? Or imagine how affordable public transportation might become compared to driving alone, and how quickly all of us would demand higher quality, affordable public transportation?

It is important to note that the shift toward getting prices right would be more difficult for some than others. Governments would need to help smooth out the transition, especially for those unable to afford such high gasoline prices. Nor would public transportation improve overnight in such a way as to immediately meet increased demand. Such changes would be gradual. Such changes would not be easy; then again, for many today the present is already "not easy." Full cost accounting helps address the "trouble" with the externalities and free services described above. How about Gross National Product (GNP)?

Ecological economists have also developed alternative measures of economic success. Redefining Progress created the Genuine Progress Indicator (GPI). Its creators use the same accounting framework the government does in producing the GNP. But they subtract for costs associated with pollution, for example. And they add value to the GPI for the benefits associated with, for example, volunteer work and caring for children at home (both of which are ignored by the GNP). Redefining Progress concludes that American GPI has decreased since the early 1970s. (While, as we know, GNP increased.)

Other alternative economic measures include the United Nations' Human Development Index which measures economic growth along with two additional indicators: life expectancy and education.[12] The kingdom of Bhutan has, delightfully, created its own measure: Gross National Happiness. All of these alternative measures seek to provide a signal "that would tell us whether economic activity was making us better off or worse off."[13]

A Final Note: A Profane, Violent Economy

Two further characteristics of the Big Human Economy deserve mention. First, that economy assumes we live in a profane world. Life becomes valuable only to the extent that it feeds the economy's production line. As such the Big Human Economy has to answer to the world's religious traditions which declare the world a sacred place.

Second, the Big Human Economy is violent at its core. That may sound harsh. Perhaps to appreciate that, we need to, as best we can, reside for a time in the shoes of another.

Consider African-Americans. For generations, American economic wealth was based on their slave labor; many today are still structurally excluded from economic well-being and full inclusion in American society.

Consider American family farmers. They're pressured to "get big or get out." They compete against subsidized corporate agribusiness. There are now fewer full-time farmers than there are prisoners in the United States.

Consider polar bears. Now they're endangered. Even strong swimmers need ice to rest upon, the very ice now melting due to an economic engine fired with fossil fuel combustion.

Consider Native Americans. The United States' economic power was based on stolen land and broken treaties. Columbus' arrival was the advent of genocide.

Consider most any other indigenous tribal group, say Brazilian or Indonesian rainforest dwellers. Once the Big Human Economy has passed through their land, their way of life is forever altered, potentially permanently destroyed.

Consider a subsistence farmer in any country. "Free" trade opens your market to heavily subsidized agricultural products. You can't compete. Your ability to support your family is lost. You move to an urban slum, hoping to find work.

From perspectives such as these, perhaps we all can understand, at least to a certain extent, how the Big Human Economy is a violent one.

I believe that we move in the right direction to the extent that we move toward living in an economy that, first, sees the world as a sacred place and, second, an economy that does not rely on the destruction of that very world to feed its own insatiability. Tools such as the Genuine Progress Indicator and full cost accounting can be seen as helpful to the extent that they move us toward that sort of economy. Such movement will also propel us in the direction of an economy characterized by both greater ecological sustainability and equity.

1. Many have written very insightfully about our current economy. I am particularly indebted to, and enthusiastically refer you to:
   - Paul Hawken, *The Ecology of Commerce: A Declaration of Sustainability* (New York: HarperCollins, 1993).
   - Sallie McFague, *Life Abundant: Rethinking Theology and Economy for a Planet in Peril* (Minneapolis, Minnesota: Fortress Press, 2001).
   - Larry Rasmussen, *Earth Community, Earth Ethics* (Maryknoll, New York: Orbis Books, 1996).
   - Bill McKibben, *Deep Economy: The Wealth of Communities and the Durable Future* (New York: Times Books, Henry Holt and Company, 2007).
   - John Cobb, *Sustaining the Common Good: A Christian Perspective on the Global Economy* (Cleveland, Ohio: The Pilgrim Press, 1994).

– Wendell Berry. Almost anything by Berry—see his collections of essays *Home Economics* and *Sex, Economy, Freedom, and Community*.

2. Paul Hawken, *The Ecology of Commerce* (New York: HarperCollins, 1993), 12.

3. Ibid.

4. Larry Rasmussen, *Earth Community, Earth Ethics* (Maryknoll, New York: Orbis Books, 1996), 113. Rasmussen also notes that there is one further source of energy, besides solar, and that is heat radiated from the breakdown of radioactive minerals deep in Earth.

5. John Cobb, Lecture Notes.

6. McFague, *Life Abundant*, 103.

7. John Cobb, Lecture Notes.

8. McFague, *Life Abundant*, 102.

9. McKibben, *Deep Economy*, 28.

10. Ibid., 27.

11. Ibid., 27.

12. McFague, *Life Abundant*, 113.

13. John Cobb, quoted in McKibben, 28.

Prelude to "After Growth"

by Michael Schut

In the previous essay, I provide a critique of and a background with which to assess our current economic paradigm.

The most important questions, however, more likely have to do with whether or not that economic paradigm is working: whether or not it's making us better off, happier. After all, most of us are much more likely to change our own lives, or advocate for societal change, based in and on how our lives feel to us, rather than on some rational critique.

And that's where Bill McKibben's book *Deep Economy* comes in. Bill writes so clearly and in such an inviting manner that he makes potentially difficult topics exciting and accessible. Bill's book begins: "For most of human history, the two birds More and Better roosted on the same branch." More and Better, McKibben suggests, at least for the world's well-off, no longer share the same roost.

He makes three central arguments to support that point:

• First, "growth is no longer making most people wealthier, but instead generating inequality and insecurity."

• Second, constant growth is profoundly colliding with ecological limits such that our planet's ability to sustain growth may not be possible and "the very attempt may be dangerous."

- Third, new research supports what many of us feel intuitively: more, growth, greater wealth…is not making us happier. (McKibben, pages 1-2)

His third argument, concerning happiness, appears in the following essay. Before turning our attention to that, highlights of McKibben's first two arguments follow.

First, "growth is no longer making most people wealthier, but instead generating inequality and insecurity." In spite of significant growth in Gross National Product throughout most of the world, most of us are not "better off." McKibben cites the following:

- The median wage in the United States is the same as it was 30 years ago.
- The bottom ninety percent of American taxpayers have seen real income decline from $27,060 in real dollars in 1979, to $25,646 in 2005.
- Even for those with college degrees, "earnings fell 5.2 percent between 2000 and 2004 when adjusted for inflation, according to the most recent data from White House economists."
- Finally, "more than eighty countries have seen per capita incomes fall in the last decade." (McKibben, pages 11-12)

Now let's briefly consider McKibben's second argument, about economic growth profoundly bumping up against ecological limits. McKibben distinguishes between two types of environmental destruction. The first results from something going wrong, say air or water pollution. Once countries achieve a modicum of growth, that type of environmental degradation decreases because countries can then afford to pay for the environmental cleanup. "A little regulation, and a little money, and the problem disappears."

The second type of environmental destruction results from doing too much of something, when things go "more or less as they're supposed to, just at much too high a level." This sort of environmental degradation, McKibben says, is deeper and more problematic. The prime example is global warming, which results from things going as they're supposed to: in this case, carbon dioxide is emitted when fossil fuels are burned.

So increased economic growth often leads to a reduction in the first type of degradation. Countries use their increased economic clout to pay for and mitigate environmental destruction. But that's not the case for the second type. In fact, as economies grow, so do their carbon emissions (to keep our focus on global warming). (McKibben, pages 22-23) For example, let's look at China. If China's economy continues to grow at its current rate, its 1.3 billion people will, by 2031, be about as rich as Americans. If the Chinese then consume at the rates we Americans do:

- They'd consume (in 2031) the equivalent of two-thirds of the world's entire 2004 grain harvest.
- They'd use 99 million barrels of oil a day, 20 million more than the entire world consumes presently.

- They'd consume roughly double the current world production of paper.
- They'd have 1.1 billion cars on the road, half again as many as the current world total.

And that is just China. Then there's India, then there's the rest of the world. Therefore, McKibben emphasizes, "If you want to argue that an economy structured like ours (the US) makes sense for the whole world, [these] are the kind of numbers you need to contend with." (McKibben, pages 18-19)

With that, let's now focus on McKibben's third argument: growth is not making us any happier. His essay follows.

After Growth

by Bill McKibben

> Bill McKibben is well-known for many things. One of his lesser-known pieces of writing, but one for which I am particularly grateful, is his "Foreword" to my first book *Simpler Living, Compassionate Life: A Christian Perspective*! McKibben writes regularly for *Harpers, Orion, The Atlantic Monthly* and *The New York Review of Books*. Author of ten books, including *The End of Nature, The Age of Missing Information* and *The Comforting Whirlwind: God, Job and the Scale of Creation*, McKibben is a scholar in residence at Middlebury College. In late summer of 2006, McKibben helped lead a five-day walk across Vermont to demand action on climate change. He also founded the *www.stepitup07.org* campaign, which on April 14, 2007 generated over 1,400 events across the United States, asking Congress to enact legislation to cut carbon dioxide emissions by 80 percent by 2050.

Traditionally, ideas like happiness and satisfaction are the sorts of notions that economists wave aside as poetic irrelevancies, questions that occupy people with no head for numbers who have to major in something else at college. An orthodox economist can tell what makes someone happy by what they do. If they buy a Ford Expedition, then ipso facto a Ford Expedition is what makes them happy. That's all you need to know.

The economist calls this behavior "utility maximization"; in the words of the economic historian Gordon Bigelow, "The theory holds that every time a person buys something, sells something, quits a job, or invests, he is making a rational decision about what will...provide him 'maximum utility.' 'Utility' can be pleasure (as in, 'Which of these Disney cruises will make me happiest?' or security (as in, 'Which 401(k) will let me retire before age 85?') or self-satisfaction (as in, 'How much will I put in the offering plate at church?'). If you bought a Ginsu knife at 3 A.M., a neoclassical economist will tell you that, at that that time, you calculated that this purchase would optimize your resources."[1] The beauty of this notion lies in its simplicity: it reassures the economist that all the complex math he builds on top of the assumption adds up to something real. It reassures the politician that all his efforts to increase GNP are sensible and rational even when they may seem otherwise. It is perhaps the central assumption of the world we live in: you can tell who I really am by how I spend.

But is the idea of utility maximization simple, or simpleminded? Economists have long known that people's brains don't work quite as rationally as the model might imply. When Bob Costanza was first edging into economics in the early 1980s, for instance, he had a fellowship to study "social traps," for example, a nuclear arms race, "where short-term behavior can get out of kilter with longer broad-term goals." It didn't take long to demonstrate, as others had before him, that, if you set up an auction in a certain way, people will end up bidding $1.50 to take home a dollar. Other economists have shown that people give too much weight to "sunk costs"—that they're too willing to throw good money after bad, or that they value items more highly if they already own them than if they are thinking of acquiring them. Building on such insights, a school of "behavioral economics," pioneered by researchers like Princeton's Daniel Kahneman, Stanford's Amos Tversky, and Harvard's Andrei Shleifer, has emerged as a "robust, burgeoning sector" of mainstream economics, "opening the way for a richer and more realistic model of the human being in the marketplace."[2]

The real wonder, in a sense, is that it took so long. Each of us knows how irrational much of our behavior is, and how unconnected to any real sense of what makes us happy. I mean, there you are at three A.M. thinking about the Ginsu knife. You're only thinking about it in the first place because someone is advertising it, devoting half an hour of infomercial time to imagining every possible way to make you think that your life will be more complete with this marvel of the cutler's trade—that you will be hosting dinner parties full of witty conversation and impressing potential mates with your suave carving ability, your paper-thin tomato slices. There you are at the car lot thinking about the Ford Expedition. If you are like 95 percent of other buyers, you will never drive it off a paved road. By any objective and rational assessment, the Expedition is a very poor decision, given that it will harm the earth in irreparable ways, and given the fact that it's more dangerous than a car, not only to everyone else on the road but even to yourself—not to mention what its thirst for fuel will cost you. But you are wondering, in

some back part of your cortex, if the manliness inherent in such a very large con-
veyance will perhaps win you new and robust friends, as has been suggested by a
number of recent commercials you have had the pleasure of observing. Or maybe
you were completely freaked out by 9/11 and there's something mysteriously com-
forting about the yards of unnecessary sheet metal surrounding you. Such thoughts
are not rational; in fact, they set us up for as much unhappiness as pleasure.

So the orthodox economist's premise that we can figure out what constitutes a
good economy by summing the *rational individual* actions of consumers is suspect.
"Rational" is a stretch; and, as we shall see, "individual" may cause even more trouble. But until fairly recently, that orthodox economist had a pretty good comeback to
these kinds of objections, namely "Well, what other way is there?" I mean, it seems
unlikely that you'd get any closer by appointing someone (me, say) to decide that everyone had to have a Juiceman in the kitchen and that if they did, happiness would reign.
The misery of centrally planned economies testifies to that.

Each of us knows how irrational much of our behavior is, and how unconnected to any real sense of what makes us happy. I mean, there you are at three A.M. thinking about the Ginsu knife...that you will be hosting dinner parties full of witty conversation and impressing potential mates with your suave carving ability, your paper-thin tomato slices.

In recent years, however, something new
has happened. Researchers from a wide variety of disciplines have begun to figure out
how to assess satisfaction more directly, and
economists have begun to sense the implications that ability holds for their way of look-
ing at the world. In 2002, Daniel Kahneman won the Nobel Prize in economics
even though he was trained as a psychologist. To get a sense of some of his preoc-
cupations you can pick up a book called *Well-being* in which, with a pair of coau-
thors, he announces the existence of a new field called hedonics, defined as "the
study of what makes experience and life pleasant and unpleasant. It is concerned
with feelings of pleasure and pain, of interest and boredom, of joy and sorrow, and
of satisfaction and dissatisfaction. It is also concerned with the whole range of circumstances, from the biological to the societal, that occasion suffering and enjoyment."[3] If you are worried that there might be something altogether too airy about
this, be reassured that Kahneman thinks like an economist. Indeed, in the book's
very first chapter, "Objective Happiness," as he attempts to figure out how accurately people can determine their own mental states, Kahneman describes an
experiment that compares "records of two patients undergoing colonoscopy." Every
sixty seconds, he insists they rate their pain on a scale of 1 to 10, and eventually he
forces them to "make a hypothetical choice between a repeat colonoscopy and a
barium enema."[4] Dismal science, indeed.

As more and more scientists turned their attention to the field, researchers have studied everything from "biases in recall of menstrual symptoms" to "fearlessness and courage in novice paratroopers undergoing training." On occasion, the findings have a distinctly academic ring: there is one paper entitled "The Importance of Taking Part in Daily Life," and in another a researcher "note[s] that there is no context in which cutting oneself shaving will be a pleasant experience." But the sheer variety of experiments is intriguing: subjects have had to choose between getting an "attractive candy bar" and learning the answers to geography questions; they've been made to wear devices that measured their blood pressure at regular intervals; their brains have been scanned. And by now most observers are convinced that saying "I'm happy" is more than just a subjective statement. In the words of the economist Richard Layard, "We now know that what people say about how they feel corresponds closely to the actual levels of activity in different parts of the brain, which can be measured in standard scientific ways."[5] Indeed, people who call themselves happy, or who have relatively high levels of electrical activity in the left prefrontal region of the brain, are also "more likely to be rated as happy by friends," "more likely to respond to requests for help," "less likely to be involved in disputes at work," and even "less likely to die prematurely." In other words, conceded one economist, "It seems that what the psychologists call subjective well-being is a real phenomenon. The various empirical measures of it have high consistency, reliability, and validity."[6]

The idea that there is a state called happiness, and that we can dependably figure out what it feels like and how to measure it, is extremely subversive. It would allow economists to start thinking about life in far richer terms, allow them to stop asking "What did you buy?" and to start asking "Is your life good?"

It won't happen overnight, but it will happen eventually. Because if you can ask someone "Is your life good?" and count on the answer to mean something, then you'll be able to move to the real heart of the matter, the question haunting our moment on earth: *Is more better?*

In some sense, you could say that the years since World War II in America have been a loosely controlled experiment designed to answer this very question. The environmentalist Alan Durning found that in 1991 the average American family owned twice as many cars, drove two and a half times as far, used twenty-one times as much plastic, and traveled twenty-five times farther by air than did the average family in 1951.[7] Gross domestic product per capita has tripled since 1950.[8] We are, to use the very literal vernacular, living three times as large. Our homes are bigger: the size of new houses has doubled since 1970, even as the average number of people living in each one has shrunk. Despite all that extra space, they are stuffed to the rafters with belongings, enough so that an entire new industry—the storage locker—has sprung up and indeed has reached huge size itself. We have all sorts of other new delights and powers: we can communicate online, watch a hundred cable stations, find food from every corner of the world. Some people have clearly taken more than their share of all this new stuff, but still, on average, all of us in the West are living lives materially more abundant than most people did a genera-tion ago. As the conservative writer Dinesh D'Souza noted recently, we have cre-ated not just the first middle class but "the first mass affluent class in world history."[9]

What's odd is, none of this stuff appears to have made us happier. All that mate-rial progress—and all the billions of barrels of oil and millions of acres of trees that it took to create it—seems not to have moved the satisfaction meter an inch. In 1946, the United States was the happiest country among four advanced economies; thirty years later, it was eighth among eleven advanced countries; a decade after that it ranked tenth among twenty-three nations, many of them from the third world.[10] There have been steady *decreases* in the percentage of Americans who say that their marriages are happy, that they are satisfied with their jobs, that they find a great deal of pleasure in the place they live. Ever since World War II, the National Opinion Research Council has once a year polled Americans with the fundamental question: "Taken all together, how would you say things are these days—would you say that you are very happy, pretty happy, or not too happy?" (It must be somewhat unsettling to receive this phone call.) The proportion of respondents saying they were very happy peaked sometime in the 1950s and has slid slowly but steadily in the years since. Between 1970 and 1994, for instance, it dropped five full percentage points, dipping below the mark where one-third of Americans were able to count themselves as very happy. As Richard Layard points out, this trend is even more remarkable than it seems. "People must seek anchors or standards for such evaluations, and it is natural for them to compare their cur-rent situation with their situation in the recent past: if last year was bad, than an average current year would appear to be good. Such annual corrections would tend to wipe out any trend."[11] Yet there the trend is, as plain as can be and continuing to the present. In the winter of 2006, the National Opinion Research Center pub-lished data about "negative life events" covering the years 1991 to 2004, a period dominated by the rapid economic expansion of the Clinton boom. "The anticipa-tion would have been that problems would have been down," the study's author said. Instead the data showed a rise in problems—the percentage of respondents who reported breaking up with a steady partner doubled, for instance. As one reporter summarized the findings, "There's more misery in people's lives today."[12]

All in all, we have more stuff and less happiness.

The phenomenon isn't confined to the United States; as other nations have followed us into mass affluence, their experiences have begun to yield similar, though less dramatic, results. In the United Kingdom, for instance, per capita gross domestic product grew 66 percent between 1973 and 2001, yet people's satisfaction with their lives changed not at all.[13] Japan saw a fivefold increase in per capita income between 1958 and 1986 without any reported increase in satis-faction.[14] In one place after another, in fact, rates of alcoholism, suicide, and depression have gone up dramatically even as the amount of stuff also accumulated. The science writer Daniel Goleman noted in the *New York Times* that people born in the advanced countries after 1955 are three times as likely as their grandparents to have had a serious bout of depression.[15] Indeed, one report in 2000 found that the *average* American child reported now higher levels of anxiety than the average child under *psychiatric care* in the 1950s: our new normal is the old disturbed.[16] The British researcher Richard Douthwaite noted that between 1955 and 1988, the doubling of the UK's national income had coincided with increases in everything from crime to divorce.[17] That's not to say that getting richer caused these problems, only that it didn't alleviate them. All in all, we have more stuff and less happiness. *The experiment we've undertaken has yielded a significant, robust, and largely unexpected result.*

The reasons for the failure of stuff to make us happier are much less clear, and will be one of the chief subjects of this book. You could argue, for instance, that we've simply begun to run out of useful or fun new things—that despite vast numbers of patents, there's not much we can buy that really runs much chance of making us happier. Those who fly frequently (a good slice of the most affluent) will be familiar, for example, with the ubiquitous SkyMall catalogue, thoughtfully placed in the seatback pocket in front of you in order to tease your acquisitive impulse during long flights. The catalogue is a testimony to satiation: there's nothing in it a normal person would ever need, or even really want. For instance, should anyone who requires a "revolutionary new laser technology system" in order to figure out if they're parking in the right spot inside their own garage really be allowed behind the wheel in the first place? Compared with the other tasks of a driver—making right-hand turns, making left-hand turns, deciphering the red-amber-green code of a stoplight—safely positioning your auto within the confines of your own garage seems like a fairly straightforward task, the kind of thing that might not require a laser.

If satiation isn't what has cast a pall over our satisfaction, then perhaps the pall is the *effect* of all that economic buildup: if growth has filled the field behind your house with megamansions and you can't see the horizon anymore, maybe that loss cancels out the effect of the flat-screen TV. Or maybe the pall is cast by the fact that more of us have had to work more hours to afford all that new stuff. Or perhaps we're worried about keeping thieves from taking our stuff—or, more likely, wondering how we'll be able to hold on to it as an increasingly insecure old age looms. Most of all, perhaps the very act of acquiring so much stuff has turned us ever more into individuals and ever less into members of a community, isolating us in a way that runs contrary to our most basic instincts.

For the moment, however, the why is less important than the simple fact. We're richer, but we're not happier. We have more music, more education, more communication, and certainly more entertainment than any people who have ever lived—we can be entertained literally around the clock, and we can carry our entertainment with us wherever we go as long as we remember the Nano and the earbuds. But if satisfaction was our goal, then the unbelievable expenditures of effort and resources since 1950 to accomplish all this (and by most measures humans have used more raw materials since the end of World War II than in all of prior human history) have been largely a waste. "Estimates suggest," said one team of economists, "that 20 percent of the American population are flourishing and over 25 percent are languishing, with the rest somewhere in between."[18]

...the more we study the question, the less important affluence seems to be to human happiness.

In fact, the more we study the question, the less important affluence seems to be to human happiness. In one open-ended British questionnaire, people were asked about the factors that make up "quality of life." They named everything from "family and home life" to "equality and justice," and when the results were totted up, 71 percent of the answers were nonmaterialistic.[19] The best predictor of happiness was health, followed by factors like being married. Income seemed not to matter at all in France, Holland, or England, and it was only the seventh or eighth most important predictor in Italy, Ireland, and Denmark.[20] In one classic study of how various "domains" contributed to life satisfaction, "goods and services you can buy" came in twelfth among thirty areas, behind even "political attitudes" and swamped by "feelings about recreation and family."[21]

How is it, then, that we became so totally, and apparently wrongly, fixated on the idea that our main goal, as individuals and as nations, should be the accumulation of more wealth?

The answer is interesting for what it says about human nature. *Up to a certain point*, none of what I've just been saying holds true. *Up to a certain point*, more really does equal better.

Consider the life of a very poor person in a very poor society. Not, perhaps, a hunter-gatherer—it may not make much sense to think of hunter-gatherers as poor. But, say, a peasant farmer in China, trying to survive on too little land. (China has one-third of the world's farmers, but one-fifteenth of its arable land; in many places the average holding is less than a sixth of an acre, an area smaller than the footprint of the average new American home.) You lack very basic things, including any modicum of security for when your back finally gives out; your diet is unvaried and nutritionally lacking; you're almost always cold in the winter.

To compensate you for your struggles, it's true that you also likely have the benefits of a close and connected family, and a village environment where your place is clear. Your world makes sense. Still, in a world like that, a boost in income delivers tangible benefits. I remember one reporting trip when I visited a shower-curtain factory in rural China, staffed by people who had grown up on such farms. I wandered through the workrooms, watching kids—almost everyone was between eighteen and twenty-two, as if the factory was some kind of shower-curtain college

—smooth out long bolts of polyester on huge cutting-room tables, and sew hems and grommets, and fold them up in plastic bags, and pack them into cartons. It's hard to imagine a much simpler product than a shower curtain, basically, a big square of fabric with a row of holes along the top.

The workday here was eight hours; because of the summer heat everyone was working from seven-thirty to eleven-thirty in the morning and then again from three to seven in the afternoon. I'd been there a few minutes when all labor ceased and everyone poured down the stairs into the cafeteria for lunch. Rice, green beans, eggplant stew, some kind of stuffed dumpling, and a big bowl of soup: 1.7 yuan, or about 20 cents. While the workers ate, I wandered into the dormitory rooms. Each one had four sets of bunkbeds, one set of which stored suitcases and clothes. The other beds were for sleeping, six to a room. MP3 players sat on most pillows; in the girls' rooms, big stuffed animals graced most beds. There were posters of boy bands, and stacks of comic books, and lots of little bottles of cosmetics. One desk to share, one ceiling fan. Next to the dormitory, a lounge housed a big-screen TV and twenty or thirty battered chairs; the room next door had a Ping-Pong table.

Virtually all the workers came from Junan County in Shandong province, a few hundred kilometers to the south, where the factory owner had grown up. He let me select at random and interview as many workers as I liked. He was especially pleased with my first pick, Du Pei-Tang, who was twenty years old—a goofy grin, nervous, but with very bright and shining eyes. His father had died and his mother had remarried and moved away, so he'd grown up with his grandparents. His first job had been as a guard at an oil company in Shandong province, but it only paid a few hundred yuan a month and there was no food or dormitory. One of his relatives had introduced him to the shower-curtain factory owner, who had the reputation of being nice to his workers, so he'd come to work, earning about 1,000 yuan a month. From that, he'd been able to save 12,000 yuan in a little less than two years. And here's the thing you need to understand: 12,000 yuan—call it $1,200— is actually a pretty big sum of money, enough to be life changing. In a year or two more, he said, he'd have enough to build a small house back in his hometown and to get married. For fun, Du played table tennis and watched videos on the factory TV—which was good because, as the owner pointed out, buying a single Coke every night would come near to halving his savings. I asked him if he'd seen any movie that showed him a life he might aim for. He got very quiet, and said yes, he'd recently seen a film "about a young man successful in both business and family life. That's important to me because I grew up lacking the family atmosphere. I hope I would have that kind of life—not be that person, but have a good wife, a good family, a good business."

My next pick was Liu-Xia, eighteen years old, a lovely young woman nervous as hell about talking to a strange American who inexplicably and impertinently wanted to know about her life. "There are four people in my home—my parents, my elder brother, and me," she said. "My parents aren't healthy. They do farm work, but my father has a bad knee so my mother carries most of the load. I really wanted to help her. And my brother could go to college, but it is a very big cost. He is in the Shandong School of Science and Technology, studying mechanical engineering." In fact, it turned out, he had graduated the week before, thanks to her earnings at the curtain factory. Making small talk, I asked her if she had a stuffed animal on her bed like everyone else. Her eyes filled ominously. She liked them very much, she said, but she had to save all her earnings for her future.

It may well be that moving away to the factory for a few years will disrupt the lives of these young people in unforeseen ways and leave them rootless and unhappy; it may well be that the world can't afford the ecological implications of everyone in China making lots of plastic stuff, or lots of money. The only point I'm trying to make is that China's relentless economic growth—9 percent a year for the last couple of decades, the fastest in the history of the planet—was indeed lifting lots of people out of poverty and in the process making their lives somewhat happier.

And it wasn't, as it turns out, just my anecdotal impression. In general, researchers report that *money consistently buys happiness right up to about $10,000 per capita income, and that after that point the correlation disappears.*[22] That's a useful number to keep in the back of your head—it's like the freezing point of water, one of those random numbers that just happens to define a crucial phenomenon on our planet. "As poor countries like India, Mexico, the Philippines, Brazil, and South Korea have experienced economic growth, there is some evidence that their average happiness has risen," Richard Layard reports. But *past the $10,000 point*, there's a complete scattering: when the Irish were making a third as much as Americans they were reporting higher levels of satisfaction, as were the Swedes, the Danes, the Dutch.[23] Costa Ricans score higher than Japanese; French people are about as satisfied with their lives as Venezuelans.[24] In fact, past the point of basic needs being met, the "satisfaction" data scramble in mind-bending ways. A sampling of *Forbes* magazine's "richest Americans" has happiness scores identical with those of the Pennsylvania Amish and only a whisker above those of Swedes, not to mention Masai tribesmen. The "life satisfaction" of pavement dwellers—that is, homeless people—in Calcutta was among the lowest recorded, but it almost doubled when they moved into a slum, at which point they were basically as satisfied with their lives as a sample of college students drawn from forty-seven nations.[25] And so on.

On the list of important mistakes we've made as a species, this one seems pretty high up. A single-minded focus on increasing wealth has driven the planet's ecological systems to the brink of failure, without making us happier. How did we screw up?

The answer's pretty obvious: we kept doing something past the point where it worked. Since happiness had increased with income in the past, we assumed it would do so in the future. We make these kinds of mistakes regularly: two beers made me feel good, so ten beers will make me feel five times better. But this case was particularly extreme and easy to understand, because human beings have spent so much of their history trying to satisfy their basic needs. As the psychologists Ed Diener and Martin Seligman observe, "At the time of Adam Smith, a concern with economic issues was understandably primary. Meeting simple human needs for food, shelter and clothing was not assured, and satisfying these needs moved in lockstep with better economics."[26] Consider, say, America in 1820, two generations after Adam Smith. The average American earned, in current dollars, less than $1,500, which is somewhere near the current African average. As the economist Deirdre McCloskey explains, "Your great-great-great grandmother had one dress for church and one for the week, if she were not in rags. Her children did not attend school, and probably could not read. She and her husband worked eighty hours a week for a diet of bread and milk—they were four inches shorter than you."[27] Even in 1900, the average American lived in a house the size of today's typical garage.[28] Is it any wonder, then, that we built up a considerable velocity trying to escape the gravitational pull of that kind of poverty? Richard Layard calls it a "cultural lag": "Market democracies, by the logic of their own success, continue to emphasize the themes that have brought them to their current position."[29] An object in motion stays in motion; our economy—and the individual expectations that make it up— is a mighty object indeed.

You could call it, I think, the Laura Ingalls Wilder effect. I grew up reading her books—*Little House on the Prairie, Little House in the Big Woods*—and my daughter grew up listening to me read them to her, and I have no doubt she will read them to her children. They tell the ur-American story. A life rich in family, rich in con- nection to the natural world, rich in adventure—but materially deprived. That one dress, that same bland dinner. At Christmastime, a penny—a *penny*! And a stick of candy, and the awful deliberation about whether to stretch it out with tiny licks or devour it in an orgy of happy greed. A rag doll was the zenith of aspiration—it was like the Chinese girl I met at the shower-curtain factory who teared up when she thought about how nice it might be to own a stuffed animal. In that world, posses- sions still deliver. When I returned to the factory with the largest stuffed dog avail- able in that corner of northern China, the girl was as pleased as I've ever seen a person. Not only that, but the other kids living in the factory seemed enormously happy for her as well.

My daughter would have appreciated the same stuffed animal, but not with any- thing approaching the same intensity. Her bedroom boasts a density of Beanie Babies (made, doubtless, in some other Asian factory) that mimics the manic biodiversity of the deep rainforest. Another stuffed animal? Really? So what? Its marginal utility, as an economist might say, is low. And so with all of us. Which is why, for instance, our current approach to Christmas doesn't work very well. Pollsters find that at least two-thirds of Americans dread the onset of the holiday season, because it simply adds more stuff to our lives. A few years ago a group of us in the Methodist churches in my part of the Northeast started a campaign called Hundred Dollar Holidays to persuade people to celebrate the Nativity a little differently—with homemade gifts, gifts of service and time, and so forth. When we started it, we were thinking as pious environmentalists: we could rid the world of all those batteries! But the reason the campaign worked so well was because so many people were desperate for permission to celebrate Christmas in a new way that fit better what we actually need out of the holidays. We need time with family, we need silence for reflection, we need connection with nature—all the stuff that the Ingalls family had in abundance. We don't need candy; we have candy every day of our lives. We just haven't figured that out, because the momentum of the past is still with us: we still imagine we're in that Little House on the Big Prairie, when most of us inhabit the Oversized House on the Little Cul de Sac.

In the immortal words of Mr. Jagger and Mr. Richards, "I can't get no satisfaction." Bling won't do it anymore; that's why all those sterile mansions on *Cribs* look so amazingly empty. But we can't figure out where else to look. We've run out of ideas. When Americans in one survey were asked what single factor would most improve the quality of their lives, the most frequent answer was more money.[30] This isn't the fault of economists: economists built us a wonderful set of tools for getting More. And those tools work. We can steer our way around recessions, smooth out bumps in our upward climb. It's easy to understand why they, and the political leaders they advise, would be pleased to try and keep using those tools— pleased to keep us becoming ever more efficient, achieving ever greater economies of scale. But there's something profoundly unrealistic and sentimental about that approach, given what we've discovered about the limits on growth's ability to produce human happiness. As Richard Layard says in the conclusion to his book *Happiness*, "Utilitarianism is the guiding philosophy of our time, but theories of what produces happiness have changed since Bentham. Both utilitarian philosophers and their critics speak in the language of the past."

We need, in short, a new utilitarianism. When More and Better shared a branch, we could kill two birds with one stone. Since they've moved apart, we can't. We in the rich countries no longer inhabit a planet where straight-ahead Newtonian economics, useful as it has been, can help us. We need an Einsteinian economics, a more complicated and relativistic science that asks deeper questions...

1. Gordon Bigelow, "Let There Be Markets," *Harper's*, May 2005, 44.

2. Craig Lambert, "The Marketplace of Perceptions," *Harvard Magazine*, March-April 2006, 50.

3. Daniel Kahneman, Ed Diener, and Norbert Schwartz, *Well-being: The Foundation of Hedonic Psychology* (New York: Russell Sage Foundation, 1999).

4. Ibid, 5.

5. Richard Layard, *Happiness: Lessons from a New Science* (New York: Penguin, 2005), 10-11.

6. Robert Frank, *Luxury Fever* (New York: Princeton University Press, 2000), 70-71.

7. Eben Goodstein, *Economics and the Environment*, 3rd ed. (New York: Wiley, 2002), 202-3.

8. Alan Durning, *How Much is Enough?* (New York: W. W. Norton & Company, 1992), 1.

9. Dinesh D'Souza, *The Virtue of Prosperity: Finding Values in an Age of Techno-Affluence* (New York: FreePress, 2001), 16.

10. Layard, *Happiness*, 10.

11. Ibid., 22.

12. Sharon Jayson, "Unhappiness Quotient Rises in the Past Decade," Burlington Free Press (Vt.), 1.

13. New Economics Foundation, *Real World Economic Outlook 2003*, 135.

14. Frank, *Luxury Fever*, 73.

15. Layard, *Happiness*, 22.

16. Ed Diener and Martin Seligman, "Beyond Money: Toward an Economy of Well-Being," *Psychological Science in the Public Interest*, vol. 5. no. 1 (July 2004), 30.

17. Richard Douthwaite, *The Growth Illusion* (Totnes, Devon, UK: Green Books, 1999), 4-5.

18. New Economics Foundation, *Real World Economic Outlook 2003*, 5.

19. Douthwaite, *Growth Illusion*, 10.

20. Ibid., 13.

21. Layard, *Happiness*, 176-77.

22. Diener and Seligman, "Beyond Money," figure 2, 5.

23. Layard, *Happiness*, 33.

24. New Economics Foundation, *Real World Economic Outlook 2003*, 7.

25. Sharon Begley, "Wealth and Happiness Don't Necessarily Go Hand in Hand," *Wall Street Journal*, August 13, 2004.

26. Diener and Seligman, "Beyond Money," 2.

27. Deirdre McCloskey, "Capital Gains: How Economic Growth Benefits the World," *Christian Century*, May 4, 2004.

28. John McMillan, *Reinventing the Bazaar: A Natural History of Markets* (New York: W. W. Norton & Company, 2003), 212.

29. Layard, *Happiness*, 60.

30. Frank, *Luxury Fever*, 5.

The Ecological Economic Worldview and the Ecological Society

by Dr. Sallie McFague

Dr. Sallie McFague was Carpenter Professor of Theology at Van-derbilt Divinity School where she taught for thirty years. She then became Distinguished Theologian in Residence at the Vancouver School of Theology in British Columbia. One of the leading the-ologians working in the area of ecology and theology, her influen-tial books include *Models of God, The Body of God* and *Super, Natural Christians.*

The following piece is excerpted from Dr. McFague's *Life Abun-dant.* McFague focuses on two essential qualities of the circle of Earth's Economy: sustainability and distributive justice. Her com-ments not only flesh out that particular economic vision, but also ask whether or not that vision is "attainable." (Please note: Dr. McFague refers to "neo-classical economics," which is essentially comparable to my "Big Human Economy." Her "Great Economy" and "Ecological Society" are essentially my "Earth Economy.")

Who Are We? We Are Members of the Household

Whereas neo-classical economics begins with human desire, the desire to amass wealth, ecological economics begins with human need, the need for a productive and permanent dwelling in which to live. Ecological economics begins with *sus-tainability* as the preeminent and irreplaceable *sine qua non.* That we must maintain the health of the planet that gives us everything we need to live—from breathable air to food, clothing, shelter, as well as the means for all emotional, intellectual, and creative experience—seems too obvious to bear mentioning. It is, however, the big hole in neo-classical economics. Contemporary economics does not recog-nize the Great Economy, the household of planet Earth, as the overall reality within which all other functions—and economies—must fit. At most, it considers nature as "natural resources"—in terms of their availability and cost. The big pic-ture is lost; it is as if the human economy takes place in a vacuum, in isolation from any setting, any limits, any laws other than its own.[1] Hence, the difference of "who we are" in these two economic paradigms is striking: the one begins with individual human beings and their desire for material goods, while the other begins with human beings as a species, a very needy one, dependent on a complex but vulnerable living space. The first view says we are consumers of nature's wealth; the other view, that we are members of nature's household.

Assessing who we are in the scheme of things is one of the most important judgments we make, because from that judgment everything else follows. We have seen the implications of neo-classical economics' judgment; we now turn our attention to the significance of ecological economics' position. It means first of all that the design principle for economics changes from a line (of "progress") to a circle (of sustainability). We see ourselves now not as striving in a linear fashion toward a golden future of material comfort that each of us must reach on our own, but as living within a circle composed of networks of interrelationship and interdependence with all other beings, human and otherwise. These two pictures within which to imagine our lives—an upward line that we each must climb versus a closed circle within which we all must live—are not only fundamentally different understandings of human life, but they also *feel* different. Since a sense of who we are at this deep level is felt as much as (or more than) thought, it is important that we note how different these pictures are at this level. In the first, each of us feels alone to find our own way and rewards; in the other, we are forever with others for whom we are responsible and to whom we can turn for help.

That we must maintain the health of the planet that gives us everything we need to live...seems too obvious to bear mentioning. It is, however, the big hole in neo-classical economics.

This circular design principle means, then, that we focus on sustainability. What is *"sustainability"*? Some of the synonyms for "to sustain" are suggestive here: aid, bear, befriend, carry, comfort, continue, defend, feel, foster, help, keep alive, lend a hand, nurse, nurture, relieve, save, support. These are words we might use among family members, among those who live in the same household. Environmental economist S. Viederman gives us a rich, suggestive definition of sustainability.

> Sustainability is a community's control and prudent use of all forms of capital—nature's capital, human capital, human created capital, social capital, and cultural capital—to ensure, to the degree possible, that present and future generations can attain a high degree of economic security and achieve democracy while maintaining the integrity of the ecological systems upon which all life and production depends.[2]

There are several things to note here. First, sustainability is a social vision—it is "a community's control and prudent use of all forms of capital." In other words, the community makes the basic decisions concerning how to maintain the good of the community; economic decisions are for corporate good, not for individual benefit (or, to phrase it differently, the individual's benefit can only occur within corporate good). Prior to allocation of resources must come the community's conception of the good life, the overall goal for the whole. This is a political vision in the broadest sense: What is for the good of the polis, the cosmos? It is an envisionment of how we would *like to* live, given how we *can* live. Thus, the second and equally important implication of our definition is that *all* forms of capital must be considered in the notion of the good life and first in the list is "nature's capital." The good life is not, as neoclassical economics maintains, dependent only on human capital and its products, but more fundamentally on nature's capital.[3] Thus, physical limits combine with social vision to suggest the kind of good life we would like and can have. Whatever we may want and however clever our technology, human-made capital cannot substitute for nature's capital: what good is a fishing boat if there are no fish or a saw if there are no trees?[4] What is increasingly limited and precious is not human know-how, but the health of nature's basic resources and processes.

A third insight from our definition of sustainability is that while the physical base (nature's capital) is essential, it is not enough. Our definition of sustainability as the principle that grounds the good life includes *all* kinds of capital—whatever it takes to make the good life good for all. For human beings, this includes not only a decent basic standard of living and a democratic form of government, but also opportunities for cultural, technological, educational, social, and spiritual development. The good life is not limited to economic efficiency in the narrow sense of economic security, but includes as well social, emotional, and creative growth both for ourselves and for future generations. This comprehensive vision of the good life—one that is based on "maintaining the integrity of ecological systems upon which all life and production depends"—is cultural, sociopolitical, and inclusive of all human beings alive now and in the future.

Is this vision of the good life attainable? Is it merely a pleasant utopia, idealistic and naive in its assumptions of cooperation and responsibility? Perhaps—but all interpretations are: the neoclassical vision assumes that all individuals will be able, by their own efforts, to realize "the American dream."

If we are persuaded that we are isolated individuals with insatiable desires in a dog-eat-dog world, we are likely to act that way. If we become convinced and begin to feel that we are, willy-nilly, all in this together... where cooperation and responsibility are not just nice but necessary traits, we might also begin to act within these terms.

What is seldom factored into this interpretation are issues of class and privilege or race and gender. Visions are seldom entirely realistic or attainable, but they *do* matter: we become, in part, who we think we are. If we are persuaded that we are isolated individuals with insatiable desires in a dog-eat-dog world, we are likely to act that way. If we become convinced and begin to feel that we are, willy-nilly, all in this together, marooned on a finite planet with

limited resources, where cooperation and responsibility are not just nice but necessary traits, we might also begin to act within these terms. We can only act individually and concretely—no one can change the world—but how we act individually
and concretely rests to a large degree on our deepest feelings about who we are.
One of the purposes of this book is to persuade readers that the ecological image of
the good life is both "good" and "good for you." The first critical dimension of that
image is *sustainability*: a vision of the good life that sees our good as within the good
of the planet, now and always.

Therefore, embracing sustainability rests on a kind of self-interest. Just as the
neo-classical economic worldview depends on a kind of self-interest—consumer
aggrandizement—so does the ecological economic worldview. In fact, it recognizes
both long-term and short-term self-interest. The good life certainly depends on the
indefinite viability of the planet, but it also claims that its vision of satisfactory living is more desirable than consumerism.

But sustainability is only possible if there is also distributive justice. This follows
logically; for the planet and its various life-forms to continue indefinitely in a
healthy state, all must have access to the earth's resources upon which survival—
and flourishing—depend. Thus, the second critical economic component we must
deal with is distributive justice.

Distributive justice is a contentious issue between neo-classical and ecological
economics. Conventional economics believes that the distribution of material
goods will "trickle down" from the jobs created by entrepreneurs to the workers
who will eventually benefit. "Distribution" is covered by the "invisible hand" of
market capitalism, which guarantees that everyone will profit, though to different
degrees. The two fallbacks for any inadequacies in the system are taxes and philanthropy. Ecological economics takes a different view on distributive justice. Because
sustainability is its goal, it sees the sharing of material goods (nature's resources) as
a necessity; it is the principal means *to* sustainability. To have a sustainable economy, there must be limits to inequality in terms of minimum and maximum
incomes and also in terms of how much of nature's wealth we use now versus hold
available for future generations.[5] In other words, since both poverty and excessive
wealth destroy nature (for example, the poor denuding their environment for cooking fuel and the rich polluting the air with greenhouse gases), a median lifestyle for
all human beings is desirable. While one billion of us live too high on the energy
scale, another billion live too low; we all need to move toward the middle. But
that is not happening; in fact, the opposite is true. The income gap between the
richest fifth of the world's people and poorest fifth, measured by average national
income per head, increased from 30 to 1 in 1960 to 74 to 1 in 1997.[6] Or, another
telling statistic is that the world's richest 200 people more than doubled their net
worth between 1994 and 1998 to one trillion dollars.[7]

Distributive justice does not mean that all (or even most) people would have
the same income; a scale is necessary to recognize the *individual*-in-community. An

extreme communist anthropology would insist on absolute parity in material goods, while an extreme individualistic anthropology—as we increasingly have in the global market economy—resists all forms of limits to inequality.[8] An ecological anthropology opposes these extremes, believing that the best way for individuals and the community to thrive—or, to put it more accurately, the best way for the community that is composed of billions of individuals of all species to thrive—is to assure that all have the basics to survive and flourish. Sustainability is not possible if people devastate nature either through excessive wealth or excessive poverty. Nor is the good life possible if some have too much and others too little (remember Goldilocks!).As we have seen, the good life is not necessarily the high consumer life; in fact, happiness does not seem to correlate with excessive consumerism.

But *can* "all have the basics to survive and flourish"? Of course all life-forms cannot. However questionable the truth of the Darwinian phrase "the survival of the fittest," it is painfully evident that in the natural world, most individuals do not survive and those that do experience vast differences in justice. However, until our numbers and lifestyle became the dominant force, nature was in a more or less sustainable condition. Can all of *us* survive and flourish? Certainly not at the level of consumption we desire nor at the level of our projected population. So, what does it mean to have a goal of distributive justice in which "all have the basics to survive and flourish"?

From a theological perspective, it means a picture of reality that we believe is desirable and right. It is not an "economic plan" that can be attained, any more than the fulfillment of the insatiable desires of all individuals can be. Both are images of *how things should be*; both are goals toward which societies and persons can work; both are ways of criticizing our present and envisioning a different future. To be sure, economists who embrace one or the other picture have devised strategies and suggested laws that will help us reach these goals, but the more basic issue for all of us is the question, "Which one do we *want*"?[9] Which vision of life on our planet are we willing to work *toward*, realizing that it will never be reached but that approximations are possible?

To sum up: who are we? As members of the household called Earth, we are relational beings, defined by our needs that make us dependent on others and by our joys that make us desire one another. We are not just self-interested individuals; in fact, according to the ecological economic picture of reality, we are basically and primarily communal beings who become unique individuals through help from and response to others.[10] Each baby, if fortunate, is born into communities of love and guidance that not only are necessary for her to become a human being but also the particular human being she becomes. Each of us, if fortunate, takes from nature not only our food, clothing, shelter, and other physical gifts too numerous to mention, but also the very words we use to describe our emotional and spiritual lives: the lion as an image of courage; the phoenix as a glimmer of hope; an ancient tree as the model of perseverance; the sea as a symbol of eternity. We would not even know that we are individuals if it were not for the similarities and differences we see with all other life both human and non-human, in which we are immersed. If, then, we are *beings-in-community* at every level—physical, mental, emotional—how can my good not be related to your good or your diminishment not diminish me? Can I flourish alone? Will I not suffer if you do?

> Communal relations are mutual relations in which the norm is not that one loses when another gains, but that each loses in the other's losses and gains in the other's gains…. The proper service of community in this case is not sacrificing one's life but enriching the community through means that enrich oneself as well.[11]

The implications are clear: our joy and sorrow, our gain and loss, our "for better or worse," are tied to our need and our responsibility for one another….

1. Stephen C. Hackett puts the matter succinctly: "Private property regimes and market systems of allocation rest on an ethical foundation of individualism, which states that all values, rights, and duties originate with individuals and not in society as a whole. In contrast, the sustainability ethic holds the interdependent health and well-being of human communities and earth's ecology over time as the basis of value" (*Environmental and Natural Resources Economics*, 209).

2. S. Viederman, "Sustainability's Five Capitals and Three Pillars," in Dennis C. Pirages, Ed., *Building Sustainable Societies: A Blueprint for a Post-Industrial World* (Armonk, N.Y.: M. E. Sharpe, 1996), 46.

3. Robert Costanza insists that a critical element of ecological economics' view of the good society begins with "the vision of the earth as a thermodynamically closed and nonmaterially growing system, with the human economy as a subsystem of the global ecosystem. This implies that there are limits to biophysical throughput of resources from the ecosystem, through the economic subsystem and back to the system as wastes…" (*An Introduction to Ecological Economics*, 79).

4. As Herman Daly notes, "Economic logic remains the same—economize on the limiting factor," but now the limiting factor is natural, not human-made, capital (*Beyond Growth: The Economics of Sustainable Development* [Boston: Beacon, 1996] 8).

5. Ibid., chap. 14.

6. United Nations, *Human Development Report 1999*, as quoted in the *Vancouver Sun* (July 12, 1999), sec. A, 6.

7. Ibid.

8. Economists vary on their estimates of what limited inequality must be for sustainability, but the figure of a ten to twenty times differential is common. For instance, the CEO of a company would be paid ten to twenty times more than the lowest-paid worker; thus, if the worker received $25,000 a year, the CEO would have a salary between $250,000 and $500,000 (certainly a handsome income). At the present time the differential in most large companies is several times that figure, often (counting stock options and other benefits) in the multi-millions.

9. For suggestions on specific strategies, laws, alternative taxes, subsidies, etc. to encourage the goals of sustainability and distributive justice, see Costanza, *An Introduction to Ecological Economics*; Daly and Cobb, *For the Common Good*; Daly, *Beyond Growth*; and Hackett, *Environmental and Natural Resources Economics*.

10. "Libertarian economists look at *Homo economicus* as a self-contained individual who is infinitely mobile and equally at home anywhere. But real people live in communities, and in communities of communities. Their very individual identities are constituted by their relations in community" (Daly, *Beyond Growth*, 163).

11. Daly and Cobb, *For the Common Good*, 188.

Corporations Are People Too?

But corporations aren't like us. Because their powers
are determined by laws, not by nature, it is possible to
engineer them with all sorts of qualities.... In theory,
that programming can go either way: society can
make corporations stronger by removing restraints
and adding new legal powers, or it can make them
weaker by doing the reverse. The key lesson is
this: corporations are only as powerful as they
are legally designed to be.

—*Ted Nace*

Did you ever expect the corporation to
have a conscience, when it has no soul to
be damned, and no body to be kicked?

—*Baron Thurlow*

Introduction—V

The previous section's readings raised questions about connections between happiness and economic growth, and pointed out several significant problems with the engine of that economic growth, what I referred to as the "Big Human Economy (BHE)." The entity perhaps benefiting most from the BHE's structure is the large, limited liability corporation.

Corporations, and their CEOs, are too easy a target for those disgusted with the world's vast inequities in wealth and power, and with increasing ecological degradation. In corporations, just as in any other institutional structure—whether a church, a local non-profit, or government—some are committed to the common good, while others are committed to personal gain and consolidation of power.

But let's begin with two key assumptions: that all of God's creation is "very good" and that Jesus' life and teaching continually challenge economic inequity and injustice—which led Catholic Social Teaching to emphasize the "preferential option for the poor." If we then consider any historical period and ask whether or not a certain institution honors and values creation and engenders greater equity, we would discover powerful institutions that do not. In many historical periods, of course, branches of the Church itself would not be exempt from such critique.

Today, however, it is fair to focus a great deal of attention on corporations, particularly large multinationals, as those entities responsible for a great deal of ecological damage and concentration of wealth. But corporations owe their very existence to humankind. We created them; they have become what they are as a result of a series of human decisions and choices. It follows, then, that we can change our minds and make new choices about how corporations operate.

The corporation reflects what our society values: money, wealth, prestige, economic growth. The corporation could reflect a profoundly different set of values, say, as emphasized here, greater equity and the goodness and intrinsic value of all creation. Provide a new set of operating values, implement laws reflecting those values, and a new set of results will follow.

Ideally, *Money and Faith* would allow for more discussion of corporations (and related issues of free trade and globalization). So this section is really a primer. But it is an important section in a book that advocates for an economy that embodies compassion, honors the sacredness of creation and bears particular concern for the preferential option for the poor.

This section begins with my short essay highlighting corporations' legal status as persons. William Greider describes further characteristics of corporate structure. Following Greider, Ted Nace relates an empowering story of real people—specifically, North Dakota farmers—confronting a "corporate person."

Corporate Personhood

by Michael Schut

Corporations Are People Too!

When I first learned corporations were considered persons under the law, I was astounded.

This book does not have space to focus on this issue, but a fascinating book by Thom Hartmann does. Called *Unequal Protection*, Hartmann details how corporations gained the legal status of persons in an 1886 Supreme Court case titled *Santa Clara County v. Southern Pacific Railroad Company*. Although the case was a simple tax case, "having nothing to do with due process or human rights or corporate personhood, the attorneys for the railroad nonetheless used much of their argument time to press the issue that the railroad was a person and should be entitled to human rights under the Fourteenth Amendment."[1]

The Fourteenth Amendment was ratified in 1868, granting citizenship to "all persons born or naturalized in the United States." The amendment, originally adopted to protect emancipated slaves, forbade states from denying any person "life, liberty or property, without due process of law." It has much more commonly been used by corporations seeking the rights of natural persons as the following 1938 quote by Justice Hugo Black makes clear: "Of the cases in this court in which the Fourteenth Amendment was applied during its first fifty years after its adoption, less than one half of one percent invoked it in protection of the Negro race, and more than fifty percent asked that its benefits be extended to corporations."[2]

Particularly confounding about the Santa Clara case, according to Hartmann, is that the Supreme Court actually did *not* formally decide that corporations were persons in the Santa Clara case; the language in question is actually found in the case's "Headnotes" which are not legally binding. In addition, Hartmann cites two Supreme Court Justices since then, Black and Douglas, agreeing that the Fourteenth Amendment did not mean to protect corporations legally as persons.[3]

This (apparent) ruling has had profound, worldwide consequences. As "persons" under the law, corporations have benefited from the protections in the Bill of Rights. Corporate free speech is protected (First Amendment), allowing them to spend whatever they wish on lobbyists. Entitled to "privacy and freedom from unreasonable searches" (Fourth Amendment), corporations "do not have to submit to random inspections." Which raises a question: how are meaningful health, environmental and safety regulations enforced without random inspections?

Hartmann's book provides many more examples and includes chapters on unequal regulation, unequal taxes, unequal access to creation's resources, unequal media and influence, and so on. All emanate from corporate personhood. All end up favoring the corporate person over actual persons. This is not surprising, considering that a corporate person has certain advantages over most actual persons:

- corporations can operate/exist in more than one place at a time;
- many corporations have millions, some billions, at their disposal;
- a corporation need not heed the guidance (and potential limitations) of a soul or a conscience;
- corporations are potentially immortal.

Revoking a corporation's right (whether or not that "right" was actually ever lawfully granted) to enjoy the protections afforded to real people is surely one of the more important structural changes *actual persons* need to take on! If, that is, we adopt the two key assumptions highlighted in this section's introduction: that all of God's creation is "very good" and "the preferential option for the poor."

1. Thomas Hartmann, *Unequal Protection: The Rise of Corporate Dominance and the Theft of Human Rights* (New York: Rodale Press, 2002), 97.

2. Ibid., 157.

3. Ibid., 105 and 107.

Command and Control

by William Greider

William Greider, a prominent political journalist and author, has been a reporter for more than 40 years. For 17 years Greider was the National Affairs Editor at *Rolling Stone* magazine. He is also a former assistant managing editor at the *Washington Post*, where he worked for fifteen years as a national correspondent, editor and columnist. He is the author of the national bestsellers *One World, Ready or Not*; *Secrets of the Temple* and *Who Will Tell the People*. Greider has also served as a correspondent for six *Frontline* documentaries on PBS, including "Return to Beirut," which won an Emmy in 1985.

One of the most powerful entities in our economy today is the corporation. In order to understand the way our economy works, we need to better understand how corporations consolidated so much power within themselves. The following essay is particularly helpful in that it reveals that the present-day corporate structure came about through a series of political decisions. Therefore, a series of political decisions could just as well shift corporate structure in an entirely new direction.

Greider's essay empowers us to see that the corporation of today need not be the corporation of tomorrow. He specifically addresses the following characteristics (among others) of corporate structure: corporate personhood, limited liability, majority shareholder rule and concentration of wealth. He concludes with modest suggestions for reform.

...the corporation originated in early American history as a government-authorized exception to the everyday routines of commerce. Following the English model, the first American corporations existed only if specially chartered by government (instead of the king). They were given explicit privileges and public obligations because these private organizations were able to undertake large projects, like building canals or railroads, that promised great public benefit (George Washington was among the early incorporators; he was chartered to build the C & O Canal westward from the nation's capital). A well-financed collaborative could organize and sustain large tasks and complex business activities beyond the capacity and scattered resources of small independent businesses. Popular resistance to the corporation was fierce throughout the nineteenth century because merchants, mechanics and farmers well understood the greater implications of giving competitive advantages to these large growing business organizations. Nevertheless, by the end of the century the corporation was the preferred form, proliferating because it was so effective and achieving national scope with the rise of the transcontinental railroads.[1]

State-issued charters are still required to incorporate (the reason these private organizations are called "public" corporations), but the obligations to fulfill specified public objectives have disappeared. In the 1890s, states were eager for development and began competing to attract new companies by steadily weakening the requirements in corporate charters—a "race to the bottom" that ended in Delaware which set the least demanding rules for incorporation. This virtually erased any meaningful public demands on corporate purpose. Open chartering was, in a real sense, democratizing because incorporation was thereby liberated from political influence and the usual favoritism toward powerful elites. Anyone can incorporate a new business for any purpose they imagine, no questions asked. But the relaxed terms also enabled corporations to claim open-ended power for themselves. They became unchecked and undefined institutions unless people somehow mobilized enough political muscle to stop them.

Society, in other words, was put permanently on defense, playing catch-up with new and unanticipated corporate developments, always responding after the fact.

The weakness of the public's position is especially relevant to the ecological crisis. Because citizens are unable to define reliable limits on the corporation's purposes and performance in advance, people must passively experience the environmental consequences of exotic new industrial substances or production techniques until the harm becomes visible around them. Then citizens must gather elaborate scientific proof and persuade politicians to take their complaint seriously, while the corporation typically scoffs, denies anything is amiss, and mobilizes its own political resources to block any corrective action. Eventually, if the evidence becomes overwhelming, the company may agree to stop dispensing the dangerous materials into air, land, and water (though some determined companies, like General Electric, may fight clean-up obligations for a generation or longer).

Biotechnology is only the latest example of these mass-market experiments with nature and human well-being. Genetically altered seed, foodstuffs, and animals may be harmless to the future. The Companies say so and persuade government regulators to assent, but the truth is, no one actually knows. And history suggests that corporate assurances of harmlessness are quite unreliable, from lead additives in gasoline to DDT, from carcinogenic food dyes to PCBs. We will find out the truth about biotechnology some years hence when, if there are destructive consequences, the damage already will be widely present in our lives, routinized in commerce and nature.

To ecologists, this approach is dangerously irresponsible, as well as grossly wasteful, since cleaning up environmental mistakes is always far more expensive than preventing them. Public health and environmental leaders advocate a disciplinary concept known as "the precautionary principle" that would require a heavy burden of proof *before* such experiments are commercialized. If that obligation were written into every corporate charter or state laws governing corporate behavior, it would no doubt slow down the process of introducing new products and production practices that seem to promise cost savings or higher quality. But it would assign the unmeasured risks to the proper party—the people who expect to profit—rather than the unwitting public. Managers and investors would be on notice that they are responsible.

> Unlike real people, a corporation may exist in many places at once. Or it can reconfigure its body parts and re-create itself in an entirely new form. Unlike real people, a corporation can live forever.

The formation of corporate power also was advanced decisively by the Supreme Court during the late nineteenth and early twentieth centuries (the same conservative court that upheld the South's legally sanctioned racial segregation in its notorious *Plessy v. Ferguson* decision). In 1886, the Supreme Court held, with no public argument and little explanation, that the corporation shall henceforth be treated as a "person" for purposes of law, and be entitled to the same constitutional protections previously accorded only to the citizens who are human beings.

In particular, corporations could invoke the Fourteenth Amendment's right to "due process," which was adopted after the Civil War to protect the newly emancipated slaves. Personhood was legal fiction, obviously, but it became a most powerful tool for corporate lawyers fending off the demands of citizens and governments.

Over the next fifty years, the Supreme Court made numerous decisions involving Fourteenth Amendment rights, and half of these were devoted to protecting corporations, with less than 1 percent to the rights of African-Americans. The corporate power relationship with citizens was thus shifted to a startling level of inequality, since the corporate organization already has inherent advantages over individuals. Unlike real people, a corporation may exist in many places at once. Or it can reconfigure its body parts and re-create itself in an entirely new form. Unlike real people, a corporation can live forever.[2]

The ascendant corporations, eager to expand in scope and scale, also moved to seize power (and property rights) from their putative owners—the shareholders. Shareholders were a major obstacle to reorganizing the American industrial base, the grand project of acquiring scores of competing firms and amassing them in giant holding companies (conglomerates, we would call them now). Common law at that time still treated each shareholder like a true partner in the firm, and thus unanimous approval was required from the shareholders before a corporation could acquire another company or sell its own assets entirely or make other major structural changes. Led by New York in 1890, states began enacting a remedy for ambitious empire builders: Henceforth, a company could execute its mergers and acquisitions with only majority approval from the shareholders. This change effectively alienated shareholders from their property and secured control of the firm for the insiders, including the largest stakeholders.

This alteration also ignited the first great wave of consolidations and takeovers that led to the gargantuan scale of the largest corporate organizations. That was the objective. The early industrial titans—Carnegie, Mellon, Rockefeller, Du Pont—understood the competitive advantage of utterly dominating a sector. One very large producer could ride out the downturns, while the smaller companies ate the losses. Two or three of these giants together astride a market sector could conspire to set prices and drive competitors into ruin or bleed the customers who had nowhere else to turn. These monopolistic alliances were known then as "trusts" and blanketed everything from trolley cars and cigarettes to oil and steel.

During the recent boom and breakdown we witnessed yet another explosive wave of mergers and buyouts, topping out at $1.4 trillion in acquisition deals during 2000. It was the fifth or sixth such frenzy during the last century (depending on how one counts them). These episodes of consolidation typically are followed by periods of break up and dissolution in which the swollen companies sell off or close down elements of production they have just acquired (the conglomerates may themselves be attacked by financial raiders questioning the rationality of their size and scope). It is as though America has decided that proper corporate structure and scale can best be determined by periodic tournaments of gladiatorial combat.

This time around, the failed conglomerations included dozens of red-hot technology firms, led by WorldCom, that expanded revenue and profit almost entirely by acquisitions, with no real strategy for how to manage all the disparate parts profitably. They flamed out when stock prices collapsed, and many have disappeared. Perhaps the most spectacular failure was the merger of AOL Time Warner, supposedly undertaken on the basis of "synergies" but actually envisioned as a forbidding media empire that would stand astride everything from television and publishing to the Internet. It did not work so well for shareholders, who lost $170 billion in market value, or for the new megacompany itself that was compelled to take an initial write-down of $50 billion, with more to come. Meanwhile, authorities investigated AOL for allegedly cooking its revenue numbers.

More significantly, the modern era of consolidation has created a new galaxy of oligopolies dominating a dozen or more sectors in which a few companies own most of the marketplace and can intimidate or crush minor competition (all of these new formations passed legal muster with the federal government). Three companies own two-thirds of cable television. Five companies control 71 percent of wireless phones. Three mammoth companies, along with two smaller ones, own defense manufacturing. Eight "Baby Bell" telephone companies turned into four. Airlines, semiconductor memory chips, pharmaceuticals, college textbooks, food production, and food retailing—the concentration in these and other sectors seems an ironic outcome for an era that celebrated deregulation and set out to reinvigorate "free market" competition. But this too is an old story. Interludes of intense competition always are followed by the high stakes rush to reconcentrate market power among a few. Corporations, like human beings, seek stability in their lives and use their predatory size to secure it.[3]

The antitrust laws that originated during the "robber baron" era to contain the overbearing size of industrial giants have been largely neutered. They were never altogether effective, but the social meaning of the legal doctrine has been whittled away steadily (most audaciously during the Reagan era) so that the deep-rooted American skepticism toward bigness and its impact on democratic society has been virtually lost in the law. A restoration and reformulation of the theory and doctrine is urgently needed and might start by changing its name, from the archaic "antitrust" to something fresh and optimistic, like "social trust" policy.

David Morris, the advocate for small, local, innovative enterprises, sees "the deck always stacked against them." The first step, Morris suggests, is to restore the legal presumption that bigger and bigger is always suspect, inherently not better for a free society, and not even for advancing capitalism: "If we just recognized [that] the central principle antitrust embodies is that the burden of proof has to be on those who want to get bigger, there are very few, if any, of these deals that we would approve."

In the early 1900s, as the broad ranks of shareholders were separated from corporate control, the insiders were rewarded with greater rights to be irresponsible through introduction of the "limited liability" corporation. The new doctrine was adopted state by state over stiff resistance in state legislatures. It meant that if the company went bankrupt investors would lose the value of their shares, but no more. Thus, their personal wealth was insulated from any further liabilities stemming from the company they had owned. That may sound logical and necessary to modern sensibilities—a way to encourage entrepreneurial explorers—but it has had the effect of authorizing recklessness. The reform was undertaken, not in behalf of the small shareholders, but for the major investors and other insiders. They could walk away from their failures and start again elsewhere while bankruptcy courts picked over the corporate carcasses they had left behind.

"Limited liability basically shifts the risk of enterprise from the owners to the creditors, including construction companies, suppliers, lenders, and laborers," William G. Roy wrote in his social history of the large industrial corporation. The full costs of failure (whether from stupidity or fraud) are thus "socialized," as Roy put it. That is, the costs are spread across many other parties in society—including wrecked communities—while the architects of the disaster are excused.

...the corporation functions as a principal source of American inequality, concentrating both power and wealth at the top.... The production of inequality is not inherent to the corporate institution itself, but it cannot be altered unless corporations are reorganized internally.

Doubtless, this doctrine does encourage a more adventurous capitalism, but it also assigns the losses to people and interests who typically have already been victimized by the failure. We can observe the injustices of "limited liability" in the laborious legal cleanups following the debacles of Enron, WorldCom, Global Crossing, and many other bankruptees. The insiders held onto their mansions and personal fortunes. The losers—creditors, suppliers, shareholders, employees—fought over the scraps, with their claims stacked in descending order of priority—bankers first, employees last. In bankruptcy court, employees always come in last. Indeed, they may have no standing at all unless they can prove fraud or they have an enforceable union contract.

The concept of "limited liability" has also slyly damaged American culture by diluting the ideal of personal responsibility for one's actions. My own family history includes the cautionary tale of a learned great-uncle, Cicero McClure, a farmer in western Pennsylvania who died well before I was born. Uncle Cicero was a director and investor in a small community bank that failed during the great banking panic of 1907. For long years afterward he worked nights as a watchman at an electric power substation in order to repay depositors who had lost their money. They were friends and neighbors. He felt the obligation, whether or not the law required it. I do not recommend such extreme sacrifice for failed investors—it would be unthinkable today—but his story does suggest how much our system of personal values has been degraded by the conventions of modern capitalism.

These various legal premises established long ago all undergird the command-and-control authority of the corporate insiders, especially over the workforce. I use "command and control" ironically because it is the ideological catchphrase always invoked against state-centered socialism or, for that matter, against federal regulatory laws. In the U.S. legal structure, however, it is not the state alone but the corporation where command-and-control is located. This includes intimate powers to tell workers what to do and what not to say. While obviously convenient for managers at the top, their concentrated power distributes many unseen costs throughout the society.

Inherent to this command structure, the corporation functions as a principal source of American inequality, concentrating both power and wealth at the top. It does this by aggregating the surplus value produced from what employees contribute to the firm through their labor and knowledge, then redistributes that value upward and outward to others. Naturally, the insiders do not grant employees a voice in this distribution if they can avoid it. The steep pyramid in incomes—CEOs making more than 500 times what their company's workaday employees earn—would be inconceivable if control of how the surplus returns are distributed was not so closely held. The production of inequality is not inherent to the corporate institution itself, but it cannot be altered unless corporations are reorganized internally.

"The accumulation of wealth and power through large organizations is the modern device for generating inequality," sociologist Charles Perrow explained in *Organizing America*, his study of corporate capitalism. "The bigger the organization, the bigger the surplus is likely to be.... It is likely that the larger the organization, the greater the multiple of earnings of top officials over the lowest rank, further centralizing wealth. If an organization buys up other firms, the profits from those employees go to the top. In addition, the larger the firm, the more market power it will have, further increasing profits, and the more political power it is likely to have because of its control of resources (jobs, capital, plants, and equipment, etc.) that are vital to governments."

This fundamental relationship between inequality and the corporation is so thoroughly obscured by business lore and economic mythology that even very sophisticated citizens may not grasp the connection. At a town meeting with management, some five hundred Dow Jones employees, including reporters for *The Wall Street Journal*, complained bitterly about the company's harsh cutbacks in 2002, when scores of senior journalists were fired while senior management and shareholders "didn't suffer any pain," as one employee put it. Dow Jones Chairman Peter Kann was taken aback by the openness of their anger. "It's not an egalitarian place," Kann explained. "No corporation is." Why not? Kann seemed visibly flustered by the question. "That's one of the dangers you face living in a capitalist society," he replied. The employees thought in hard times the sacrifice should be shared by all. Their boss was simply explaining the fundamentals of corporate organization.

When this power alignment first unfolded in history, people did rebel—furiously. From the outset of the modern corporation, working people organized collectively in unions to fight for better wages, control of the workplace, and safe, secure working conditions. Social reformers, likewise, campaigned for standards of decency, respect for human life. Politicians from both parties repeatedly legislated new public rules and requirements to constrain corporate behavior. Mostly forgotten now, these social struggles against corporate power represented the largest mobilization of citizens across fifty years of history, from the Populists in the 1890s to New Deal reformers during the Great Depression.

Early on, however, as the reform efforts were gaining political momentum, the Supreme Court threw a huge log across their path. The property rights of business, the court declared, protected companies from government economic and social regulation. In 1905, the court's *Lochner* decision invoked this logic to invalidate a pioneering labor law enacted by New York state to require a ten-hour workday and safer working conditions in bakeries. The statute was unconstitutional, the justices explained, because it intruded without the "due process" of law guaranteed by the fourteenth amendment—on business's right to produce profit from its private property. Property over people. The concept generated great outrage, but the court stood its ground. For the next three decades it used the *Lochner* doctrine to block virtually any new social and economic reforms. More than two hundred state and federal laws were invalidated: minimum-wage standards, health and safety codes, workers' right to organize, and many others.

The judicial stranglehold on public action was not broken until deep into the New Deal, when a liberal majority finally was established on the Supreme Court in 1937. The court promptly upheld the new National Labor Relations Act and declared the government has broad powers to protect society's general health and welfare by regulating business activity. That moment opened the modern era of government and its expansive use of regulatory powers, including for environmental protection. Many great accomplishments endure, and corporate behavior and accountability were improved significantly. Yet many reforms also have been effectively gutted, as regulators were captured by counterattacking corporations or regulatory standards fell victim to political reinterpretation, their meaning held hostage to the next election.

...Modern government, meanwhile, continues to elaborate new legal privileges for corporate "personhood," and in some exotic ways that were revealed in the wake of the Enron scandal. A corporation, the public discovered, may turn itself into a citizen of Bermuda for purposes of avoiding U.S. taxes without losing any of the benefits and protections of being American. A corporation may split off elements of itself into "special purpose entities," and these off-balance-sheet partnerships permit a kind of dematerialized accounting. Bank loans become "revenue" on the company's books. Its debts mysteriously turn into "assets." The illegitimacy of these legal deceptions is made obvious when one asks: What if families tried to arrange their financial affairs or tax returns in this manner? They likely would be prosecuted. Congress could clear away all of these corporate tricks by imposing one simple requirement: Companies must report the same set of numbers (revenue, profit, and loss) to the tax collector as they report to their shareholders. It is hard to imagine Congress undertaking such a revolutionary step.

In all these ways the corporation became a uniquely powerful institution and proceeded to use these advantages to become still more powerful. Richard Grossman, codirector of the Program on Corporations, Law and Democracy, a citizens group campaigning for deep reforms, offered a provocative metaphor to summarize the story: "People create what looks to be a nifty machine, a robot, called the corporation. Over time the robots get together and overpower the people. They redesign themselves and reconstruct law and culture so that people fail to remember they created the robots in the first place, that the robots are machines and not alive. For a century, the robots propagandize and indoctrinate each generation of people so they grow up believing that robots are people too."[4]

A handful of Midwestern and Western farm states prohibit corporations from owning farmland in agricultural production in order to block the concentration of farm ownership or to discourage notorious practices like the hog factories.

The basic question of reform is: Can the corporation be refashioned into a more responsive, less powerful institution without destroying the qualities that make it effective as a business organization? Obviously, altering any of the historic legal premises—moving the boundary markers in society's favor—will be most difficult, but perhaps not as hopeless as generally assumed. Governments do still possess the capacity to redefine the chartering terms for incorporation or to modify other legal protections. The difficulty is finding a state legislature with the will to do so. But some states have acted in limited ways when they saw sufficient cause. A handful of Midwestern and Western farm states prohibit corporations from owning farmland in agricultural production in order to block the concentration of farm ownership or to discourage notorious practices like the hog factories. During the takeover frenzy of the 1980s a larger number of states enacted anti-takeover provisions that enabled boards of directors to stymie the corporate raiders, thus protecting local companies and jobs from the destructive grasp of the conglomerates.

A reform idea with superficial appeal is the wholesale rechartering of corporations by the federal government, proposed by Ralph Nader a generation ago and first championed by some progressive reformers early in the last century. That sounds like a swift, straightforward solution, but aside from the political implausibility, it skips over some hard questions without answering them: To what end will the corporation be redefined? And who will control the new terms? A mammoth federal regulatory agency, the courts, popular plebiscites? Blanket rechartering, in other words, could encounter the same vulnerabilities that undermine the regulatory system. Without first establishing the functional principles in bedrock—what society wants and needs from corporations—the vision is easy prey to the same political manipulations. It seems the wrong place to start.

A more practical approach would begin, less grandiosely, by thinking about the real-world distinctions that already exist in the corporate realm and exploring how these distinctions might be used as leverage points for altering the underlying legal premises. In other words, there are concrete differences in corporate behavior—good, bad, and terrible—that could become the basis for modifying corporate legal privileges, not in search of utopian perfection, but in order to reward what is better and penalize what's worse....

Measuring a corporation's social responsiveness or the internal accountability of its operating structure and culture cannot be easily reduced to scores and percentages or even legal definitions. But these qualities and others can be gauged concretely by systematic research and reporting. That would start by asking the various contributors or communities how the company behaves. Studying a corporation's actual performance, past and present, alongside its proclaimed values may reveal telling comparisons about which designs for corporate governance consistently produce the better results. Making distinctions, getting beyond generalized bromides, is a way to gain leverage for changing the status quo.

All shareholders are not equal, for instance, despite the conventional lore that pretends otherwise. It is the large-scale investors who become the intimate insiders with management and who control the large decisions that often injure, rather than serve, the broader ranks of distant shareholders (not to mention society). The company treats these big guys differently, since they are often the controlling owners, and so should the law. The "limited liability" protections, for instance, could be modestly scaled back for the inside stakeholders, proportionate to the size of their holdings in the firm and their proximity to power. This would raise the level of risk for those who stand to gain the most from their insider status.

Congress actually took a small step in this direction with the accounting reform legislation enacted in 2002, with a provision that makes it marginally easier to win personal restitution from corporate executives for fraudulent conduct. The same approach could be broadened to cover egregious management failures that do not reveal criminal intent but are profoundly destructive for other parties. The AOL Time Warner merger, for example, is a stunning case of horrendous error by the insiders, betting two large and strong corporations on dubious premises and severely damaging both enterprises, their employees, and shareholders. Yet there is no recourse by which to hold the architects accountable, unless a crime can be proven. Business and finance, meanwhile, campaign to shrink their liabilities still further. Under the banner of "tort reform," they lobby relentlessly for legal ceilings on the damage lawsuits filed against them by injured citizens (and Congress sometimes goes along).

Reducing "limited liability" protection for the designated insiders—increasing their exposure to personal loss—would instill a measure of personal responsibility at the commanding heights. Let those who control things share in the downside costs of their adventures. This new measure of discipline (if one can imagine its adoption) also would provide the leverage for encouraging structural reforms by corporations themselves. Companies, for instance, might be permitted to retain the full scope of their "limited liability" protection *if* they restructure internally to disperse power and ownership so that other contributors become authentic insiders themselves, starting with the employees. Management thus would have to accept greater internal accountability, including legal obligations for disclosure and deliberations with other contributing elements, including the supporting communities, in exchange for retaining their own "limited liability" protection. If they chose not to reform, insiders would face greater financial risk for the consequences of their actions....

> **The missing political question is: Why are the corporate "persons" treated so much more generously than living, breathing citizens, especially when the corporate privileges often are used to damage the interests of the human "persons"?**

Like shareholders, corporations are not all alike either. They exist variously in size, shape, and internal configurations, indeed, in hybrid formats too numerous and complex to describe. The law already recognizes most of these differences in excruciating detail, especially in the tax code, since the obscure distinctions and exceptions typically are enacted at the behest of business interests (much like the corporate legal privileges adopted originally). The usual justification for these myriad exceptions is that whatever makes a corporation more effective (profitable) is bound to improve the overall economy and, therefore, benefit everyone. But is this actually true?

What is largely missing from the political deliberations is the social presence that would ask different questions about what's valuable and what's harmful. A thorough reconsideration of the loopholes and exceptions in the corporate tax code, for instance, would ask whether any of these esoteric arrangements, like the so-called "special purpose entities," actually produce real value for the economy or exist mainly to legalize tax evasion and other antisocial maneuvers. The missing political question is: Why are the corporate "persons" treated so much more generously than living, breathing citizens, especially when the corporate privileges often are used to damage the interests of the human "persons"?

The social inquiry, more broadly, would examine the vast differences in corporate governance, structure, and scale, and seek to discover which corporate arrangements really do provide the greatest benefits, not to the bottom line alone, but for society's non-economic imperatives. Once such distinctions are established and made clear to the public, government might then begin to exercise preferences and to shrink the operating boundaries for corporate types that consistently injure or neglect or destabilize the society that chartered their existence.

Since the political system obviously lacks the courage, this inquiry will have to be taken up initially by nonofficial "public auditors"—respected authorities, scholars, community leaders, perhaps supported by private philanthropy—who can be trusted to do honest examinations. This "public audit" would require a supple and difficult search—one that depends on field-tested results—but also could open up productive conversations with numerous corporations about how they perform, how they are held accountable. Some of us have strong convictions that a more democratic corporate design works best for society and are confident that a thorough inquiry will confirm this. Everyday Americans might like our logic, but they will want to see living proof.

In any case, these modest suggestions for initiating corporate reform, though intentionally gradualist, are probably not yet ready for prime-time politics. They would be batted away swiftly by business and finance interests with their usual warning to politicians: Don't mess with the golden goose. The corporation, they would caution, functions as the main vessel of our economic prosperity, and anyone who tampers with it will be punished severely by campaign contributors and also by the voters if things go awry. That admonition usually shuts down any serious political discussion. They have a point. It is too easy for critics to assume the modern corporation exists only because of some long ago power grab.

1. For the history of corporate power, I have drawn upon Morton J. Horwitz, *The Transformation of American Law, 1870-1960, The Crisis of Legal Orthodoxy*, Oxford University Press, 1992; Mary A. O'Sullivan, *Contests for Corporate Control: Corporate Governance and Economic Performance in the United States and Germany*, Oxford University Press, 2000; David Kairys, editor, *The Politics of Law: A Progressive Critique*, Basic Books, 1998; Charles Perrow, *Organizing America: Wealth, Power and the Origins of Corporate Capitalism*, Princeton University Press, 1992; and William G. Roy, *Socializing Capital: The Rise of the Large Industrial Corporation in America*, Princeton, 1997.

2. The Consequences of the Supreme Court's Santa Clara decision of 1886 were reviewed in the 1930s by Justice Hugo Black, who determined that corporations, not emancipated slaves, were the principal beneficiaries; see my book, *Who Will Tell the People: The Betrayal of American Democracy*, Simon & Schuster, 1992.

3. A dramatic account of the new oligopolies astride so many sectors was provided by Yochi J. Dreazen, Greg Ip, and Nicholas Kulish in the *Wall Street Journal*, February 25, 2002.

4. Richard Grossman and the Program on Corporations, Law and Democracy (POCLAD) have led a nationwide campaign of education and agitation around the subject of corporate power. Among other ideas, POCLAD argues for the rechartering of all corporations. His remarks on "robots" are from "Can Corporations Be Accountable, Part 2," originally published in *Rachel's Environment & Health Weekly*, August 6, 1998.

Breadbasket of Democracy

by Ted Nace

Ted Nace is the author of Gangs of America: The Rise of Corporate Power and the Disabling of Democracy. Nace is the founder of Peach-pit Press, the world's leading publisher of books on computer graphics and desktop publishing. He has also worked as a freelance writer and served as staff director of the Dakota Resource Council, helping rural communities deal with the impact of strip mines and power plants.

Nace visits North Dakota's rich farm country in the Red River Valley. There, in the heart of conservative America, he finds an economy that "cannot be described as corporate, but neither can it be described as socialist. Perhaps the best way to describe it is with a term that doesn't appear too often in economics textbooks: democratic." The story highlights North Dakota wheat farmers asserting their right to practice what farmers have done throughout the millennia: save their seed. That practice had been legally chal-lenged by Monsanto, and the farmers had had it.

North Dakota farmers organizing against the Monsanto Corpora-tion is an important story. It reveals the power of an organized citi-zenry to state emphatically one of this book's underlying themes: that the economy ought to serve the well-being of communities (human and other-than-human), rather than communities serving the well-being of the economy.

∞

In the new red-blue lexicon of American politics, the Red River Valley of North Dakota seems aptly named. This is football-on-Friday-night country, where Clear Channel Radio sets the tone, and patriotic themes blend smoothly with corporate ones. Broad and pancake-flat, with topsoil measured in feet rather than inches, it possesses some of the most prized agricultural land in America. The roads run straight, the pickup trucks are big, and the immense Massey Ferguson tractors that ply the fields come equipped with global positioning system guidance, satellite radio, and quadraphonic sound. In 2004, George Bush carried North Dakota with 63 percent of the vote. It seems like the last place that one might go looking for a revolt against the powers that be.

Nor does a man like Todd Leake seem like the type of person to participate in any such uprising. "Extreme traditionalist" might be closer to the mark. Lean and soft-spoken, Leake has spent the past twenty-eight years farming the homestead established by his great-grandfather, a Canadian immigrant who arrived here over 120 years ago. Leake even farms the same crop as his great grandfather: hard spring wheat. "I guess you'd describe me as an umpteenth-generation wheat farmer," he says, "because as far back as we can tell, on both sides of the family, it's been farmers. And as far back as we can tell, it's also been wheat."

On a crisp, windy November day, Leake reflects on the events that turned him into a thorn in the side of the agribusiness establishment, especially the Monsanto Company. It's the time of year when farmers, having completed the harvest, begin overhauling their machinery and making plans for the next spring's planting. From Leake's kitchen, the view to the east is unimpeded—a dozen miles of Red River Valley farmland that must have looked like paradise to refugees from rocky eastern Canada.

Leake begins by gesturing toward two symbols. The first, just visible through his kitchen window, is the outline of the North Dakota Mill, the only grain-handling facility owned jointly by the citizenry of any state. "Sort of the epitome of farmers cooperating," he notes.

The other symbol offers a less inspiring vision, one of farmer fragmentation and disempowerment. It is a simple refrigerator magnet inscribed with the words "Monsanto Customer Support 800-332-3111."

"They call it customer support," says Leake. "It's actually a snitch line, where you report that your neighbor is brown bagging. Or where somebody reports you, and a week or two later you find a couple of big guys in black Monsanto leather jackets standing in your driveway."

Brown-bagging is an old term in rural America. It refers to replanting seed from your own harvest, rather than buying new seed. Until recently, it simply described a common agricultural practice. But lately the term has come to possess a second meaning, that of a crime, a consequence of the U.S. Supreme Court's 1980 decision in *Diamond v. Chakrabarty* allowing private companies to obtain patents for life forms, and the Court's 2001 decision in *J.E.M. Ag Supply v. Pioneer* affirming that the saving of seed constituted a patent violation.

Monsanto Customer Support 800-332-3111...It's actually a snitch line...where somebody reports you, and a week or two later you find a couple of big guys in black Monsanto leather jackets standing in your driveway.

When Todd Leake first became aware of genetic engineering in the mid-1990s, the prospects sounded enticing, including heady promises that new biotech crops capable of producing industrial chemicals and even pharmaceuticals would expand agricultural markets and thereby raise farm incomes. "But when they finally came out with actual product," he said, "it was all about selling more Roundup."

Roundup, Monsanto's leading product, is the trade name of an herbicide based on the chemical glyphosate. Normally, herbicides cannot be applied once crops have sprouted. But by using genetic engineering to create glyphosate resistance in common crops, Monsanto made it feasible for farmers to apply Roundup directly to fields at any time in the growing season, killing weeds without killing crops.

> When Leake talks about wheat, his tone shifts subtly, becoming almost reverential. "Wheat's an amazing plant," he notes...."In many languages, the word for 'wheat' is the same as the word for 'life.'"

By 2000, Monsanto had successfully intro-duced "Roundup Ready" corn, alfalfa, canola, soybeans, and cotton in the United States and elsewhere. Meanwhile, the company began field-testing and pursuing USDA permits for Roundup Ready spring wheat. Wheat is the world's most widely cultivated food, and Mon-santo wanted to introduce it as the crown jewel of genetically modified (GM) crops. North Dakota, which accounts for 47 percent of the U.S. acreage for spring wheat, was vital to the company's plans.

As Leake began contemplating the proposed introduction of Roundup Ready wheat, he found himself wondering whether the new seed would end up actually hurting farmers. One worrisome possibility was that "Frankenfood"-averse Euro-pean or Japanese markets would reject GM wheat, causing the price to collapse. Something similar had happened in the late 1990s, when the Japanese had begun rejecting soybean shipments containing transgenic material.

Another concern was Monsanto's record of suing scores of farmers whose crop was found to contain patented genetic material, even miniscule amounts that had arrived via spillage, wind-blown seed, or pollen drift. He found himself sympathiz-ing with Percy Schmeiser, the Canadian farmer who had been sued by Monsanto in 1998 for violating the company's patent on Roundup Ready canola. Schmeiser had never bought Monsanto's seed. He had only planted seed saved from his own fields. Apparently, his fields had been contaminated through seed blown from passing trucks, but it didn't matter: brownbagging had turned him into a common thief.

When Leake talks about wheat, his tone shifts subtly, becoming almost reveren-tial. "Wheat's an amazing plant," he notes. "It's a combination of three Middle Eastern grasses, and that gives it a huge genome. In many languages, the word for 'wheat' is the same as the word for 'life.' There's a ten-thousand year connection between wheat and human beings, each generation saving seed. Now it's in our hands."

In January 2000, Leake began urging various organizations in North Dakota to oppose the introduction of genetically modified wheat. One of the groups he approached was the Dakota Resource Council, a statewide network of local groups that originally formed in the late 1970s to deal with strip mines and power plants. By the mid-1980s, the DRC had expanded into a variety of other rural issues, from toxic waste dumps to industrial hog operations. (For full disclosure, I should note that I spent several years working for the council in the early days, first as a field organizer and later as staff director, until I left in 1982.)

Leake's concern about GM wheat fit naturally within the DRC's scope, but questions remained: what tactics should be adopted, and what objectives should be pursued? A reasonable political strategy might start from the assumption that GM wheat would inevitably come to be a presence in fields, freight cars, and grain elevators; hence, those concerned about negative effects would try to shore up protective regulations so that GM wheat would not contaminate non-GM wheat. They would hire specialists to write proposals for new rules improving grain segregation and testing, then hire PR and lobbying specialists to get the new fine print enacted. All this technical tweaking of the grain handling and marketing system could be done by traditional marketing and farm-service organizations.

But Leake and the DRC opted to seek a different solution: an outright ban on GM wheat in North Dakota until all outstanding concerns were addressed. In the end, the radical strategy worked; the organizers had enough support in the state to thwart Monsanto's plans. And the story of why Leake and other opponents of GM wheat chose the riskier and more militant goal, and how they fought to achieve it, is one with implications beyond the issue of genetic engineering. It is also a story about a little-known strain of U.S. history, and about the ability of Americans to control their destinies.

America's primary decision-making system, known as representative democracy, is two centuries old. Structured according to the terms and judicial interpretations of the U.S. Constitution, it nominally governs decisions on all elements of public life, from elections and schools to privacy and environmental regulations. But whatever its strengths, the Constitution leaves a fundamental issue open to interpretation: who controls important economic decisions, and how will they be made?

This ambiguity allowed the rise of America's other major form of decision making, known as corporate capitalism, which is scarcely over a century old, having emerged in the period between the Civil War and the First World War. That system is not democratic, nor does anyone claim it to be. It has given the managers of a few hundred extremely large corporations the power to make many of the big decisions that will shape the future—what energy technologies should be invested in, what medical research should be pursued and turned into pharmaceutical products, how aggressively timber or mineral resources should be extracted, how workplaces should be organized, whether hundreds of independent radio stations should be consolidated, whether major crops should be genetically engineered, and so forth.

According to the generally accepted rationale, corporate managers respond to

> Today, we rarely hear such simple questions as, "What is an economy for?" or "Should we trust our future to corporations?"

markets, and markets in turn respond more or less to public preferences as expressed through buying decisions. At times one even hears markets described as a sort of democracy, with customers voting via their dollars. But because for-profit corporations are legally mandated to maximize shareholder return, their managers tend to shut out considerations vital to the larger society: public health, worker safety, equitable income distribution, and the well-being of natural communities, animals, plants, and the atmosphere. In the revealing language of neo-classical economics, such effects are labeled "externalities," or marginal considerations rather than central ones.

In any case, as the conventional wisdom goes, what's the alternative? Surely a market system, whatever its imperfections, is preferable to an economy rigidly controlled by monolithic bureaucracies: that is, state socialism. And here the conversation typically ends.

Today, we rarely hear such simple questions as, "What is an economy for?" or "Should we trust our future to corporations?" But these were exactly the sort of questions that wheat farmers in North Dakota decided to ask during the debate over GM wheat. As one farmer, Steve Pollestad, expressed it, North Dakotans had a choice. They could put the future of wheat "in the hands of people who are accountable to the citizens of North Dakota. Or, we could let Monsanto decide. And maybe we also could get Enron to run our utilities and Arthur Anderson to keep the books."

It's no coincidence that such sentiments grow out of the fields of North Dakota. Beneath the state's conservative surface are surprising currents of history, some quite radically divergent from the course of mainstream America. North Dakota's economy cannot be described as corporate, but neither can it be described as socialist. Perhaps the best way to describe it is with a term that isn't appearing too often in economics textbooks: democratic. For residents from Amidon to Walhalla, civic participation means not just serving on political bodies such as the county commission or the school board, but also taking part in running economic institutions such as the local electric co-op or grain elevator. Farmers see nothing extraordinary in buying gas from a cooperative gas station, buying electricity from a rural electric cooperative, borrowing college money from the publicly owned Bank of North Dakota, and selling their grain or milk to a producer co-operative. The theme of noncorporate economics pervades the state, extending even to agricultural processing cooperatives handling everything from noodles to tilapia. Indeed, as a matter of state law, corporate-owned farms are banned in the state.

North Dakota's unique economic arrangement grew out of a strain of radical populism that swept the state from 1915 to 1920. Like many Midwestern states, North Dakota had from its inception been a virtual colony of corporations headquartered far away, with crucial decisions arrived at by business executives in meetings at the Merchant's Hotel in St. Paul, Minnesota. Farmers complained bitterly that the system made them easy prey for gouging at the hands of the railroads and for rampant cheating and underpayment by corporate grain merchants. Their options, of course, were nil.

According to tradition, the revolt ignited in 1915 when a North Dakota state legislator named Treadwell Twichell told an assembled group of farmers seeking relief from the state, "Go home and slop the hogs." One of the farmers present, A.C. Townley, couldn't go home to his hogs; he had already lost his farm in bankruptcy court. Instead, Townley and his friend Fred Wood sat down in Wood's farmhouse kitchen and drafted an audacious political platform. In essence, their call to arms urged farmers simply to bypass the corporate agricultural system altogether by creating their own grain terminals, flour mills, insurers, and even banks.

Townley was a charismatic speaker. Farmers flocked to hear him and to contribute to his fledgling organization, the Non-Partisan League. To the delight of crowds, Townley shouted, "If you put a banker, a lawyer, and an industrialist in a barrel and roll it down a hill, you'll always have a son of a bitch on top."

He was also a brilliant organizer, and within three years the Non-Partisan League had completed its conquest of North Dakota's state government, with NPL majorities in both houses of the legislature and an NPL loyalist in the governor's office. The league then proceeded to reorganize the infrastructure of agriculture—particularly finance, grain storage, and grain milling—taking the reins away from the corporate players and handing them over to new publicly owned institutions.

The ascendancy of the Non-Partisan League was relatively short, its decline a casualty of attacks by business groups and newspapers that branded the organization as socialist, the jailing of A.C. Townley on sedition charges, and infighting among its leaders. But the institutions of that era managed to survive, and a populist undercurrent persisted in state politics. The most significant populist reform—the exclusion of corporations from farming—arrived via a 1932 ballot initiative in response to farm foreclosures, over a decade after the end of formal NPL rule. Once again, angry farmers, after examining their options, had chosen the most militant and far-reaching. Rather than passing laws to shield farms from corporate takeover, the 1932 initiative simply legislated corporations out of the picture entirely, making it illegal not just for banks to seize the land of bankrupted farmers, but for any corporation to hold any farmland whatsoever.

Take that, robber barons!

In early 2000, Todd Leake and the Dakota Resource Council launched their anti-GM wheat campaign from the steps of the North Dakota Mill in Grand Forks, the epicenter of the original farmer revolt. In choosing the mill, the council's aim was to signal that the anti-GM struggle and the original populist revolt were essentially about the same thing: preventing outside corporations from controlling wheat, the core of North Dakota's livelihood. Had they inherited a more passive mentality, they might have told themselves that Monsanto owned the genetic patents underlying Roundup Ready wheat, so the company was the one to decide whether seed for that wheat should be sold in the state—that the issue was between Monsanto and its customers. But farmers accustomed to running institutions like grain elevators and electric co-operatives didn't think that way; they considered a decision on GM wheat to be their personal business.

By January 2001, when the anti-GM campaign rolled into Bismarck, the state capital, it had collected tremendous momentum. Farmers, many of whom had traveled hundreds of miles despite rough winter driving, gathered in clusters in the halls of the state capitol. Normally, that building, a twenty-two-story skyscraper, has the dressed-up ambiance of a bank or insurance company. But with scores of parka-clad men and women crowding the art-deco atrium, exchanging newspaper clippings and Internet downloads before filing into the hearing rooms of legislative committees, the sense of business-as-usual was broken. On near unanimous votes, both houses of the state legislature enacted a new law making it illegal for corporate agents to arbitrarily enter and inspect farmers' fields. The new protective mechanism, Nelson's Bill, was named after Roger Nelson, a farmer who had cordially opened his fields to Monsanto for inspection, only to find himself up to his neck in patent-infringement litigation.

That victory served as a prelude to the action still to come: the proposal for a ban on GM wheat until all lingering issues were resolved. Here, too, the farmer-led juggernaut seemed unstoppable. In January 2001, Todd Leake and others testified before the House Agriculture Committee on the need for the moratorium, and the mood among the legislators—three of whom had PhDs in agricultural sciences and the rest of whom were farmers themselves—was so overtly favorable that when the beleaguered Monsanto lobbyist rose to testify, the chairman of the committee handed him a bottle of whisky, commenting, "Jim, I think you're going to need this." The committee voted 14-0 to support the ban, and then-representative April Fairfield, a vocal anti-GM legislator, expressed the general mood: "Clearly, before today, Monsanto and their lackeys have been running the agenda. I am inspired by how farmers and others broke the back of that agenda and sent Monsanto crawling back to St. Louis." Several days later, the entire North Dakota House of Representatives followed the recommendation of the Agriculture Committee, with Republicans and Democrats alike overwhelmingly voting to put the kibosh on GM wheat.

The polity had spoken. Democracy had flexed its muscle. Or so it seemed. By March 2001, Monsanto had marshaled its allies to block the ban in the state senate, aided by the timely intervention of U.S. Agriculture Secretary Ann Veneman, a former board member of Monsanto subsidiary Calgene, and President George Bush, who met personally with Republican members of the North Dakota state senate during a brief visit to Fargo that month. In the wake of that pressure, the ban on GM wheat was watered down to a study of the issue.

It seemed to many that agribusiness had won the day, that the populist impulse had fallen short; worse, it appeared that the efforts of Leake and company had served merely to provoke Monsanto. After the senate vote, the company began flying legislators on special "fact-finding" junkets, working its vast network of grain-marketing organizations, seed and herbicide dealers, research contracts, public relations firms, and pro-agribusiness farm organizations such as the Farm Bureau. The goal: to build public support for Monsanto's GM-wheat proposal, and to head off any ban in future legislative sessions.

But the anti-GM activists hadn't given up either. In between the other demands of farming life, they crisscrossed the state, holding town meetings and forums, writing letters to the editor, raising the issue with grain elevator boards and wheat marketing associations, and speaking to as many farmers as would listen.

By all the conventional ways that political resources are measured, Monsanto had the advantage, and yet in those small-town cafes where the political conversation never ends, the anti-GM advocates sensed they were winning. And if farmers themselves turned against GM wheat, then all of Monsanto's political success in blocking a legislative ban would be rendered meaningless. While Monsanto had experienced across-the-board rejection of its genetically engineered food products throughout Europe and Japan, the company had never faced heavy opposition from U.S. farmers themselves. It was absolutely crucial that North Dakota farmers accept Roundup Ready spring wheat. But it wasn't happening. And during the election cycle following the defeat of the GM-wheat ban, three pro-GM legislators, including Monsanto's leading ally in the state senate, Terry Wanzek, were ousted by anti-GM opponents.

Outside North Dakota, the anti-GM revolt was also spreading. By May of 2004, two more states, South Dakota and Indiana, had followed North Dakota's lead in enacting laws protecting farmers from intrusive inspections. And in Mendocino County, California, citizens used the initiative process to pass a local moratorium on genetically modified crops. Two more counties, Trinity and Marin, would soon follow suit.

Meanwhile, North Dakota farmers had already joined forces with a wide network of activists across the globe. One North Dakota farmer, Tom Wiley, traveled to Europe, Australia, and even Qatar to spread the message of revolt. In Torun, Poland, he told a radio audience, "You fought hard for your independence. Don't give up your freedom to the biotech corporations. Saving seed is a basic human right."

On May 10, 2004, Monsanto bowed to the prevailing political sentiment. It issued a curt press release announcing the withdrawal of all its pending regulatory applications for Roundup Ready wheat and the shifting of research priorities to other crops. The main factor in the decision, the company noted obliquely, was "a lack of widespread wheat industry alignment."

It may be tempting to dismiss agrarian populism as a marginal phenomenon, as something with little relevance to a corporate economy dominated by the likes of ExxonMobil, Citibank, and Google. And there would be some truth to that assessment. Nowadays the legacy of 1915 and 1932, which so inspired Todd Leake and his fellow farmers, remains an obscure chapter in American history. But populism wasn't always obscure: it had its most famous surge in the Farmers' Alliance that swept out of Texas in the 1870s and eventually reached most of the South and Midwest. At its peak, the Populist Party controlled several state legislatures and governorships; forty Populist candidates entered Congress. A.C. Townley's rise would come a generation later.

Today, North Dakotans are not the only ones drawing on that legacy.

On the campus of Boston College, activists recently gathered for a three-day weekend to participate in "Democracy School," one of thirty such teach-ins taking place across the country in 2006. Created by environmental attorney Thomas Linzey and historian Richard Grossman, Democracy School aims to reinvoke the spirit that Grossman calls "the Populist agenda of sovereignty over corporations." They call this twenty-first-century version of populism "rights-based organizing."

Arriving from various local organizing campaigns, the students traded notes. In Humboldt County, California, for example, residents have launched a full-scale citizen revolt against corporate political meddling by Houston-based Maxxam Corporation, which acquired the local logging company, Pacific Lumber, in 1986. In order to pay off debts, including the high-interest junk bonds it had used to finance the purchase, Maxxam tripled the pace of logging. The aggressive cutting depleted forest reserves, destroyed salmon runs, fouled drinking water, and caused a mudslide that buried seven houses in the community of Stafford.

In 2004, after district attorney Paul Gallegos sued Pacific Lumber for fraudulent regulatory filings, Maxxam sought to get rid of Gallegos, devoting a quarter of a million dollars to a recall initiative. Citizens fought back, mobilizing successfully to defeat the effort. And then they immediately began laying the groundwork for a ballot initiative, scheduled for the fall of 2006, designed to prohibit Maxxam, or any other non-local corporation, from spending money to influence local politics.

...Porter Township, Pennsylvania, declar[ed] that corporate "personhood" rights no longer would apply in the township. The purpose of the declaration was to deny corporate attorneys any basis to challenge the township's right to ban the spreading of industrial sludge on farm fields.

Opening a hefty brown binder, the teacher of the Boston Democracy School session, Adam Sacks, led a discussion of a recent incident in St. Thomas Township, Pennsylvania. A newly elected supervisor, Frank Stearn, arrived at his first meeting on the township board in 2004, only to be told by his fellow supervisors that he would not be allowed to vote on any matters pertaining to a proposed limestone quarry complex. The reason? St. Thomas Development Incorporated, the corporation planning the quarry, had threatened to sue the township if Stearn, who had run for office on a platform of opposition to the quarry out of concern over its environmental effects, voted on the project.

The implication of the corporation's claim—that the rights of corporations somehow trump the rights of citizens to be represented by whomever they choose—created an uproar, and Stearn's supporters mounted a counterassault. In 2004, Friends and Residents of St. Thomas Township (FROST), the citizens' organization that had sponsored Stearn's campaign, filed a class-action lawsuit against the company. The suit sought millions of dollars in damages for the attempt to intimidate an elected official from participating in a democratic body. It cited civil rights statutes that make it a federal crime to deprive others of their democratic privileges—such as the right to be represented in governmental bodies. Dismissed by the federal Middle District Court of Pennsylvania on the grounds that private corporations are not subject to civil rights enforcement, the suit is now on appeal.

In developing its lawsuit, FROST was assisted by Thomas Linzey's Pennsylvania-based Community Environmental Legal Defense Fund, a nonprofit that over the past ten years has developed a rights-based organizing approach to community empowerment. Rather than tiptoe around the reality of corporate power in America, rights-based organizing confronts it head on, often through aggressive local measures such as the 2003 ordinance by Porter Township, Pennsylvania, declaring that corporate "personhood" rights no longer would apply in the township. The purpose of the declaration was to deny corporate attorneys any basis to challenge the township's right to ban the spreading of industrial sludge on farm fields.

Linzey admits candidly that such tactics may eventually be overcome by corporate legal teams. "We've come to the realization that we can't do this work under the current Constitutional structure of this country," he says. "It's not a rights-and-liberty Constitution, it's a property-and-commerce Constitution." But rights-based organizing, according to Linzey, forces corporations to openly assert their rights over those of ordinary citizens, thereby provoking the public. "What's different about how we work is that we don't see losing as the end point, we see it as the beginning point. [Our work] could be described as 'civil disobedience through community lawmaking.' When we lose, we don't leave people behind, we bring them forward to the next step...."

Linzey's model is the Abolitionists, who uncompromisingly challenged the basis of slavery: "The Abolitionists didn't seek to create a Slavery Protection Agency to make the conditions of slaves more tolerable," he explains. "They weren't afraid to confront a legal system that classified some people as property."

In the Red River Valley, Todd Leake, too, insists that conventionally accepted notions of law and property can't be taken as a given, particularly the idea that life forms can be patented, which in turn forms the legal basis for genetic engineering of seed. "Seed?" he asks. "That's literally the future of humanity. Patents? Corporations? Those are just inventions on paper. Whatever rights corporations are claiming so that they can try to control our seed stocks," he says, "those have to be subordinated to the right of farmers to plant and replant this seed."

It is now February in the valley, the desolate core of winter, with snow blowing like sand across the stubble-tufted fields. Although preparation of those fields remains months away, Leake seems restless to begin another year of planting. More than a year has passed since Monsanto announced its abandonment of Roundup Ready wheat. And Leake knows that the central issues—Monsanto's power to introduce genetically modified wheat, and the fate of seed-saving—are far from settled.

"It's an emotional issue," he says. "Farmers are tired of being pushed. If they come out with GM wheat, what are they going to do if farmers rebel—send out the county sheriff's deputies to bust us all?" He describes a "little visit" he himself received from a pair of Monsanto enforcement representatives. "They told me they were here to check my fields for violations. I told them to get lost. They were just trying to intimidate me, that's all. They think they can go around and scare everyone into submission, but it's bad business," he concludes, "and it's ultimately not going to work."

"Breadbasket of Democracy" by Ted Nace, from *Orion* magazine, May/June, 2006. Reprinted by permission of the publisher. Visit them on-line at *www.orionmagazine.org*

Postscript on Corporations: One of the most difficult challenges in a book like this is deciding what to leave out. The first two essays in this section focused on corporate reform, on those characteristics of corporations that likely need significant change in order to shift our economy from one that exploits to one that restores. And the third essay tells the story of a group of farmers taking corporate power head on and not backing down.

However, what is not highlighted in this section are those corporations genuinely committed to sustainability. Because of their size and influence, large multinationals can be a significant force for good in the world.

Ray Anderson, the founder and chairman of Interface, Inc., experienced a conversion when he first read Paul Hawken's *The Ecology of Commerce*. Interface is the worldwide leader in carpet design and manufacture. Since his conversion, Anderson has led his company's Mission Zero promise: to eliminate any negative impact it may have on the environment by the year 2020; they are nearly 50% of the way to that goal. Their vision is to "be the first company that, by its deeds, shows the entire industrial world what sustainability is in all its dimensions..."

Interface is one of the many corporations seeking to effect positive change in the world. Find out more about Anderson's story in his book *Mid-Course Correction: Towards a Sustainable Enterprise, the Interface Model* (Atlanta: Peregrinzilla Press, 1998).

Liberation—Whose Voices Are Rarely Heard?

Successful Americans are holding themselves off in psychological and economic enclaves where they do not have to confront the wounds of humanity or the world.

—John Kavanaugh

The spirit of the Lord is on me, because God has anointed me to preach good news to the poor. God has sent me to proclaim freedom for the prisoners and recovery of sight for the blind, to release the oppressed, to proclaim the year of the Lord's favor.

—Luke 4:18-19

Introduction—VI

As highlighted in the Introduction to Section IV (page 74), *Money and Faith's* middle four sections move beyond the more personal focus of the first three sections. One way to think of the opening sections' theme could be "Money and faith in my life." The theme of these middle sections, on the other hand, could be "Money and faith within our economy." Within that latter theme, *Money and Faith* seeks to weave a prophetic voice, one that challenges largely unexamined cultural assumptions—like "more is better."

To even consider that voice requires listening—usually to voices nearly inaudible, drowned out by a chorus insisting "of course, more is better" or "your self-worth is your net worth."

When considering what faith has to say about money in this larger economic context, following in the tradition of Jesus and many of the prophets, the following two essays lift up the voices of the resource-poor—or at least those who speak for them.

This section's title "Liberation: Whose Voices Are Rarely Heard?" suggests that listening and responding to such voices is somehow linked to liberation. Which seems true, even interpersonally. To experience liberation from grief, we need to listen to the voice of grief. To feel more freedom in a relationship with a parent or a spouse, we need to listen to the soft but insistent voice saying "you really need to bring this up."

On a much larger scale, to experience liberation from what for many is an oppressive economic system, we need to listen and respond to the voice of those oppressed.

The following essays present the perspective of a former Haitian president and a Brazilian liberation theologian. Following the previous section's focus on corporate power, these writers represent some of those most impacted by that power.

*G*lobalization:
A Choice between Death and Death

by Jean-Bertrand Aristide

Jean-Bertrand Aristide is a former Roman Catholic priest and served as President of Haiti in 1991, again from 1994 to 1996, and then from 2001 to 2004. Aristide was the second elected leader of Haiti and was popular among its poor inhabitants. He was overthrown twice, first in a military coup d'état in September, 1991, and subsequently in a coup d'état in 2004 in which former soldiers prominently participated.

Free trade policies are one of the primary tools supported by those pushing for evermore economic globalization. Here, Aristide writes about free trade from his country's perspective. Popular among the poor, first as a priest and then as Haiti's first elected president, he describes how certain globalization/free trade policies affected Haiti's rice crops and Creole pigs.

A morgue worker is preparing to dispose of a dozen corpses. One living soul lifts himself off of the table, shakes his head and declares, "I am not dead!" To which the morgue worker answers, "Yes you are. The doctors say that you are dead, so lie down."

In today's global marketplace trillions of dollars are traded each day via a vast network of computers. In this market no one talks, no one touches. Only numbers count.

And yet today this faceless economy is already five times larger than the real, or productive, economy.

We know other market places. On a plain high in the mountains of Haiti, one day a week thousands of people still gather. This is the marketplace of my childhood in the mountains above *Port Salut*. The sights and the smells and the noise and the color overwhelm you. Everyone comes. If you don't come you will miss everything. The donkeys tied and waiting in the woods number in the thousands. Goods are displayed in every direction: onions, leeks, corn, beans, yams, cabbage, cassava, and avocados, mangoes and every tropical fruit, chickens, pigs, goats, and batteries, and tennis shoes, too. People trade goods, and news. This is the center; social, political and economic life roll together. A woman teases and coaxes her client. "*Cherie*, the onions are sweet and waiting just for you." The client laughs and teases back until they make a deal. They share trade, and laughter, gossip, politics, and medical and child-rearing tips. A market exchange, and a human exchange.

We are not against trade, we are not against free trade, but our fear is that the global market intends to annihilate our markets. We will be pushed to the cities, to eat food grown on factory farms in distant countries, food whose price depends on the daily numbers game of the first market. "This is more efficient," the economists say. "Your market, your way of life, is not efficient," they say. But we ask, "What is left when you reduce trade to numbers, when you erase all that is human?"

Globalization, the integration of world markets, has promised to "lift all boats," rich and poor, to bring a global culture of entertainment and consumer goods to everyone—the promise of material happiness. And indeed, since 1980 most third world countries have embraced globalization. They have opened their economies to the world, lowered tariffs, embraced free trade, and allowed goods and services from the industrialized world to flow in. It seems the world is brought closer together. In fact the gap between the thumb and the little finger has never been larger.

What happens to poor countries when they embrace free trade? In Haiti in 1986 we imported just 7000 tons of rice, the main staple food of the country. The vast majority was grown in Haiti. In the late 1980s Haiti complied with free trade policies advocated by the international lending agencies and lifted tariffs on rice imports. Cheaper rice immediately flooded in from the United States where the rice industry is subsidized. In fact the liberalization of Haiti's market coincided with the 1985 Farm Bill in the United States which increased subsidies to the rice industry so that 40% of U.S. rice growers' profits came from the government by 1987. Haiti's peasant farmers could not possibly compete. By 1996 Haiti was importing 196,000 tons of foreign rice at the cost of $100 million a year. Haitian rice production became negligible. Once the dependence on foreign rice was complete, import prices began to rise, leaving Haiti's population, particularly the urban poor, completely at the whim of rising world grain prices. And the prices continue to rise.

> **We are not against trade, we are not against free trade, but our fear is that the global market intends to annihilate our markets.**

What lessons do we learn? For poor countries free trade is not so free, or so fair. Haiti, under intense pressure from the international lending institutions, stopped protecting its domestic agriculture while subsidies to the U.S. rice industry increased. A hungry nation became hungrier.

In a globalized economy, foreign investment is trumpeted as the key to alleviating poverty. But in fact, the top beneficiary of foreign investment from 1985-95 was the United States, with $477 billion. Britain ran a distant second at $199 billion, and Mexico, the only third world country in the top ten, received only $44 billion in investment. When the majority of this money fled the country overnight during Mexico's financial meltdown in 1995, we learned that foreign investment is not really investment. It is more like speculation. And in my country, Haiti, it's very hard to find investment statistics.

We are still moving from misery to poverty with dignity.

Many in the first world imagine the amount of money spent on aid to developing countries is massive. In fact, it amounts to only .03 % of GNP of the industrialized nations. In 1995, the director of the U.S. aid agency defended his agency by testifying to his congress that 84 cents of every dollar of aid goes back into the U.S. economy in goods and services purchased. For every dollar the United States puts into the World Bank, an estimated $2 actually goes into the U.S. economy in goods and services. Meanwhile in 1995, severely indebted low-income countries paid one billion dollars more in debt and interest to the International Monetary Fund (IMF) than they received from it. For the 46 countries of Subsaharan Africa, foreign debt service was four times their combined governmental health and education budgets in 1996. So, we find that aid does not aid.

The little finger knows that she is sinking deeper into misery each day, but all the while the thumb is telling her that profits are increasing, economies are growing and he is pouring millions of dollars of aid into her country. Whose profit? Whose economy? What aid? The logic of global capitalism is not logical for her. We call this economic schizophrenia.

The history of the eradication of the Haitian Creole pig population in the 1980s is a classic parable of globalization. Haiti's small, black, Creole pigs were at the heart of the peasant economy. An extremely hearty breed, well adapted to Haiti's climate and conditions, they ate readily-available waste products, and could survive for three days without food. Eighty to 85% of rural households raised pigs; they played a key role in maintaining the fertility of the soil and constituted the primary savings bank of the peasant population. Traditionally a pig was sold to pay for emergencies and special occasions (funerals, marriages, baptisms, illnesses and, critically, to pay school fees and buy books for the children when school opened each year in October).

In 1982 international agencies assured Haiti's peasants their pigs were sick and had to be killed (so that the illness would not spread to countries to the North). Promises were made that better pigs would replace the sick pigs. With an efficiency not since seen among development projects, all of the Creole pigs were killed over a period of thirteen months.

Two years later the new, better pigs came from Iowa. They were so much better that they required clean drinking water (unavailable to 80% of the Haitian population), imported feed (costing $90 a year when the per capita income was about $130), and special roofed pigpens. Haitian peasants quickly dubbed them "*prince a quatre pieds*," (four-footed princes). Adding insult to injury, the meat did not taste as good. Needless to say, the repopulation program was a complete failure. One observer of the process estimated that in monetary terms Haitian peasants lost $600 million dollars. There was a 30% drop in enrollment in rural schools, there was a dramatic decline in the protein consumption in rural Haiti, a devastating decapitalization of the peasant economy and an incalculable negative impact on Haiti's soil and agricultural productivity. The Haitian peasantry has not recovered to this day.

Most of rural Haiti is still isolated from global markets, so for many peasants the extermination of the Creole pigs was their first experience of globalization. The experience looms large in the collective memory. Today, when the peasants are told that "economic reform" and privatization will benefit them they are understandably wary. The state-owned enterprises are sick, we are told, and they must be privatized. The peasants shake their heads and remember the Creole pigs.

The 1997 sale of the state-owned flour mill confirmed their skepticism. The mill sold for a mere $9 million, while estimates place potential yearly profits at $20-30 million a year. The mill was bought by a group of investors linked to one of Haiti's largest banks. One outcome seems certain; this sale will further concentrate wealth—in a country where 1% of the population already holds 45% of the wealth of the country.

If we have lingering doubts about where poor countries fall in this "new" economic order, listen to the World Bank. In September 1996, the *London Guardian* cited a draft World Bank strategy paper that predicted that the majority of Haitian peasants—who make up 70% of Haiti's population—are unlikely to survive bank-advocated free market measures. The Bank concluded: "The small volume of production and the environmental resource constraints will leave the rural population with only two possibilities: to work in the industrial or service sector, or to emigrate." At present the industrial sector employs only about 20,000 Haitians. There are already approximately 2.5 million people living in *Port-au-Prince*, 70% of them are officially unemployed and living in perhaps the most desperate conditions in the Western Hemisphere. Given the tragic history of Haiti's boat people, emigration, the second possibility, can hardly be considered a real option.

The choices that globalization offers the poor remind me of a story. Anatole, one of the boys who had lived with us at *Lafanmi Selavi**, was working at the national port. One day a very powerful businessman offered him money to sabotage the main unloading forklift at the port. Anatole said to the man, "Well, then I am already dead." The man, surprised by the response, asked, "Why?" Anatole answered, "Because if I sneak in here at night and do what you ask they will shoot me, and if I don't, you will kill me." The dilemma is, I believe, the classic dilemma of the poor; a choice between death and death. Either we enter a global economic system, in which we know we cannot survive, or, we refuse, and face death by slow starvation. With choices like these the urgency of finding a third way is clear. We must find some room to maneuver, some open space simply to survive. We must lift ourselves up off the morgue table and tell the experts we are not yet dead.

* *Lafanmi Selavi* is the center for street children in *Port-au-Prince* founded by Aristide in 1986.

From Jean-Bertrand Aristide's EYES OF THE HEART, "Globalization: A Choice between Death and Death" (Monroe, ME: Common Courage Press, 2000). Reprinted by permission of the publisher.

Liberation Theology and Ecology

by Leonardo Boff

Leonardo Boff was born in Brazil in 1938, received a doctorate from Munich in Germany in 1970, and for the following 20 years was Professor of Theology at the Jesuit Institute for Philosophy and Theology in Petropolis. Since 1993 he has been a Professor at the State University of Rio de Janeiro. Boff, the author of more than 60 books, was one of the founders of liberation theology. He has worked closely with the Brazilian Landless Movement. In 1991 he received the Right Livelihood Award. (*www.rightlivelihood.org*) Boff's recent work has sought to integrate ecology into liberation theology. His book, *Cry of the Earth, Cry of the Poor* is a synthesis of deep ecology thinking with social critique.

Boff writes that the core of liberation theology has always been the "option for the poor, against their poverty and for their liberation." This essay begins to lay a theoretical framework for the interconnectedness of liberation theology and ecology. Both "start from bleeding wounds": the pillage of Earth and the cry of the poor and hungry. Liberation theology, when reflecting on our economic system (and remember, economics is most basically about who gets what) says we must take the perspective of the "resource-poor," as the Catholic Church does when it argues for the "preferential option for the poor." This essay isn't always easy-sledding, but it is short, powerful and worth the effort.

Liberation theology and ecological discourse have something in common: they start from two bleeding wounds. The wound of poverty breaks the social fabric of millions and millions of poor people around the world. The other wound, systematic assault on the Earth, breaks down the balance of the planet, which is under threat from the plundering of development as practiced by contemporary global societies. Both lines of reflection and practice have as their starting point a cry: the cry of the poor for life, freedom, and beauty (cf. Ex 3:7), and the cry of the Earth groaning under oppression (cf. Rom 8:22-23). Both seek liberation, a liberation of the poor by themselves as active subjects who are organized, conscious, and networked to other allies who take on their cause and their struggle; and a liberation of the Earth through a new covenant between it and human beings, in a brotherly and sisterly relationship and with a kind of sustainable development that respects the different ecosystems and assures a good quality of life for future generations....[1]

Hearing the Cry of the Oppressed

Where does liberation theology stand with regard to ecological concern? We must acknowledge that the initial setting within which liberation theology emerged was not that of ecological concern as we have sketched it above. The most salient and challenging fact was not the threat to Earth as a whole but to the sons and daughters of Earth exploited and condemned to die prematurely, the poor and oppressed...."[2] That does not mean, however, that its basic intuitions have little to do with ecology. The relationship to ecology is direct, for the poor and the oppressed belong to nature and their situation is objectively an ecological aggression. But all of this was considered within a more restricted historical and social framework and in the context of classical cosmology.

Liberation theology was set in motion back in the 1960s by ethical indignation (true sacred wrath of the prophets) in the face of the dire poverty of the masses, especially in the Third World. This situation seemed—and still seems—unacceptable to the Christian conscience, which reads in the faces of the poor and the outcast the reembodiment of the passion of the Crucified One, who cries out and wants to arise for the sake of life and freedom.

The option for the poor, against their poverty and for their liberation, has constituted and continues to constitute the core of liberation theology. To opt for the poor entails a practice; it means assuming the place of the poor, their cause, their struggle, and at the limit, their often tragic fate.

Never in the history of Christian theologies have the poor become so central. To seek to build an entire theology starting from the perspective of the victims and so to denounce the mechanisms that have made them victims and to help overcome those mechanisms by drawing on the spiritual storehouse of Christianity, thereby collectively forging a society that offers greater opportunity for life, justice, and participation: this is the unique intuition of liberation theology.

That is why for this theology the poor occupy the epistemological locus; that is, the poor constitute the point from which one attempts to conceive of God, Christ, grace, history, the mission of the churches, the meaning of the economy, politics, and the future of societies and of the human being. From the standpoint of the poor, we realize to what extent current societies are exclusionary, to what extent democracies are imperfect, to what extent religions and churches are tied to the interests of the powerful.

From the beginning Christianity has cared for the poor (cf. Gal 2:10) but never have they been accorded so central a place in theology and for political transformation as they have been given by liberation theology.

The understanding of the poor in liberation theology has never been reduced to a single focus on them as poor. The poor are not simply beings made up of needs, but they are also beings of desire for unrestricted communication, beings hungering for beauty. Like all human beings, the poor—as the Cuban poet José Roberto Retamar puts it nicely—have two basic hungers, one for bread, which can be sated, and another for beauty, which is insatiable. Hence, liberation can never be restricted to the material, social, or merely spiritual realm. It is only true when it remains open to the full sweep of human demands. It has been the merit of liberation theology to have maintained its comprehensive scope since its origins; it did so because it was correctly interpreting what human liberation is about, not because of the demands of doctrinal authorities in the Vatican.

To be genuine, liberation must not only remain comprehensive in scope, but it must also and primarily be achieved by the poor themselves. Perhaps this is one of the unique features of liberation theology when compared with other practices of tradition, which have also shown concern for the poor. The poor are generally regarded as those who do not have food, shelter, clothes, work, culture. Those who have, so it is said, must help those who do not, so as to free them from the inhumanity of poverty. This strategy is full of good will and is well meaning; it is the basis for all assistance and paternalism in history. However, it is neither efficient nor sufficient. It does not liberate the poor, because it keeps them in a situation of dependence; worse yet, it does not even appreciate the liberating potential of the poor. The poor are not simply those who do not have; they *do* have. They have culture, ability to work, to work together, to get organized, and to struggle. Only when the poor trust in their potential, and when the poor opt for others who are poor, are conditions truly created for genuine liberation....

The Most Threatened Beings in Creation: The Poor

At this point the discourses of ecology and of liberation theology must be brought together for comparison. In analyzing the causes of the impoverishment that afflicts most of the world's population, liberation theology became aware that a perverse logic was at work. The very same logic of the prevailing system of accumulation and social organization that leads to the exploitation of workers also leads to the pillaging of whole nations and ultimately to the plundering of nature. It no longer suffices merely to adjust technologies or to reform society while keeping the same basic logic, although such things should always be done; the more important thing is to overcome such logic and the sense of being that human beings have held for at least the last three centuries. It will not be possible to deal with nature as our societies have tried to do, as though it were a supermarket or a self-service restaurant. It is our common wealth that is being mercilessly plundered, and that inheritance must be safeguarded.

Moreover, conditions for nature's further evolution must be assured for our own generation and for those to come, for the whole universe has been working for fifteen billion years so that we could come to the point at which we have arrived. Human beings must educate themselves so that far from being the Satan of Earth they may serve as its guardian angel, able to save Earth, their cosmic homeland and earthly mother.

The astronauts have accustomed us to see the Earth as a blue-and-white spaceship floating in space, bearing the common fate of all beings. Actually, on this spaceship Earth, one-fifth of the population is traveling in the passenger section. They consume 80 percent of the supplies for the journey. The other fourth-fifths are traveling in the cargo hold. They suffer cold, hunger, and all kinds of hardships. They are slowly becoming aware of the injustice of this distribution of goods and services. They plan rebellion: "Either we die passively of hunger or we make changes that will benefit everyone," they say. It is not a difficult argument: either we are all saved in a system of participatory common life in solidarity with and on spaceship Earth or in an explosion of wrath we could blow up the ship, sending us all falling into the abyss. Such an awareness is on the rise and can be terrifying.

The most recent arrangements of the world order led by capital and under the regime of globalization and neoliberalism have brought marvelous material progress. Leading-edge technologies produced by the third scientific revolution (computerization and communications) are being employed and are increasing production enormously. However, they dispense with human labor and hence the social effect is perverse: many workers and whole regions of the world are left out, since they are of little relevance for capital accumulation and are met by an attitude of the cruelest indifference.[3]

Recent data indicate that today globally integrated accumulation requires a Hiroshima and Nagasaki in human victims every two days.[4] There has been huge progress, but it is profoundly inhuman. The individual and peoples with their needs and preferences do not stand at its center, but rather the commodity and the market to which everything must submit. Hence, the most threatened creatures are not whales but the poor, who are condemned to die before their time. United Nations' statistics indicate that each year fifteen million children die of hunger or hunger-related diseases before they are five days old; 150 million children are undernourished, and 800 million go hungry all the time.[5]

This human catastrophe is liberation theology's starting point for considering ecology. In other words, its starting point is social ecology, the way human beings, the most complex beings in creation, relate to one another and how they organize their relationship with other beings in nature. At present it all takes place under a very exploitative and cruelly exclusionary system. We are faced with the cry of the oppressed and the excluded. A minimum of social justice is most urgently sought in order to assure life and the basic dignity that goes along with it. Once this basic level of social justice (social relationship between human beings) has been achieved, it will be possible to propose a possible ecological justice (relationship of human beings with nature). Such justice entails more than social justice. It entails a new covenant between human beings and other beings, a new gentleness toward what is created, and the fashioning of an ethic and mystique of kinship with the entire cosmic community. The Earth is also crying out under the predatory and lethal machinery of our model of society and development. To hear these two interconnected cries and to see the same root cause that produces them is to carry out integral liberation.

The social and political framework for this kind of integral liberation is an extended and enriched democracy. Such democracy will have to be biocracy, socio-cosmic democracy; in other words, a democracy that is centered on life, one whose starting point is the most downtrodden human life. It must include elements of nature like mountains, plants, water, animals, the atmosphere, and landscapes as new citizens participating in human common life and human beings sharing in the cosmic life in common. There will only be ecological and societal justice when peace is assured on planet Earth....

Liberation and Ecology: The Bridge between North and South

Two major issues will occupy the minds and hearts of humankind from now on: what is the destiny and future of planet Earth if the logic of pillage to which the present type of development and consumption have accustomed us continues? What hope is there for the poor two-thirds of humankind? There is a danger that "the culture of the satisfied" will become enclosed in its consumeristic selfishness and cynically ignore the devastation of the poor masses of the world. There is also a danger that the "new barbarians" will not accept their death sentence and will set out on a desperate struggle for survival, threatening everything and destroying everything. Humankind may find itself facing violence and destruction at levels never before seen on the face of the Earth unless we collectively decide to change the course of civilization and shift its thrust from the logic of means at the service of an exclusionary accumulation toward a logic of ends serving the shared well-being of planet Earth, of human beings, and of all beings in the exercise of freedom and cooperation among all peoples.

These two issues, with different accents, are shared concerns in the North and South of the planet. They are also the central content of liberation theology and of ecological thought. These two directions of thought make possible dialogue and convergence in diversity between the geographical and ideological poles of the world. They must be an indispensable mediation in the safeguarding of everything created and in rescuing the dignity of the poor majorities of the world. Hence liberation theology and ecological discourse need each other and are mutually complementary....

1. Cf D. Hallmann, Ed., *Eco-Theology: Voices from South and North* (Maryknoll, New York: Orbis Books, 1994); Th. S. Derr, *Ecology and Human Liberation* (Geneva: World Council of Churches, 1973).

2. H. Assmann, "Teologia da solidariedade e da ciudadania, ou seja, continuando a teologia da libertacao," *Notas, Jornal de Ciencias da Religiao*, no. 2 (1994), 2-9.

3. See F. J. Hinkelhammert, "La logica de la expulsion del mercado capitalista mundial y el proyecto de liberacion, " in *Pasos* (San Jose, 1992).

4. R. Garaudy, *Le Debat du Siecle* (Paris: Desclee de Brower, 1995), 14.

5. Cf. UNDP, *Human Development Report* (Oxford and New York: Oxford University Press, 1990).

What Is the Jubilee?

If we are going to dismiss the Jubilee because Israel practiced it only inconsistently, we should also ignore the Sermon on the Mount because Christians have rarely embodied Jesus' instruction to love our enemies. But it is time to move beyond such a rationalizing theology in our churches. We must rediscover the gospel as good news for the poor, and the economic disciplines of Sabbath as the path of humanization.

—*Ched Myers*

Trickle-down economics, which holds that so long as the economy as a whole grows everyone benefits, has been repeatedly shown to be wrong.

—*Joseph Stiglitz*, Nobel Prize Winning Economist

Introduction—VII

The Jubilee, as central as many believe it is to the Old Testament and to Jesus' ministry, is relatively obscure. Rooted in the foundational truth that "The Earth is the Lord's" (Psalm 24:1), the Jubilee, as described by Walter Brueggemann in Maria Harris' essay, means "finding out what belongs to whom and giving it back." (Following the Jubilee would certainly be good news to the Haitian peasants read about in the previous section.) Put another way, Jubilee entails the notion of "return" in the sense of returning to God what is not ours in the first place.

One of the following readings is a sermon. For those of you reading *Money and Faith* on your own, and not necessarily using the study guide, see page 266 for a litany written by Pastor Rich Lang for the Sunday service in which he preached the sermon appearing in this section.

Jubilee Justice

by Maria Harris

Maria Harris was an internationally known teacher, religious education consultant and writer who died in 2005. Her books include *Women and Teaching: Themes for a Spirituality of Pedagogy* and *Fashion Me a People: Curriculum and the Church.* One of her most popular books is *Dance of the Spirit: The Seven Steps of Women's Spirituality.* Toward the end of her career, she began to see the idea of Jubilee as a way to combine her passion for justice and the practice of deep spirituality. Early in the 1990s she saw that the year 2000 offered a powerful opportunity to proclaim Jubilee. She published *Proclaim Jubilee* in 1996. Once a Sister of St. Joseph, she later left the order and eventually married Gabriel Moran with whom she co-authored a number of books.

In her thought-provoking essay, Maria Harris describes how Jubilee is fundamentally a practice of justice. Citing Walter Brueggemann, who wrote that Jubilee justice entails finding out what belongs to whom and giving it back, Harris writes "the particular meaning of justice that Jubilee stresses is the notion of "return,"...as relinquishing, giving back, and handing over what is not ours to God." Harris also rightly emphasizes that any practice of justice impacts the way we "do economics." She offers five guidelines toward economic justice and then concludes with a brief reflection on mourning, which just may be the "sanest" response "in a planet gone mad through acquisition."

∞

...it is Walter Brueggemann's terse phrase that provides the clearest and closest rendering of Jubilee justice: you find out what belongs to whom and give it back. Brueggemann fleshes out this meaning by telling a prosaic story of a very proper woman who went to a teashop one day, sat down, ordered tea, and got ready to eat some cookies that she carried in her purse.

Because the teashop was crowded, a man took the other chair and also ordered tea. As it happened, he was a Jamaican black, though that is not essential to the story. The woman was prepared for a leisurely time, so she began to read her paper. As she did so, she took a cookie from the package. As she read, she noticed that the man across also took a cookie from the package. This upset her greatly, but she ignored it and kept reading. After a while she took another cookie. And so did he. This unnerved her and she glared at the man. While she glared, he reached for the fifth and last cookie, smiled and offered her half of it. She was indignant. She paid her money and left in a great hurry, enraged at such a presumptuous man. She hurried to her bus stop just outside. She opened her purse to get her fare. And then she saw, much to her distress, that in her purse was her package of cookies unopened.[1]

Brueggemann concludes the story by making the point that we are not very different from that woman. Sometimes we possess things so long that we come to think of them as ours, even though they don't belong to us. But at other times, "by the mercy of God, we have occasion to see to whom these things in fact belong. And when we see that, we have some little chance of being rescued from our misreading of reality."[2]

For those of us who are so privileged we have forgotten who owns what, Jubilee justice comes as a gift; for the particular meaning of justice that Jubilee stresses is the notion of "return," not in the Jubilee journey sense of a return home but return as relinquishing, giving back, and handing over what is not ours to God and to those crying for justice throughout the whole, round earth.

Implications of Jubilee Justice

The Jubilee text of Leviticus 25 offers several descriptions that elaborate on what finding out and giving back entail:

> When you buy from your neighbor, you shall pay only for the number of years since the jubilee; the seller shall charge you only for the remaining crop years. If the years are more, you shall increase the price, and if the

years are fewer, you shall diminish the price; for it is a certain number of harvests that are being sold to you.(vv. 15-16)

The land shall not be sold in perpetuity, for the land is mine; with me you are but aliens and tenants.(v. 23)

Throughout the land that you hold, you shall provide for the redemption of the land.(v. 24)

If anyone of your kin falls into difficulty and sells a piece of property, then the next of kin shall come and redeem what the relative has sold. If the person has no one to redeem it, but then prospers and finds sufficient means to do so, the years since its sale shall be computed and the difference shall be refunded to the person to whom it was sold, and the property shall be returned.(vv. 25-27)

Clearly, these texts make two striking points. One is their provision of an answer to the question "How long does my ownership last?" where the reply is "No more than fifty years." Because everything in the universe is gift, you're allowed to buy only a certain number of harvests, for—as Yahweh succinctly puts it—"the land is mine." The other point, however, is that at the time the Jubilee was first proclaimed, what the modern world refers to as "capital" was equivalent to land. Land that originally belonged to others must be returned to them.

Most commentators agree this rendering of Jubilee's meaning—the restoration of land—can't always be applied exactly today, although obviously there are occasions when land can and should be returned. But to see this as the only expression of Jubilee justice would entail limiting the modern meaning of capital or possessions to land; perhaps even more difficult—indeed, impossible—it would also assume a continuously equal population throughout the world, with the same number of people alive from one century to the next.

Commentators are also agreed that we can make contemporary applications of Jubilee justice, seeking to embody its moral principles today—the fact that the scripture cannot always be taken literally does not sanction washing our hands of the vocation to justice....

Justice and the Economic Realm

The commentary on Jubilee's implication for religious justice in the Anchor Bible series also speaks to what God required of Israel economically. It describes "what in principle God desires for humanity—broadly equitable distribution of the resources of the earth, especially land, and a curb on the tendency to accumulate, with its inevitable oppression and alienation. The Jubilee stands as a critique not only of massive private accumulation of land and related wealth, but also of large-scale forms of collectivism or nationalization which destroy any meaningful sense of personal or family ownership...."[3]

Economics

"Economics" refers here to the most commonly assumed aspect of the economy, the arena of capital, wealth, land, and goods—including money but not limited to money. It also refers to the economically translatable value of the schooling, education, skills, health, opportunities, and privilege that bring these to some but not to all.

One of the privileges often accorded Nobel Prize-winning economists is the assumption they are the only ones who understand economics—an assumption that is not the fault of the economists. A recent *New York Times* account helped to question this with the following story, filed under the heading "Camp Lemonade Stand":

> The season is late summer. Billy and Sue decide to sell lemonade in front of the house. They measure out water and sugar. They make a sign all by themselves and prop it up on a crate.
>
> Or: They go to lemonade camp…On the principle that successful entrepreneurs need early encouragement and training, Loyola College in Maryland created Camp Lemonade Stand. This summer, in two separate weeklong sessions, groups of 6-to-10-year-olds were taught researching, marketing, advertising, business strategies and a few recipes.
>
> 'Kids this age are very entrepreneurial,' says a dean of the college. So are colleges. The camp costs $250 per child, and children learn the differences between net and gross when they pay back $10 in seed money out of their proceeds.
>
> But it's all for a good cause. Underlying this capitalism is philanthropy. All proceeds from Camp Lemonade Stand go to Project Mexico—two orphanages the college sponsors in Mexico.[4]

This is preparation for understanding and becoming involved in the economic life of one's own country and of other countries. Indeed these youngsters may be at the beginning of understanding just how much the U.S. relations with Mexico is tied to the land that belonged to Mexico until the nineteenth century, when warfare, expansion, and sale made Mexican land part of the United States. It may be difficult to imagine a legal means of restoring such land today, but to be unaware of the Jubilee connection is to miss the creation of just possibilities.[5]

For the ordinary person, the beginnings of this creativity lie in guidelines being developed throughout today's world that assist people in determining how they might find out what belongs to whom and give it back. Among these guidelines are the following:

1. **There are limits to growth.** Environmentally concerned scientists throughout our world have given widespread publicity to this principle via the "limits to growth" theory, concerning what is and is not sustainable life on this planet.[6] But further education is undoubtedly needed concerning the metaphor of growth itself. On the one hand is the image of growth embodied in all living creatures, both human and nonhuman: we are born; we grow to a certain height, weight, and fruitfulness; we decline; we die. Such is the organic, healthy meaning of the metaphor. On the other hand we have a cancer metaphor of growth: growth as the unlimited proliferation of diseased cells. Although disease-as-metaphor has its own problems, the imagery of the unhealthy proliferation of cancer cells helps develop understanding of the dangers of unlimited growth in the same ways as do unstoppable giantism or obesity.

2. **There are limits to earning.** A recent conversation with friends led to two different proposals on this issue. Catherine said that everyone in the nation, including those working at home giving care to children, ought to get the same salary. Dick proposed that the highest salaries should go to those doing the most menial and least desired labor, whereas those whose work is most intrinsically satisfying should receive the least. But both believed in a salary cap.

Herman Daly, an economist with years of service at the World Bank, talks as many others do of ratios in earning, what is sometimes called "limited inequality." Daly points out that the military and civil service in this country both earn at a ratio of around ten to one: the highest paid member of the military makes no more than ten times the lowest paid member. In academic circles the ratio is around seven to one, with distinguished professors earning no more than seven times the salary of the lecturers who have not yet finished their dissertations (unless the lecturer is an adjunct professor, often the serf of academia, who is generally grossly underpaid by the feudal university).[7] These ratios are in sharp contrast to CEOs' salaries—the chair of General Motors versus the assembly-line auto worker—or to entertainers' salaries—David Letterman and Oprah Winfrey both earn more than ten times the bit player in a TV soap. Salary imbalances became a national issue during the baseball strike of the mid-1990s, not only when it became clear that the star with the contract for $7 million a year earned many times more than the large number of players making $120,000 but when it became impossible to find out the salaries that owners paid to themselves.

3. **There are limits to accumulation.** As we have seen, the Jubilee is pertinent and practical here, answering the question "How much can I acquire?" with the response "Only what you can accumulate in fifty years." This means that a will can either be a Jubilee document or create further division of rich and poor, especially in the case of inherited but unearned wealth. But Jubilee can also guide businesses and corporations. In October 1994, for example, a consortium of semiconductor companies *volunteered* to give up (return, relinquish, give back) a $90

million-a-year federal subsidy. The consortium, Sematech, was created seven years earlier to encourage U.S. production of semiconductors. As a result, it began to produce them, and by 1994 the future of the industry was assured. So Sematech decided to stop the subsidy on the principle that they did not need it anymore.[8]

This guideline is pertinent to the accumulation of land. As I have noted, it is sometimes possible to restore actual land even today: among the most dramatic examples in this century are the returns to the original inhabitants of former colonial nations in Africa, the British withdrawal from the subcontinent of India, and the U.S. relinquishment of the Philippines. This Jubilee tradition is about land redistribution whenever possible, whether to North American natives; to natives of countries richer nations have despoiled, including those whose economies they have devastated; or to countries taken as spoils of war.

Sarah Epperly, a California writer, suggests other aspects of restoring land: "Society might begin to live in such a manner that the reverence for life of native tribes would reemerge. We might begin on a personal level by eating only the amount of food required to live a healthful life, so that we want not but also waste not. We might use laundry detergents that don't pollute streams. We might imitate white-water rafting practices that must leave the water and shoreline exactly as it was, even to carrying off ashes from the campfire."[9]

4. **There are no limits to all people having the right to certain benefits: education in basic skills, including basic economics, a job, life, liberty, and the pursuit of happiness.** One of these rights is health care; it is difficult to understand how congressional lawmakers continue to evade this, since their own health care and that of their families is so extensive. Still another basic is the right to water. One of the first articles of agreement when Israel and Jordan signed the draft of their wide-ranging peace treaty in this decade was the simple headline "Will Share Water."

5. **There are also—apparently—no limits to two other things.** The first is human resistance when faced with the theology of relinquishment, where the demand on our lives is to simplify and to give back in order to redress massive inequality. But the other unlimited factor is the human imagination—especially the North American human imagination, with its can-do dimension—in finding out how to live this Jubilee tradition by sorting out what belongs to whom and returning it.

Some of the people I have met who talk about Jubilee in their lives provide simple yet eloquent examples here: the woman who told me that she and her husband had sold their second house because two homes in this needy world seemed an obscenity; the couple who have given up on stocks and bonds to invest in the schooling of a child in a family not their own, because that child is poor; the lawyers at our local soup kitchen, who make their pro bono services available to everyone who needs them; the Salvadoran peasants who receive all visitors as ambassadors from the Divine and give up the best spots on their earth floor to their guests while they sleep outside. All are aware that "the earth is the Lord's," and all have found ways to honor this and to give back whatever they can.

Justice and the Social Realm

This brief sketch of some of the economic implications of Jubilee justice already foreshadows many of its social implications. Still, one social unit must be stressed and highlighted, the same one stressed in the biblical teaching: the family. Essentially, Jubilee articulates a specific, practical concern for the family, one we have already encountered in considering forgiveness from debt.

Families' lives are badly damaged if they are split up by economic forces that make them powerless, making restoration of social dignity to families through economic viability still another aim of Jubilee justice. Further, the economic collapse of a family in one generation ought not be the circumstance, as it is in much of our world today, that condemns all future generations to perpetual debt.

Although economics can never be completely separated from family life, Jubilee justice does apply to families in other personal and intimate areas. For older family members, the principle of finding out/giving back turns attention to the generations coming after us. In Richard Ford's novel *Wildlife*, for example, a mother tries to teach this Jubilee tradition to her son. As her marriage is ending, she says to the sixteen-year-old, "Your life doesn't mean what you have, sweetheart, or what you get. It's what you're willing to give up. That's an old saying, I know. But it's still true." When he responds that he feels that's a problem for him, since he doesn't want to give up anything, she goes on, "Oh well. Good luck." Then she elaborates: "That's really not one of the choices," she says. "You have to give things up. That's the rule. It's the major rule for everything.[10]

One of my colleagues, a New Jersey educator, describes what this has meant in her family. She told me that finding out what belongs to whom and returning it became real for her when her oldest daughter came home after her first year in college. "The first weeks she was home," my colleague said, "I found myself encountering reluctance on her part to account for her time, especially how long she'd be gone in the evening and when she was coming in. I finally realized that accountability now belongs to her; that made it possible for me to give it back."

At the same time, adult children experience the relevance of finding out and giving back with reference to the generations preceding them, especially toward their parents. Often a bittersweet moment comes in adult life when we need to return to our parents their wishes for us, their dreams for us—of schooling, of a mate, of lifework, for example—so that we might pursue our own. Even more poignant and powerful, a finding-out moment also occurs with their deaths, as we return their bodies or their ashes to the earth.

This Jubilee teaching even reveals individual, intrapersonal dimensions that we may not have suspected or, more likely, have not had time to consider. Often these also occur as we age, especially as we enter the later years of adult life only to discover parts of ourselves life itself has taken away or reserved until now. Women who have spent the first decades of their adult lives raising a family or caring for a home may eventually discover unused gifts of academic inquiry or musical creation or service beyond their families, as Lillian Carter did at sixty-eight when she joined the Peace Corps. And men pushed to excel and to shut down their emotions may start opening closed doors and crossing thresholds into affective areas they have not entered until now. These too fall under the counsel to find out what belongs to whom and give it back.

Finally, there are two family situations that are a direct concern of Jubilee justice. Grace Harding, director of the Office for Persons with Disabilities in the Diocese of Pittsburgh, drew my attention to the first. Listening to me a decade ago as I delivered one of the first lectures I ever gave on Jubilee, she reminded me that the words of Isaiah and of Jesus in citing the Jubilee were not only, not even primarily, metaphorical. "Sight to the blind" means precisely and especially that: attending to those with the inability to see. Then Harding pointed out that those texts also refer to the proclamation of hearing for the deaf, and ramps, wide doorways, and accessible bathrooms for those who must use wheelchairs. These persons demand primary Jubilee attention, as do their parents and the rest of their families.

The other situation is the family made up of the widow and her fatherless children. My brother and I have some experience here: as the small children of a mother widowed after only ten short years of marriage, Tom and I knew something of the isolation, loneliness, and fear that the presence of sudden death brings and much of the trauma and bruising it can carry. Amazingly, we also knew Jubilee through the Jewish family who lived next door. Toward us, they lived the prescriptions of Torah fully and explicitly. Throughout my childhood they remembered us and cared for us through gifts of food, time, friendship, laughter, and prayer.

A Coda on Mourning

A surprising, although not unexpected, reaction often occurs as people begin finding out what belongs to whom and giving it back. They begin to mourn, although their reasons for mourning may differ. Sometimes the mourning is the natural response to the sobering corrective of suffering. Sometimes it is the natural response to the inexplicable loss accompanying the pain of the world. Sometimes it is the response to recognizing we are entering the pathos of God. And sometimes it is the resistance that accompanies the realization that we—and our possessions—must decrease if justice is to increase.

At other times our mourning is a passage through the stages learned from Elizabeth Kubler-Ross, who outlines a movement from denial to anger to bargaining to depression to acceptance, a movement that seems to take up residence within us.[11] If it does, the anger that is part of the mourning rhythm can be instructive. Theologian Beverly Harrison has written that anger signals attention to our awareness that all is not right with the world, and so it can be an ally. She extols the power of anger in the work of love, and in the work of justice.[12]

Sometimes our mourning has physical manifestations. It can include the characteristics that Erich Lindemann discovered in interviewing survivors and bereaved after the Coconut Grove nightclub in Boston burned in 1942.[13] This was a flash fire that left 492 dead in less than an hour, and those who were left manifested similar reactions: a disconcerting lack of warmth, somatic distress (pains in the stomach), preoccupation with the image of what had been lost, guilt, disorganized patterns of conduct, and the feeling one no longer fits. These same responses can appear as we take on the work of Jubilee.

Some would unthinkingly label these symptoms aberrant. But if we grieve the loss in the world, if we are in bodily distress due to its poisons, and if we feel we are out of place and no longer fit, we may be acting as the sanest ones of all, in a planet gone mad through acquisition.

Indeed, this may explain why we sometimes experience our mourning as endless. Although we know it is possible to get "stuck" in mourning, the sheer immensity of the world's grief and need bogs us down, and the heaviness may not lift until, mysteriously, we embrace mourning as a natural and necessary component of Jubilee justice and take it into ourselves.

Our precise relation to mourning, however, really does not matter, for once a person or a community or a nation mourns truly, its hands no longer clutch and it becomes free. Those free hands symbolize the ability to give back and return, as well as the power to let go. And once a person or community or nation has learned to find out what belongs to whom and give it back, it is itself released. It is set free *by* Jubilee justice and *toward* Jubilee justice into the vocation of proclaiming Jubilee throughout a broken world.

1. Brueggemann, "Voices of the Night," 6.

2. Ibid.

3. bid.

4. "Camp Lemonade Stand," *New York Times Magazine*, September 4, 1994, 15.

5. See Rodolfo Acuna, *Occupied America: The Chicano's Struggle toward Liberation* (San Francisco: Canfield Press/Harper & Row, 1972).

6. See Donella H. Meadows, Dennis L. Meadows, and Jorgen Randers, *Beyond the Limits: Confronting Global Collapse, Envisioning a Sustainable Future* (Mills, Vt.: Chelsea Green Publishing Co., 1992).

7. See Herman Daly, "A Biblical Economic Principle and the Steady-State Economy," *Epiphany Journal 12* (Winter 1992): 12ff. The comment about the adjunct professors is mine, not Daly's.

8. Editorial, "Palms Down," *New York Times*, October 12, 1994, sec. A, 14.

9. Sarah Epperly, in a private communication with the author.

10. Richard Ford, *Wildlife* (New York: Atlantic Monthly Press, 1990), 123.

11. Elizabeth Kubler-Ross, *On Death and Dying* (New York: Macmillan, 1969).

12. See Beverly Harrison's inaugural lecture, "The Power of Anger in the Work of Love: Christian Ethics for Women and Other Strangers," *Union Theological Seminary Review* supplement (1981), 41-57.

13. Erich Lindemann, "Symptomatology and Management of Acute Grief," in Robert Fulton, Ed., *Death and Identity* (New York: John Wiley & Sons, Inc., 1965), 186-201; reprinted from *American Journal of Psychiatry 101* (1944), 141-48.

On Being a Jubilee Church

by Rev. Rich Lang

Rev. Rich Lang is the Pastor of Trinity United Methodist Church
in Seattle. He has published articles in *Yes! Magazine* and the
Progressive Christian, and is a regular columnist for Seattle's weekly
homeless community paper, *Real Change*. His ministry has been
recognized with a Heroic Leadership Award for ministry with the
poor and street kids, the Taking the Bull By The Horns Award for
courageous social justice leadership, an Ordinary People/Extraordi-
nary Outcomes Award, and the Rauschenbusch Award for Leadership in the Social Gospel.

Introduction

Trinity United Methodist Church calls itself a Joy and Justice church. Our spiritual DNA compels us to push out against our fears and limitations, towards the
next step, the next surprise. We seek to be radically inclusive, welcoming all people
as partners and friends. We have developed a soup kitchen and a shelter whose real
goal is not only to feed and house, but to build relationships of friendship. Trinity
also organizes people to address systemic issues—for example, to cry out against
homelessness and for peace. As a Jubilee congregation, we advocate to cancel the
debt of impoverished nations.

Such works of charity and justice require a community of joy and trust. The sermon that follows was delivered on the occasion of our officially becoming a Jubilee
Congregation, committed to working for the elimination of Third World debt. As a
preacher, my goal was to develop the connection between the works of justice, the
works of mercy, and the necessity of living out that which we preach.

The Scripture for the day, Acts 2:37-47, is printed below.

> When the people heard this, they were cut to the heart and said to Peter
> and the other apostles, 'Brothers, what shall we do?'
>
> Peter replied, 'Repent and be baptized, every one of you, in the name of
> Jesus Christ for the forgiveness of your sins. And you will receive the gift
> of the Holy Spirit. The promise is for you and your children and for all
> who are far off—for all whom the Lord our God will call.'
>
> With many other words he warned them; and he pleaded with them,
> 'Save yourselves from this corrupt generation.' Those who accepted his
> message were baptized, and about three thousand were added to their
> number that day.

*They devoted themselves to the apostles' teaching and to the fellowship,
to the breaking of bread and to prayer. Everyone was filled with awe,
and many wonders and miraculous signs were done by the apostles. All
the believers were together and had everything in common. Selling their
possessions and goods, they gave to anyone as he had need. Every day
they continued to meet together in the temple courts. They broke bread
in their homes and ate together with glad and sincere hearts, praising
God and enjoying the favor of all the people. And the Lord added to their
number daily those who were being saved. (Acts 2:37-47)*

On Being a Jubilee Church

The exasperated refrain of Rodney King, "Can't we all just get along?" is a common cry heard throughout life. You see it on the playground: two kids are playing well together, co-operating and sharing, but then a third friend shows up, and before you know it, two begin to gang up on one. What we see in child's play is intensified as we grow up and move into school, employment and neighborhoods, and into state, national and international matters. We see it in all spheres of life, competition and interpersonal ego needs. We see it in families, friendships, politics, marriage, partnerships, economics and churches. "Can't we all just get along?" is a cry heard from our own lips.

In a way the entirety of the Bible is a handbook addressing the same cry. It is similar to Cain's question, "Am I my brother's keeper?" From Genesis through Revelation, the Bible tells stories and offers guidance and encouragement for the purpose of trying to help us all get along.

The Bible offers a double blessing of salvation and liberation. We are saved from our sins, the inner demons that turn us into less than ourselves. We are liberated from the political and economic institutions that oppress us as we work together for justice. God cares for both our eternal character and our concrete, day-to-day lives.

The text in Acts is a Jubilee text. It chronicles how the Jesus movement began, with an announcement that Jesus, not Caesar, was lord of life. It announced that the way of Jesus, not the way of Caesar, was the way to life, freedom, abundance and fulfillment. The people responded in specific, concrete actions: they devoted themselves to the teachings of the Apostles, they bonded together learning to trust each other, they ate together in memory of Jesus eating with sinners and saints and they developed the inward discipline of prayer.

As a result, many signs and wonders began to emerge. Folks had experiences of God's grace. They got healed, welcomed and offered a shot at new life. Those who followed Jesus became extraordinarily generous. They funded their values: their money was placed at the service of their mission. They looked out for one another. The early church understood itself as a large extended family: everyone belongs.

Looking way back, we can see that the Jews were formed as a people when they fell into captivity to Egyptian empire. Under the heavy burdens of empire, their identity and self-respect were crushed: they were "less than," they were "unworthy," they were pawns to be used and abused by folks greater than themselves. They were "no people," slaves, nobodies. In their affliction they cried out to God but not to the God known as Yahweh. They just cried out to any god, any power that could help them, that could release them from their afflictions and anguish. Yahweh heard their cry. Yahweh moved into history and inspired, empowered and directed a movement out of Empire and into Promised Land. Because Yahweh helped them, the slaves bonded themselves to Yahweh in a specific covenant: an eternal agreement to be the people of Yahweh, the family of Yahweh in history.

The Jubilee...was legislation, politics with a spiritual base. A just economic order was a way of life that cared for the poor and put limits on the rich.

The Jubilee was Yahweh's blueprint answering the economic cry of "can't we all get along?" In a nutshell, the answer, at least economically, was that the way to get along is to share and co-operate. Folks who get too rich need to redistribute their wealth back into the community. Those who fall through the cracks need to be caught and given a second, third, fourth and fifth chance. Wealth, in those days, didn't come in the form of dollar bills. Rather, wealth was in the concrete form of land. The way of Yahweh was simple: Yahweh alone owned the land. The people of Yahweh were simply stewards caring for Yahweh's land.

The Jubilee, in other words, was legislation, politics with a spiritual base. A just economic order was a way of life that cared for the poor and put limits on the rich. The Jubilee idea was to completely redistribute Yahweh's wealth every fifty years: basically every other generation got a fresh start. This is hard for us to grasp because we are a bunch of individuals. But, back then, there were no individuals: you were part of a family, a clan, a tribe. You were not yourself without others.

So what does all this have to do with us today? As our litany [please see page 266] attests, the Jubilee is rooted throughout the scripture. Jesus was calling his people back to a Jubilee lifestyle. The story in Acts reflects this call of creating a community of commonwealth, not segregated wealth. It reflects the necessity that those who follow Jesus become an extended family. I am not myself without you. The movement of Jesus is a relational dance that keeps opening up to more and more partners: welcoming everyone to participate, share, become part of, equal with, a society of mutual aid, mutual benefit and mutual blessing.

Is that possible today? I think it is. I think our becoming an official Jubilee Congregation is an enormous act of spiritual maturity. It focuses us on thinking globally. We are one world, and those who follow Jesus believe that this is God's world. Afghani people are just as sacred as American people. The babies of Iran are just as precious as the babies of Seattle. Being a Jubilee Congregation commits us to the spiritually-based political commitment of debt cancellation, economic opportunity, economic justice and global economic welfare for the common good.

How does a focus on Jubilee shape our spirituality? Again, looking at Acts, when the first church heard the good news of salvation they responded by devoting themselves to the teaching, hanging out together, eating together, praying together, sharing possessions—and day by day others came to the party and danced.

In the kind of individualized world we inhabit today, the world where dollar bills, not land, equal wealth, the kind of world where we ourselves are the Empire, many of us in captivity to debt, many of us enslaved to our jobs…in this world how do we all get along?

I think that the foundation of Jubilee spirituality, a Jubilee politics of justice, is the bonding of a people. It is saving those who feel they are individuals in the world, and incorporating them into an extended family. To be specific, here inside this congregation, the first foundational step is to bond with each other. It is to see oneself and all of us as a tribe, a clan, a family that has chosen to be in covenant with the God whom we know through Jesus.

For example, how do we live in such a way that if one of our elders loses her apartment then we will rally around and care for her, and house her? If one of us loses his job, how do we support him through the agony of unemployment until better days arrive? If a divorce shatters a family, how do we care for both spouses, and the kids, so that none fall through the cracks, so that none face their suffering alone? How do we network so that every person in our homeless shelter finds a job, and graduates into a home? How do we love one another in spirit, and in the concrete political acts of feeding, sheltering, clothing and living abundantly in an Empire that instructs us to live affluently? How do we stay true to one another as the expression, sign and wonder that brings awe upon everyone?

To be a Jubilee Church is a spiritually-based political action. But it is also a spiritually-based lifestyle of mutual aid, mutual benefit and mutual blessing. If I had one wish for our congregation it would be this: that you love one another in such a way that every one of you knew that, in this place, amongst these people, I belong, and in this place, amongst these people, I will be cared for; in this place, amongst these people, my gifts are welcomed and received. That each of us might be able to say, "These people I have loved, and been loved by; with these people I have poured out my life, and been poured into; with these people I have been given abundance, with these people I have seen the Risen Christ."

If we can learn to do such a little thing, then God will shower us with even greater signs and wonders, and we will live to see the day when a global Jubilee is proclaimed amongst the nations, who have learned, finally, to get along. To live in this faith is what it means to be a Jubilee congregation: an awesome sign of enlightened hope in the darkness of Empire.

Used by permission of the author, Rich Lang.

Practicing Abundance—
Sabbath and Tithing

Christian stewardship is the *practice* of the Christian
religion. It is neither a department of life nor a sphere
of activity. It is the Christian conception of life as a
whole, manifested in attitudes and actions.

—W.H. Greever

Being faithful to God is always manifest
practically in a transfigured distribution
of resources.

—Tom Beaudoin

Introduction—VIII

Walter Brueggemann's essay "The Liturgy of Abundance, the Myth of Scarcity" (see page 25) recounts what he calls the Biblical "liturgy of abundance." He reflects on Jesus' life, parables and teachings and says: "Many people both inside and outside of the church haven't a clue that Jesus is talking about the economy. We haven't taught them that he is. But we must begin to do so now...the creation is infused with the Creator's generosity, and we can find practices, procedures and institutions that allow that generosity to work."

Money and Faith's final four sections emphasize those very "practices, procedures and institutions" to which Brueggemann refers; in other words, the following sections ask the question, "How shall we then live?" in ways pertinent to both the personal and societal.

Questioning sacred cows—like the GNP, economic growth and corporate personhood—is understandably overwhelming. One of the reasons for that, however, is our belief in the myth "That's just the way it is."

The essays throughout the rest of this book challenge that myth. They highlight practical steps individuals, governments and corporations can and are taking which demonstrate, "That's *not* just the way it is."

The essays in the following section highlight Sabbath and tithing as particularly powerful practices to challenge money's power in, and claim on, our lives. Muller and Myers reflect on the Sabbath, a practice the ever-growing, always-consuming money machine certainly does not understand. And Killian Noe's essay considers the equally counter-cultural practice of tithing.

It Is Good

by Wayne Muller

Wayne Muller is an ordained minister, therapist and author. A graduate of Harvard Divinity School, he is the founder of Bread for the Journey, a national, non-profit charity serving the poor and underprivileged. He is also the founder of the Institute for Engaged Spirituality, Senior Scholar with the Fetzer Institute, and is a Fellow of the Institute of Noetic Sciences. His books include the national bestseller *Legacy of the Heart: The Spiritual Advantages of a Painful Childhood* and *How, Then, Shall We Live?*

∞

And God saw everything that he had made, and behold, it was very good.

—Genesis 1:31

Our willingness to rest depends on what we believe we will find there. At rest, we come face-to-face with the essence of life. If we believe life is fundamentally good, we will seek out rest as a taste of that goodness. If we believe life is fundamentally bad or flawed, we will be reluctant to quiet ourselves, afraid of meeting the darkness that resides in things—or in ourselves.

In Genesis, a fundamental goodness is presumed throughout the creation story. At every juncture God acts, steps back, and rests. God invokes the light, separates it from the darkness—creating a conversational rhythm between light and dark—and steps back. *And God saw that it was good.* Then God makes a place for heaven and earth, separates the sea from dry land—creating a tidal rhythm—and steps back. *And God saw that it was good.*

Then God made the sun and moon, creating a seasonal rhythmicity. And, stepping back, *God saw that it was good.* And so the story continues, emptiness giving birth to form, with the creation of living creatures, the beautiful birds that claim the air as their home, the many-colored fish and great whales, the cattle and insects, all the animals wild and free upon the earth. Then God creates man and woman in the likeness of God. *And God saw everything that he had made, and behold, it was very good.*

Sabbath rest invites us to step back, *and see that it is good.* Jews believe that on the Sabbath we are given an extra soul—the *Neshemah Yeterah,* or Sabbath soul—which enables us to more fully appreciate and enjoy the blessings of our life and the fruits of our labors. With this extra soul, like God on the Sabbath we, too, are more able to pause, and see how it is good.

Since I was a child I have felt this fundamental goodness in the world—in people, in life, in the earth. It is not something I learned, apprehended, or discovered. It was something I knew, like gravity, or wind. I have felt the truth of this goodness even when no external evidence suggested its presence. This is what drew me to the field of psychotherapy, and later to the ministry and spiritual practice. In psychotherapy training I gravitated toward those forms of healing that presumed this essential strength and wisdom in people, those methods that sought to affirm what was already whole and strong. I steadfastly believed, even as I worked in the midst of the most horrific sorrow—sexual abuse, alcoholism, poverty, illness—that there remained a persistent luminosity of spirit, an unquenchable resilience.

When I was young I had no way to speak of this goodness. Later, as a therapist, I was taught no official diagnostic name for this place. Only poetry and music, art and dance seemed to know of this vast and luminous country. Only in spiritual texts would I find such phrases as Thomas Merton's "hidden wholeness" or Tibetan Buddhism's "persistent luminosity." Through my seminary training and meditation practice I would learn that the spiritual traditions of the world dearly love this inner resilience, and call it by many names: inner light, still, small voice, Buddha Nature, Kingdom of God, Holy Spirit.

If we look deeply and carefully within all that is hurtful, ignorant, and wounded, we will eventually see the light of the world shine through. When Jesus says "You are the light of the world" he is reaffirming this persistent luminosity, our hidden wholeness. As children of a good and whole creation, we remain whole and good in spite of all our sorrows, sins, and weaknesses.

The Sabbath makes this very same presupposition. Sabbath time assumes that if we step back and rest, we will see the wholeness in it all. We will naturally apprehend the good in how things are, taste the underlying strength, beauty, and wisdom that lives even in the difficult days, take delight in the gift and blessing of being alive.

If we believe our soul is naturally luminous and that we are filled with innate, natural perfection, if we are the light of the world, then when we sink into quiet we return to peace. Conversely, if we believe creation is badly flawed, then we must avoid intimate contact with it. We greet silence with fear, afraid it will show us the broken center at the core of the world and of ourselves. Afraid of what we will find there, we avoid the stillness at all costs, keeping ourselves busy not so much to accomplish but to avoid the terrors and dangers of emptiness.

Jesus began his Sermon on the Mount—arguably the most important teaching of his life—by saying *Blessed are*. Blessed are the poor. Blessed are those who mourn. Blessed are the meek. He did *not* say "Blessed will be the poor when they finally achieve a certain level of economic independence." He did not say "Blessed will be those who mourn after they have endured their period of unspeakable grief and received support from their clergy or family." He did not say "Blessed will be the meek after they graduate from assertiveness training, and claim their inner strength."

He said blessed *are*. Not "they will one day be blessed," but they are blessed *right now*. The poor are blessed, even in their poverty. Those who mourn are blessed, even in their grief. The meek, the merciful, even those who are persecuted— blessed, blessed, blessed. Not later. Not when their trials are over. Not when they are fixed. Right here, right now. There is a blessing for you here, now, in this very moment.

All Jesus' teaching seems to hinge on this singular truth concerning the nature of life: It is all right. *Do not worry about tomorrow. I have come that you might have life abundantly. Be not afraid.* Over and over, in parable, story, and example, he insists that regardless how it goes for us, we are cared for, we are safe, we are all right. There is a light of the world, a kingdom of heaven inside us that will bear us up, regardless of our sorrow, fear, or loss. Do not wait to enjoy the harvest of your life; you are already blessed. *The kingdom of God is already here. It is within you and among you.*

Like the creator who steps back and sees that it is good, Jesus just as confidently insists we are already whole. Once we become aware of this teaching in the gospels, we find it everywhere. *Whoever has eyes, let them see, and ears, let them hear.* Do not wait to be joyful; take your portion now, take your rest and savor the delicious fruits of the kingdom. *Do you not say "There are yet four months, then comes the harvest"? I tell you, lift up your eyes, and see how the fields are already white for harvest. You are the light of the world. Rejoice always. Be of good cheer. Elijah has already come. You are already blessed.*

What if, as Thomas Merton insists, we harbor a hidden wholeness? What if, as the Buddhists insist, we are saturated with an innate natural perfection? What if, as Jesus insists, we are the light of the world? What if, as God insists, it is already good, very good?

In our hurry and worry and acquiring and working, we forget. Rest, take delight in the goodness of creation, and remember how good it is.

In this light the Sabbath prescription is a loving reminder to take full advantage of a condition that already exists. At rest, our souls are restored. This is the only commandment that begins with the word "remember," as if it refers to something we already know, but have forgotten. It is good. It is whole. It is beautiful. In our hurry and worry and acquiring and working, we forget. Rest, take delight in the goodness of creation, and remember how good it is.

When people share with me their sorrow and suffering, at my best I am merely a faithful companion, watching for the wholeness embedded deep within their fear and confusion. For a time, all they can see or feel is the cold, cutting blade of their terror, the ache of despair, the burning sadness. My work is to be good company, to allow them to lean for a while on my unshakable belief in their inner fire. Even on the good days I cannot do more than this. Then, slowly, in their own time, their bodies open, they begin to feel and taste the possibility of this wholeness for themselves. This fundamental goodness always waits for us to discover it, if we will only gather together patiently, and listen.

On May 30, 1996, a fire ravaged Lama Mountain, home to many families in the hills of northern New Mexico, as well as to the Lama Foundation, a spiritual retreat center that had for years been a place of meditation and refuge for pilgrims from around the world. The fire was quick and furious. It destroyed dozens of homes and all but a few of the buildings at the retreat center. Three weeks after the fire, I walked the land with Owen Lopez, a close friend and director of the McCune Foundation in New Mexico. We were hoping, along with Bread for the Journey, to provide some emergency relief for the community, including quick restoration of water and electricity. Everywhere we looked we saw the color of charcoal, silver-gray-black, shiny, reflecting the light of the sun that filtered through charred and twisted branches. Just three weeks earlier, this was an inferno.

But on this day there spread out before us a sea of green. Small oak seedlings, six to ten inches high, blanketed the forest floor. Without any human effort to clear or seed, already the earth was pushing out life. Creation creates life at every revolution; it is incapable of doing otherwise. Were we to reduce the planet to cinders, a holocaust of ignorance and greed, still the universe would create life from the ashes of our clumsiness.

Sabbath is a day we walk in the forest, walk among the fruits of our harvest and the ruins of our desperations, and see what lives. On the Sabbath, we rest. And see that it is good.

The Gift Must Always Move
An Interview with Ched Myers on Sabbath Economics

In this interview, Myers teaches: "Sabbath represents a cautionary discipline that seeks to constrain…our fallen human impulse to work compulsively, to consume addictively, and to use and exploit resources and labor mercilessly." In other words, he pointedly suggests that practicing Sabbath is also an economic practice. He thus expands the customary understanding of Sabbath as primarily a personal/family choice associated with resting one day a week. In the movement to connect Sabbath with creating a more just economic order he proclaims, "The church ought to be leading the way rather than indulging in the middle-class fantasy that everything will somehow work out."

Following a workshop that Ched conducted…for a national gathering of the Servant Leadership Schools in Washington, DC, *Inward/Outward* co-editor, Kayla McClurg, asked Ched about the issues that led him to focus his work on Sabbath Economics.

KM: Ched, what do you mean when you say "Sabbath Economics?" Aren't those two words contradictory? Isn't "Sabbath" about letting go and receiving, and "economics" about attaining and possessing? How do they fit together?

CM: You are certainly correct in your impression that these two terms, when viewed from the vantage point of current economic orthodoxies, would seem to be mutually exclusive. I have put them together, however, precisely to argue that economics for Christians must be reinterpreted in the light of the central biblical tradition of keeping Sabbath. Conversely, I contend that Sabbath is at its core an economic ethic, not just a spiritual one.

KM: How are you defining the word "Sabbath?"

CM: Sabbath in the Bible has three essential connotations. First, the Sabbath suspension of *doing* in order to *be* is grounded in the Self-limiting character of God, who created and then rested (Gen 2:1ff). Indeed, according to the primeval Garden story, the original vocation of the human being (*'adam*) was simply to enjoy this "cosmic Sabbath" by entering into intimate relationship with an abundant and wonderful Creation (Gen 2:19f). Instead, as the Fall story goes, the human being succumbed to the fatal temptation to try to re-engineer or "improve" upon the work of God. Life outside the Garden thus consists of alienation from God, from each other, and from the Creation, all symbolized by difficult and exhausting work and a creation that, as a result, is not quite as abundant. The Sabbath is a hedge on our tragic fate, however, reminding us of the original symbiosis. This explains why the ecstatic and erotic dimensions of human activity, such as sex or singing or eating, are not only allowed on the Sabbath, but encouraged.

Second, Sabbath concerns the communal discipline of setting limits. We are commanded to cease our determined work to transform the world, in particular the "economic" activity of production and distribution of goods. Why? It is because of our Fallen human impulse to work compulsively, to consume addictively, and to use and exploit resources and labor mercilessly. Sabbath represents a cautionary discipline that seeks to constrain this addiction/compulsion (which the Bible calls Sin). Interestingly, the central question of the 21st century will be whether or not humans can set and maintain limits: on our plundering of the planet, on our increasingly Promethean technologies, and on our spiraling violence toward the biosphere and each other. If we cannot, we will perish—which is precisely what the old Sabbath traditions of Scripture warn (see e.g. Ex 31:14-17; Lev 26:2-39).

Third, the Sabbath is a tradition of economic justice. The practice is introduced in the context of the manna story in Exodus 16. This grounds it firmly in the "economic instructions" of that archetypal tale, in which the newly liberated Hebrew slaves are tutored in the old ways of sharing: everyone must gather "enough" and no one must accumulate "too much." So Sabbath is not an individual spiritual discipline only; it represents a communal practice of constraint within the context of economic sufficiency for all.

KM: And "economics?"

CM: Economics, on the other hand, is usually identified in our capitalist culture with profit, accumulation, markets, development, and trade. But our word comes from the Greek *oikonomia*, which means "law of the household." Ironically, the household today is the last space in our hypermarket society in which the traditional "gift economy" still holds: labor is cooperative, assets and possessions are shared equitably, and consumption is done without payment. Before the rise of the great civilizations and empires—which is to say, for 99% of the history of *homo sapiens*—all human communities operated this way, practicing what anthropologists call "generalized reciprocity." Indeed, prior to the rise and relentless and aggressive spread of modern capitalism beginning in the 17th century, most people on the planet still lived more or less this way. The older lifeways were based upon a cosmology that saw everyone in the community as kin, the Creation around us as commonwealth, and the Spirit world as the origin of the great Gift.

This traditional cosmology is shared by the Bible—which is why it seems so strange to our capitalist ears! The natural abundance of the Creation lasts as long as the gift circulates; conversely, to try to own or hoard or consume the gift for ourselves replaces the abundance with addiction, a warning nicely illustrated in the alternative version of the manna story found in Numbers 11:31-34. As Lewis Hyde puts it in his brilliant and highly recommended study, *The Gift: Imagination and the Erotic life of Property* (Vintage, 1983), indigenous people "...understood a cardinal property of the gift: whatever we have been given is supposed to be given away again, not kept.... The only essential is this: the gift must always move.... 'One man's gift,' they say, 'must not be another man's capital.'"

So in effect, "economics," etymologically speaking, should concern how we manage and share the gift—it is modern capitalism that has hijacked the term, not me! In sum, then, I would boil Sabbath Economics down to this basic proposition: a) we must limit and constrain our economic activity in order to b) keep the gifts of Creation circulating equitably.

KM: If symbiosis is how we were created, and dis-integration is the result of the Fall, what should be our response? Should we try to return to that earlier state of harmony—or move to something new and as yet unimagined?

CM: The old story in its wisdom reminds us that there are flaming swords that forever keep us out of the garden. We cannot go back to hunting and gathering lifeways, not because they are primitive but because we have destroyed that possibility—our numbers are too large, our plundering of nature too far advanced, our competence in the old ways too atrophied. But ironically, neither can we continue on with our addictive/compulsive way of life. Here again the old traditions prove to be more relevant than ever. The biblical prophets right up to Jesus predicate the future upon the people's ability and willingness to repent, which means to "turn around." We must turn around not because we can go back to the beginning, but because we must first *stop* heading in this destructive direction. Then we must *learn* from the old ways, and then we must use all of our creativity and commitment to *reconstruct* postmodern lifeways that are just, sustainable, and re-integrative. This will necessarily focus upon creating and maintaining limits, learning from the poor and marginalized, and embracing disciplines of sharing. This will demand of us extraordinary spiritual resources, which is why the church ought to be leading the way rather than indulging in the middle-class fantasy that everything will somehow work out (to our continuing advantage!) and that our faith meanwhile has nothing to do with economics!

KM: What about Jesus? Did he care about economic systems, or did his comment that we should "render unto Caesar what is Caesar's" indicate he wasn't concerned, as some folks argue?

CM: That verse, so notoriously misinterpreted, sums up our dilemma perfectly! We have indeed conceded the economy, and with it the Creation itself, to the dictates and designs of Caesar. But he is concerned only with trade advantages, profit-maximization, capital flows, and the consolidation of economic and political power. And the problem for the church is that the Creation belongs to Creator, not to Caesar or any other would-be proprietor: "The land must not be sold permanently, because the land is Mine, and you are but aliens and tenants" (Lev 25:23). Conscientious Christians today should no longer take refuge from moral accountability in the old "two kingdoms" copout. Admittedly, Jesus is all too often portrayed as having little to say apart from the mildest occasional moral gloss on the dominant economic system of the day (as if the best he could muster was: "Try not to be greedy," or "Give to charity once in awhile"). This is *not* the Jesus of our gospels, however.

Jesus of Nazareth was unafraid to identify the cultural phenomenon of money/capital with the principalities (even employing the ancient Babylonian name of "Mammon" to emphasize its pagan and imperial origins), whose enslaving power is omnipresent (Mt 6:24). He called the rich plainly and unequivocally to redistribute their wealth to the poor while inviting disciples to "re-communitize" their assets (Mk 10:17ff). Above all, he was immersed in that old Gift cosmology: he asserted without a hint of irony that Solomon's Temple—symbol of the socioeconomic zenith of Israel's civilization—pales in worth next to one single wildflower in the eyes of the Creator (Lk 12:27).

KM: What might "this Jesus" have to say to us in our present times?

CM: *This* Jesus' call to discipleship is identified in the gospels with "release" from our captivity to the dominant Mammon system. This is indicated by the fact that the verb used to describe the fishermen "leaving" their nets to follow Jesus is the same verb used to describe the forgiveness of sin/debt, the liberation of captives and the unbinding of the demon-possessed. This Jubilee release takes many forms: writing off debt, practicing solidarity with the poorest, making sure that everyone is included at the social table, sharing our assets with each other—and resisting the tyranny of Caesar's coin! I believe Jesus invites us to do the same today. Our task is not to rationalize why we can't follow, or to equivocate where Jesus was clear, but to figure out what his call means in concrete terms today, in a world quite different (but probably no more complex and ambiguous) than that of the gospels.

KM: Where do you see the worst consequences of the abuse of Sabbath Economics in our society? It seems we are guided as a culture by the "Myth of Progress." Is there any truth to this myth, or is it merely deceptive?

CM: I believe the terrible but inevitable consequences of our way of life are the twin global apocalypses of the broadening environmental crisis and the deepening gulf between rich and poor. The Promethean myth of Progress promised Paradise, but has delivered an end-game. Social Darwinism, which is the true subtext of Progress, has indeed been a self-fulfilling prophecy: the "fittest" have survived, enjoying unconscionable affluence while the many scramble for scraps. Meanwhile the "developed" world continues with exponential determination to exhaust the very life support systems of the planet—forests, waterways, air, topsoil—convinced that we can correct the problems we've created through technological intervention, even into the very genetic structures of life. We are like Icarus, relying on the artificial wings of our ingenuity, and unless we listen to the old wisdom stories, we too will fly too close to the sun and learn the terrible lessons of gravity.

KM: The immensity of the problem feels overwhelming. Where might we begin the task of restoring Creation and calling forth the full humanity of both the oppressed and their oppressors? What might we be doing now?

CM: It will take at least as many generations to repair the damage we have wrought as it took to wreak havoc. Yet Grace and the renewing power of Life in creation can sustain us, if we do our part. There are no blueprints, just the life-long tasks of turning away from all the personal and political delusions and dysfunction, and turning toward the recommunitization and reintegration of life. I would suggest that a good beginning point is to examine our relationship to the following areas of our lives:

1. **The land:** Is there any natural place that you care enough about to defend? Whether it's a backyard garden, a local streambed, a regional watershed or a beloved national park, we cannot rehabilitate our relationship to the earth in the abstract.

2. **The poor:** The truth of any society is embodied not by its richest, most powerful, or most beautiful members, but by those on the bottom. The marginalized will unmask our illusions about the nobility of the status quo and teach us about grace in the struggle to survive, to change, and to heal. I would include in this that we have a special responsibility to learn who the indigenous people of our area were and are, and to face the legacy of our dispossession of them.

3. **Our money:** Our paralysis because of debt servicing needs to be examined, on the household, national, and international levels. Re-examine how you and your church handle your surplus, and consider re-investing it in communities that most need access to capital. There is a current renaissance of alternative banking and community currency experiments just waiting for Christians to plug into!

4. **Our possessions:** Whether or not we suffer from "affluenza," we need to realize how fetishistic our relationship to things has become for all of us, thanks to the mystical and inescapable huckstering of Madison Avenue. Until and unless we truly are convicted that our "stuff" cannot save us or make us happy, we will be unable and uninterested in commencing the journey of "recovery" from our attachment to a consumer culture that is fundamentally addictive/compulsive and that is driving the destructive ideology of growth.

5. **Our work:** How we earn our bread, and the relationship between wage-labor and life-work, is possibly the most important nexus of examination. Our anxiety about money keeps us fretful about work, and allows it to direct our time and space in ways that may have little to do with our discipleship vocation. If our identity should not be defined by what we own, neither should it be defined by what we do.

KM: What do you see that brings you hope that we might be able to re-establish such a vision?

CM: The preceding suggestions focus upon individual and household issues because that is where most of us begin wrestling. But each area can and must be understood more widely as well, as public challenges, not just personal ones....

My hope is that we will acknowledge our profound need for Sabbath time and space to do *this* kind of examination and that we will muster the character and courage to make changes. Our struggle *against* a sick system, however, can only be animated and sustained by a commitment *to* a community of life. We will make hard personal choices and take on difficult political tasks in the long run only in the context of the love, accountability, and celebration of the church—that is, a church transformed by the biblical vision of Sabbath Economics.

"The Gift Must Always Move," an interview with Ched Myers published in *Inward/Outward*, a project of The Church of the Saviour, Washington, D.C. Reprinted by permission of Ched Myers.

The Ultimate Question: Where Is My Security?

by K. Killian Noe

K. Killian Noe has long been a student of intentional communities. She has spent time with and learned from the Missionaries of Charity in India, the Taize community in France and the Joweto Community in South Africa. Killian co-founded New Creation Community and Recovery Café in Seattle. Prior to living in Seattle she was a member of the Church of the Savior in Washington, DC, where she cofounded one of its ministries, Samaritan Inns. Killian earned a Masters of Divinity degree from Yale Divinity School and a distinguished alumni award from the school in 1998. She is the author of *Finding Our Way Home*.

Early Experience with Tithing

The practice of tithing was central in my family when I was growing up, as unshakable as paying the mortgage and taxes. The tithe check, ten percent of my family's gross income committed to the work of the church, was the first written each month. My mother referred to "first fruits" to explain why, even on months when money was tight, the tithe check had highest priority.

One of the earliest references to tithing is found in Genesis 28. Jacob had a dream in which he saw a ladder "set up on the earth, and the top of it reached to heaven; and behold, the angels of God were ascending and descending on it." When Jacob woke up he knew he had been in the presence of God so he marked the sacred place with stones, called it Bethel and made a vow to God: "Of all that thou give me, I will give a tenth back to you." Deuteronomy, Chapter 14 also refers to the practice: "You shall tithe all the yield of your seed, which comes forth from the field year by year."

My childhood understanding of tithing was that God owned all things. We merely gave back a percentage of what was already God's. I believed that payment to the church equaled payment to God. It was not until young adulthood that I began to see that the work of the church—God's work—is to stand with the suffering, poor and oppressed and to create a more just and compassionate world. I realized that payment to the church did not automatically equal payment to God.

At that stage, I became a member of the ecumenical Church of the Saviour in Washington, D.C. Members commit to spiritual practices, seeking to keep the doors of our hearts open to the transforming power of Divine Love. One of those is the practice of "proportionate giving."

From Tithing to Proportionate Giving

Soon after World War II, Church of the Saviour founders Gordon and Mary Cosby, Elizabeth Anne Campagna and others drafted their vision for a new faith community. They included a practice to help members engage more rigorously with the power of money in their lives. Their first draft read, "We commit ourselves to giving 10% of our gross income to the work of the Church."

This emerging faith community was called to contemplation and action, journeying inward to connect with God and one's truest self, then journeying outward to connect with community and authentic need. The community specifically committed to not maintain buildings for worship or a hierarchy of professional ministers, but to offer gifts and resources for the sake of the whole community, especially those suffering and excluded by the larger culture. The founding members believed that tithing 10% would address their relationship with money, fund their compassionate works and keep them engaged in the struggle for justice.

These early members took the draft of their new church's constitution to one of the most renowned theologians of their day, Reinhold Niebuhr, who taught at Union Theological Seminary. Regarding the discipline on money, Niebuhr suggested, "You should commit yourselves, not to tithing, but to proportionate giving, with tithing as an economic floor beneath which you will not go unless there are some compelling reasons." The commitment was re-written, "We covenant with Christ and with one another to give proportionately beginning with a tithe of our incomes."

In her book *Letters to the Scattered Pilgrims*, Elizabeth O'Connor wrote this challenge to the Church of the Savior's small faith communities:

> None of us has to be an accountant to know what 10% of a gross income is, but each of us has to be a person on his knees before God if we are to understand our commitment to proportionate

giving. Proportionate to what? Proportionate to the accumulated wealth of one's family? Proportionate to one's income and the demands upon it...? Proportionate to one's sense of security and...anxiety? Proportionate to the keenness of awareness of those who suffer? Proportionate to our sense of justice and of God's ownership of all wealth? Proportionate to our sense of stewardship for those who follow after us? And so on and so forth. The answer, of course, is in proportion to all these things.

Biblical Mandate for Resource Sharing

Throughout the Church of the Saviour's history, members have been instructed and inspired by the early Hebrew community, the Hebrew prophets, the life and teachings of Jesus and the earliest communities of Jesus' followers.

The early Hebrew text reveals practices that safeguarded Israel against greed and the extreme disparity between rich and poor. Every seventh year, or Sabbath Year, all outstanding debts were to be forgiven. As each seventh year grew near, laws prohibited people from refusing to provide a loan if the refusal was based on the fear that it would never be repaid.

Every fiftieth year, during the Jubilee Year, all land was to be returned to the original owner, or family of the original owner, to prevent the accumulation of tremendous wealth by any one family. Other laws mandated that a portion of every crop be left in the fields so that the poor would not starve.[1]

The Hebrew prophets cried out for justice. In Isaiah 58:6-7, the prophet asks:

> Is not this the fast that I choose: to loose the bond of wickedness,
> to undo the thongs of the yoke, to let the oppressed go free and to
> break every yoke? Is it not to share your bread with the hungry,
> and bring the homeless poor into your house?

Jesus expressed this mandate for justice and transformation of oppressive systems when he denounced the purity system practiced in strands of Judaism; a system which ranked an individual's degree of "purity" based on their income, race, employment, social standing, gender and health status, among other things. His ministry was one of radical inclusion of those excluded by the systems of his day.

Jesus proclaimed in Matthew 25 that if you have done it to the least of these you have done it to me. And if you have not done it to the "least" you have not done it to me. In short, if you have shown compassion to those excluded by our larger culture, you have shown compassion to Jesus.

We know from the Book of Acts that some of the earliest faith communities shared resources in such a way that "there was no one in need among them."

In the twenty-six years of my membership in the Church of the Saviour and the New Creation Community—founded in Seattle and rooted in the practices of

Church of the Saviour—the gap between the rich and the poor has widened in the U.S. I still do not have clear answers to the questions Elizabeth O'Connor posed. However, I would like to share four insights that our community has come to through years of wrestling with the questions.

Capping Our Needs and Desires

The first came in the way of practical advice. In response to my struggle to balance the financial needs of my young family with the needs of the larger human family, Gordon Cosby counseled:

> Take time with your husband to discuss the real needs of your family. Include in that discussion not only your housing, food, clothing and medical needs, but your need for recreation, vacation and occasional treats. After determining your family's financial need, put a cap on that need. Adjustments will be necessary as the children grow.... There will be unexpected expenses and expenses you will plan for, like college, but within reason put a cap on your needs. If you do not you will never be free. Faster than your income rises, what you think you need will rise. The need for more will always be two steps ahead of what you earn. You will never feel free enough to share financial resources with the poor and you will not know the joy of giving.[2]

When I received this advice I did not know the power of the compulsion to want more. I had not yet experienced the emptiness, isolation and short-sightedness of an elevated lifestyle with continuously rising expectations. I had no idea that practicing proportionate giving can be more difficult for those who have more than they need than it is for those who have so little. Letting go of more money, and its buying power, can be hard. It becomes possible, and therefore tempting, to either invest the money to make more money or to raise one's lifestyle and expenses significantly. I did not yet realize that the spiritual practice of proportionate giving was as important to my own freedom as it was to the call for justice. I had only begun to understand the significance of Gordon Cosby's warning, "There is a oneness in the human family that we deny at our own peril."

We in the United States live in a culture addicted to the pursuit of more. The compulsion to consume is an unrelenting force. We cannot on our own hear an alternative, more life-giving message. I have discovered I must stay planted in the soil of authentic community if I am to have any chance of breaking free from my compulsion to seek more and more of what will never satisfy my deepest longing. In the context of authentic community, I grow more free of what I "possess" and begin to view money as a resource, like all resources, to be used for the purpose of building up the whole community, the entire human family, not just my own biological family.

Authentic, Transforming Relationships with the Poor

Second, I have come to believe the practice of proportionate giving must go hand in hand with a practice of being in authentic relationships with some individual or group of people who suffer under the weight of poverty. Our deepening relationship with one individual or group of oppressed people connects us with other oppressed people throughout the globe. We begin to know ourselves as part of the human family in ways we cannot possibly know when our giving is more abstract. Real relationships have the power to transform.

As a young woman I spent some time in India. One day I sat with a mother about my age as she cradled and rocked her dying nine-year-old daughter in her arms. I was hit with the truth that this child was dying of a disease that could have been cured with a round of antibiotics, had health care been available to her. What hit me deeper still was the recognition that this mother's pain was every bit as profound as the pain I would feel if one of my daughters were wasting away.

I had long denied that the poor could possibly feel the pain and indignity of their lives in the same way I would if I were in their circumstances. I had believed that since the poor suffer so much, beyond what I could even imagine, that all their suffering must give them some immunity to pain. My denial protected my heart from the deeper pain and suffering in the world. To recognize that this mother's pain was as profound as mine would be in those same circumstances would have broken my heart in two. The time had come to let my heart break.

In the gospel of Luke, Chapter 16, Jesus tells a story of a rich man, Dives, who walks past the beggar Lazarus every day at his gate. Dives dies and finds himself in a place of agony and Lazarus dies and finds himself resting in the arms of Abraham, the father of Judaism.

Dives begs Abraham to send Lazarus to warn his brothers so that they won't end up like him. Abraham breaks the news to Dives, "No one can pass across this great chasm, [the chasm between the dead and the living and between the rich and the poor] and even if they could, it would not do any good. If your brothers will not listen to the Laws of Moses [referring to the laws safeguarding Israel against greed and disparities between rich and poor] and the Hebrew prophets, neither will they listen to one who returns from the dead." [Lazarus, or even Jesus.]

If we are truly growing in love with our excluded neighbors, if that love is deep enough and authentic enough, then we will find ourselves opposing even unjust systems of which we are the primary beneficiaries.

The sin or alienation that created the great chasm was not simply Dives' wealth. Abraham was widely recognized as the most prosperous man in antiquity and he ended up on the life-giving side of the divide in the story. Dives' sin, which created his own hell, was the sin of ignoring Lazarus, of denying that Lazarus, too, was his brother. The sin was the denial of his relationship with his suffering brother and what that required of him.

Several years ago Bill Gates made this astute observation at the United Nations' special session on children:

> We must increase the visibility of what is happening to our children. Health inequities continue to worsen. I believe this is because people who see the worst of it don't have the resources to defeat it, and the people who have the resources to defeat it don't see the worst of it. I believe that if you took the world and randomly re-sorted it so that rich people lived next door to poor people—so, for example, people in the United States saw millions of mothers burying babies who had died from measles or malnutrition or pneumonia—they would insist something be done and they would be willing to pay for it.

The New Creation Community began as a faith community committed to "following Jesus by standing with the suffering, the excluded, the poor." It has become a community mostly made up of those who have suffered, those who have been excluded and are poor. Over half of the members are recovering from homelessness, addiction and other mental health challenges and live well below the poverty line. The need to share and the joy derived from sharing is just as powerful for those members as it is for those with higher incomes and different life experiences. Together we are discovering creative ways for all members, no matter their financial situation, to participate in the sharing of financial resources. For example, we've covered a member's specific monthly expense—their electric bill or food bill, say—so that they can contribute financially to the faith community. New Creation supports work among the poorest of the world's poor and honors the importance of every member's contribution in creating a more just and compassionate world.

Movement from Sharing Resources to Confronting Systems

In 1971 Gustavo Gutierrez coined the phrase "preferential option for the poor" in reference to the Latin American Catholic movement of solidarity with the poor. Since its founding, the Church of the Saviour has been called to embrace the places of suffering and poverty in the world and in ourselves. There has been an evolution in our understanding. We have realized more deeply that it is not enough to care for the poor and develop authentic relationships with the suffering. That concern and those relationships must result in a willingness to join together to confront unjust systems that oppress, exclude and create suffering.

We do not usually begin knowing that "confrontation of systems" will be our path. We begin simply seeking mutually liberating relationships with those who are suffering. If we are truly growing in love with our excluded neighbors, if that love is deep enough and authentic enough, then we will find ourselves opposing even unjust systems of which we are the primary beneficiaries. If we do not find ourselves confronting unjust systems we may need to ask ourselves, "Do I love my suffering brothers and sisters in such an authentic way that their struggles and pain have become my struggles and pain?"

Our work for justice must flow naturally out of our being in love with those for whom there is no justice. Otherwise our activism is nothing more than a "sounding gong or a clanging cymbal."

When we are truly "with" those on the margins, or not even on the system's map at all, those real relationships will lead to the confrontation of unjust systems. When we join our hearts with the excluded we may not always witness a change in systems, but we will certainly discover that we, ourselves, are being transformed.

Therefore, the third insight is that sharing resources and engaging in compassionate works, on their own, may in fact have the unintended effect of postponing the dismantling of unjust systems. We must not let our call and focus on compassionate works result in our allowing city, state and federal governments to shirk the responsibilities of providing affordable housing, healthcare, adequate education, decent wages, unemployment benefits and so on.

In her book, *Sweet Charity*, sociologist Janet Poppendieck writes that charity can act as "a sort of moral safety valve; it can reduce the discomfort evoked by visible destitution in our midst by creating the illusion of effective action and offering us myriad ways of participating in it. It can create a culture of charity that normalizes destitution and legitimates personal generosity as a response" to injustice, rather than encouraging the work of systemic change.

We must maintain a sense of outrage over systems that leave out huge segments of our human family. Compassionate works are not enough. Compassionate works and confronting unjust systems must go together as two sides of the same coin.

David Hilfiker, a member of the Eighth Day Community of the Church of the Saviour, and founder of Joseph's House, a hospice in D.C. for people living with AIDS, wrote:

> We hear so much talk these days about 'faith-based organizations' as appropriate tools for dealing with social ills—perhaps even replacing government as the primary provider of services to the needy. But while they certainly play a useful role they cannot be a substitute for government. Only the government—that is "we the people," acting in concert locally, state-wide and nationally—can guarantee rights, can create or oversee programs that assure everyone adequate access to what they need.
>
> ...the fundamental problem for the poor in our country is not homelessness or AIDS or hunger or the like—or even any combination of these. They are just the symptoms; the problem is injustice...the inevitable result of the structures of our society—economic, governmental, social and religious—that undergird

inequality. And the way things stand now; poverty is built into these systems.[3]

Shift in Where we Find Security

Perhaps more than anything else, the practices of proportionate giving and being in relationship with the poor encourage an internal shift in where one discovers or clings to security. It encourages a movement from finding security in the external, which never really delivers, to experiencing an internal "knowing" that whatever happens on the surface of my life, God can use it to help me become who I was created to be. Whether it's illness, divorce, unemployment, humiliation, a severed relationship, death of a loved one, exposure to violence, being misunderstood, God reveals the chance for forgiveness, love, transformation and healing—experiences that are not likely discovered in the relentless pursuit of "more."

Elton Trueblood, in his book *Confronting Christ*, wrote:

> Christ does not say that it is impossible for a rich man to enter into the kingdom of God. Instead, he says that it is difficult. Part of the difficulty arises from the sense of security, with lack of need, which often marks the person of wealth. Security is itself a barrier to spiritual growth. The broken and needy are far closer to the Kingdom than are those who feel adequate and successful. God reaches us most easily when there is a crack in our armor.

In *Sojourners Magazine* (September 1978), Gordon Cosby put it this way:

> The only ultimate question is where we finally place our security. At the place of our deepest inner being, where do we let down our full weight? The assumption is often made: God can't look after me unless society is organized in its present form, with its special advantages for my nation, my business group, and my income group. So we Christians hold on with a death grip to the present way of ordering society.... We should always be moving toward a more equitable and just structure, which will spread the benefits to everybody. To be unwilling to entertain radical changes in political structures is to say that we trust the structures that insure us privilege, rather than believing God will provide our needs.

1. Edward W. Bauman, *Where Your Treasure Is* (Arlington, VA: Bauman Bible Telecast, Inc., 1980), 39-50.
2. Conversation with Gordon Cosby, 1985.
3. David Hilfiker, "When Charity Chokes Justice," *The Other Side*, September/October 2002.

Moving toward Jubilee
—Investments and Retirement

Therefore I tell you, do not worry about your life, what you
will eat or drink; or about your body, what you will wear.
Is not life more important than food, and the body more
important than clothes? Look at the birds of the air; they
do not sow or reap or store away in barns, and yet your
heavenly Father feeds them. Are you not much more
valuable than they? Who of you by worrying can add
a single hour to his life?

—Matthew 6:25-34

God's vision of abundant living is a world
where we live out of a theology of "enough,"
a theology based in the knowledge that we
are grounded in Christ, that our sense of
personal value and esteem grows from our
Christ-centered life.

—United Methodist Church
2000 Book of Resolutions

Introduction—IX

Money and Faith has by now covered a lot of ground. The following essays, as well as the previous piece on tithing, get up close and personal. They ask you to consider what you actually do with your money. If you are fortunate enough to have extra to invest, where is your money and what is it doing? And once you reach retirement age, how much is enough, and by the way, what is retirement for?

Society's messages regarding investments and retirement are pretty clear:
- Invest, invest, invest—make sure you have enough for retirement;
- The purpose of investing is to maximize financial returns;
- The purpose of retirement is to relax, travel and enjoy the fruits of your accumulated investments.

These messages are not wrong, but reflect assumptions and values which periodically need exposure to the light. Are you comfortable with them?

Investing, the Poor and Social Change

by Rev. Andy Loving, CFP®, AIF®

Andy R. Loving is a certified financial planner, ordained minister, investment advisor and social activist. Along with his wife and business partner, Susan Taylor, Andy runs a firm, Just Money Advisors, in Louisville, Kentucky. He specializes in "community investing" helping people and institutions invest capital in financial institutions that serve poor people. Just Money Advisors specializes in working with individuals and religious institutions trying to understand and redefine what it means to be a "responsible financial steward." Money, poverty and economic issues have been a crucial part of Andy's adult work life. He was cofounder of an award-winning magazine on hunger and economic justice as well as minister to the homeless at an inner-city Episcopal Church. He believes that how we use money is one of the best indicators of how we understand the Christian faith journey.

∞

Financial Stewardship

When Christians discuss financial stewardship, the conversations usually focus on questions of giving. How much should we give and where should we give it? As important as these questions are, they generally address our assets only up to the 10% tithe. What about the other 90%? Does God's claim on all that we are, and all that we have, require that we at least look at how we might put more of our assets to work as instruments of justice in God's world?

If we are fortunate enough to have savings, an IRA or a pension, could those monies actually be invested in vehicles that directly benefit the whole of God's creation? Fortunately, the answer is "yes."

Most of us—as individuals, local churches and church-related institutions—are addicted to our affluence, making it difficult to change the way we think of, and handle, our assets. While dramatic change is possible, it is more likely that we will learn to share with the poor if we do so with small steps. Those manageable steps can, cumulatively, have significant impact on the lives of God's people.

Socially Responsible Investing (SRI)

The SRI movement in the US and Western Europe is barely thirty-five years old. Its roots can be found in opposition to the war in Vietnam and apartheid in South Africa. In that brief time, we have seen the evolution of a myriad of financial institutions and investment options designed to nurture social change. For too long the church has focused on charitable giving as *the* financial stewardship tool. The SRI movement broadens the possible financial stewardship options to include consideration of how we deposit, loan and invest our money. Let's begin with two issues at the heart of alternative thinking about investments.

First, we have to consider not only the financial return on our capital, but what the capital itself is doing. For most of us, our money goes into the system—a bank, a mutual fund, a 401k or a pension account—and we act as if it is going into a black box. We don't really understand or perhaps even care about what goes on inside the box. All we want to know is how much we are putting in, how much risk we are taking, and how much we are going to get out. When our ultimate goal or value is only getting maximum return with minimum risk, we are worshipping the God of Maximum Return.

People of faith need to ask, "Should maximum return be the only factor, or even the primary factor, in investment decisions?" I would suggest that the human and environmental impacts of our investments should be as important as the financial return. We need to look inside the box.

Second, capital deposited in any financial institution grants that institution a measure of power; they are given the right to decide who will use that capital and power. Most financial institutions do not hand over any of that power/capital to the poor or to institutions that serve the poor. Their primary emphasis is on maximizing profit, which typically means the capital flows to the rich, who become richer.

Profit is not evil; it is necessary if capital is to be created for jobs and services. But should profit be the only value or criterion we use in making decisions about investments? Some financial institutions specifically target their capital to poor communities. I believe we must begin to deposit our assets in these new institutions.

Let's take an introductory look at Socially Responsible Investing. Believing that significant social change can result, SRI's goal is to align investors' social, ethical, moral and/or religious values with their investment portfolios and bank accounts. SRI's three characteristics, sometimes referred to as SRI's three-legged stool, include: screened investing, shareholder activism and community investing.

Screened investing is probably the most well-known of SRI's three legs. Many more people and institutions participate in it than in shareholder activism and community investing. Screened investing uses "negative" screens to exclude companies or industries that conflict with our values, and "positive" screens to proactively support companies that help create a more equitable and sustainable world. Traditional "negative" screens include avoiding alcohol, tobacco, military companies, polluters and those employing workers in sweatshops. Many church institutions have avoided investments in alcohol, tobacco and gambling for over a hundred years. Common "positive" screens include companies that hire and promote women and minorities, those with good environmental records and employee relations, and those that offer superior health care and pensions.

Dollar for dollar, screened investing has less social change impact than shareholder activism or community investments, but it is the most common entry point into SRI. Though past performance cannot predict future returns, academic studies (*www.sristudies.org*) have shown that screened investment products can perform just as well as unscreened investments. The process of selecting and implementing screens allows investors to align their investment portfolio with their values. For example, in recent years, hospital foundations have divested from tobacco companies, as the use of tobacco is incompatible with promoting health. Web sites: *www.socialfunds.com*, *www.socialinvest.org*

The second leg of the stool is **shareholder activism**: leveraging ownership in a company to influence its behavior and policy. Shareholders typically work in coalitions to file shareholder resolutions and engage in company dialogue.

The Interfaith Center on Corporate Responsibility (ICCR) has been a leader in this area for more than twenty-five years. ICCR is an association of 275 faith-based institutional investors, including denominations, religious communities, pension funds, foundations, hospital corporations, economic development funds, asset management companies, colleges and unions. ICCR engages in shareholder activism on issues like global warming, international finance and the hiring and promotion of women and minorities. The more people invest with institutions involved in this process, the more power and votes those shareholder activists wield in convincing corporations to change policies. Web sites: *www.iccr.org*, *www.sriadvocacy.org*, *www.coopamerica.org/socialinvesting/shareholderaction/*

Community investing, the last leg of the three-legged stool, holds tremendous promise for social change. Community investing directs investors' capital to poor communities, those underserved by traditional financial services. It provides access to credit, equity, capital and basic banking products previously unavailable to these communities. In the U.S. and around the world, community investing enables local organizations to provide financial services like microcredit to low-income individuals, and to supply capital for small businesses and vital community services, such as child care, affordable housing and healthcare. Dollar for dollar, community investing probably has more positive social change impact than the two other legs of the stool. But far fewer dollars are now placed in community investment vehicles.

Community investment institutions include community development banks, community development credit unions, developers of low-income housing, overseas microfinance institutions and community development loan funds. A recent study showed that such institutions have lower default rates than commercial banks in the United States. Most are less than thirty years old. In the last ten years, many have grown in size and sophistication, making them accessible to many more people. Some are federally insured; some are not. Some offer market-rate returns; others offer below-market returns.

Churches have been some of the biggest investors in community investing institutions. But when comparing the potential amount of both personal and denominational investments with the extent of the need for access to capital, we have barely begun.

As we all know, changing money habits is not easy, but taking that first step is crucial. Here are examples of first steps all of us can take to put our capital in institutions that serve the poor in the United States and around the world. Website: *www.communityinvest.org*

Community Development Financial Institutions (CDFIs)

Many of us have funds sitting in money market, checking and saving accounts in traditional banks. The same could be said of our churches. We have put our "measure of power" in institutions whose first and primary purpose is to maximize profit. We can take back at least a part of that power by depositing our money in Community Development Financial Institutions (CDFIs) whose primary purpose is to loan money to undercapitalized people and the institutions that serve them.

Please keep in mind that the following examples may or may not be appropriate for a particular individual. Listing them below does not constitute an offer to buy or sell these investment options. Before investing in any financial instrument, you should check with a financial advisor who knows your personal financial situation. Also, the financial services industry evolves quickly. While these particular instruments are available as of the publication of this book, these exact products may not be available years later. However, there will no doubt be other community investment options that serve similar purposes. A financial advisor knowledgeable in community investments can direct a reader to specific products available at that time. (*With all investments, past performance is not indicative of future results.*)

Domini Social Money Market

The Domini Social Money Market is an FDIC-insured money market account (minimum deposit of $1,000) that pays market-rate returns and offers electronic transfer and checking services. It is managed by Shorebank, the largest community development bank in the U.S. The bank has been an integral part of reinvigorating the south side of Chicago, making loans in neighborhoods largely ignored by traditional banks. Shorebank created jobs by hiring neighborhood contractors to renovate the housing stock in threatened neighborhoods. Shorebank now works in Detroit and Cleveland as well. A Domini Money Market account is a tangible, direct way to make money available to undercapitalized neighborhoods in three Midwest cities. Visit *www.domini.com*

Shorebank Direct High-Yield Savings Account

The Shorebank Direct High-Yield Savings Account is a great option for people comfortable with internet banking. Shorebank requires no minimum balance and pays competitive savings rates. All deposits up to $100,000 are federally insured. This account is available to individuals, but not to churches or other institutions at this time. Visit *www.sbk.com*

Self-Help Credit Union

Self-Help Credit Union in Durham, NC is one of the largest community development credit unions in the U.S. Self-Help loans to organizations and individuals unable to secure loans at mainline commercial banks. Self-Help has been a leader in the fight against predatory lending and in the development of affordable housing. They have CDs and money market accounts that are federally insured and feature competitive interest rates. Visit *www.self-help.org*

There are many CDFIs. Find them in your area at *www.cdfi.org* or *www.communityinvest.org* If you do not find any in your area, consider using one of those listed here and bank by mail or on the internet. The above institutions' deposits are federally insured. Their rates are usually competitive with mainline banks.

Oikocredit

Oikocredit is an international, ecumenical loan fund with about $360 million in assets. "Oiko" comes from the Greek root meaning "fellowship" or "community" so Oikocredit means "credit for the fellowship or community." Oikocredit loans to co-ops and indigenous microfinance groups in over sixty countries in Latin America, Africa and Asia. Microfinance loans are sometimes as little as $100—a small amount, but enough to change lives.

Oikocredit functions as a kind of grassroots, poor people's development bank.

Over 80% of the deposits in Oikocredit come from local churches and individuals. The rest comes from over 500 national and regional church bodies. Oikocredit, based in the Netherlands, is widely ecumenical with involvement from Catholic, Protestant, Orthodox and evangelical bodies. An individual or church can start an account with as little as $1,000. Investors choose their own interest rate, between 0% and 2%. Oikocredit then uses the capital to invest via loans in low-income communities around the world. Oikocredit has made loans for more than thirty years and has never lost a dime of investor money. However, loans made through Oikocredit are not guaranteed. Visit *www.oikocredit.org*

Calvert Foundation

Calvert Foundation is a 501(c)(3) charitable foundation that makes below-market loans to more than 240 non-profits and social enterprises. The fiscally conservative organization was created in 1995 by the for-profit Calvert mutual fund family as a separate, but related, non-profit foundation. Investors, with as little as $1,000, can focus their investment on a section of the U.S. or a particular continent overseas. The foundation makes loans in many program areas: affordable housing, small business, microfinance institutions, CDFIs and social enterprises like fair trade.

Calvert Foundation investments are not federally insured, but loan loss reserves are in place to decrease investor risk. The Calvert Foundation, like Oikocredit, can link investments to a money market account, enabling an investor to have access to invested money in only a couple of days. Visit *www.calvertfoundation.org*

CRAIX

The mutual fund Community Reinvestment Act Qualified Investment Fund (stock symbol: CRAIX) invests in low-income housing and is now available through mutual fund market entities like Charles Schwab and Fidelity. The fund offers market return and high credit quality and has an impressive five-year investment track record. CRAIX is potentially appropriate for individuals as well as church endowments and institutions. At certain investment levels, investments can be targeted to specific geographic areas: a city, a county or a state. Because this fund offers market return and investment grade securities, institutions can meet their fiduciary requirements and still support low-income housing. Visit *www.crafund.com*

Shared Interest

Shared Interest is a U.S.-based non-profit that encourages investment in low-income housing, cooperatives, microfinance and small businesses. Divestment played an important role in ending apartheid there; since then, churches in the U.S. for the most part have drifted away, but the economic struggle has really only just begun. Black South Africans have some political power, but almost all economic power remains in the hands of the white minority. Shared Interest seeks to change that by guaranteeing loans made by South African financial institutions to black-controlled companies and non-profits. Without Shared Interest's guarantees, the loans would not be approved. Shared Interest requires a $5,000, three-year, minimum investment for U.S. investors. Though not federally insured, no one has ever lost any of their investment, but remember that past performance is not indicative of future results. Visit *www.sharedinterest.org*

Financial Stewardship Revisited

These community investment options represent one way we can move beyond charitable giving and broaden our concepts of stewardship to include how we deposit, loan and invest our money. The following website highlights many other options for investing with and in poor communities: *www.communityinvest.org*

Before closing, let's consider a story highlighting "communitizing assets" as a further strategy to support one another in the process of becoming community investors. Rather than starting as an individual or family, consider doing so as a small or large group, as an inner-city church of about forty families did. They asked, "How can we create a common purse for the poor of the world, inspired by what we find in the second and fourth chapters of Acts, in which many members of our church community will participate?"

They deposited some individual savings in Oikocredit, as a common purse. The church itself created an account with Oikocredit, enabling those with less than the $1,000 minimum investment to contribute smaller amounts. Some young people even invested part of their allowance. Others opened Oikocredit accounts in their own name, then reported that to the church. None of the church members are rich; many are teachers and social workers. Yet over several years church members and friends deposited over $180,000 in Oikocredit—enough to provide microfinance loans to more than 600 families annually. Over the last several years, this church has provided loans to more than 3,000 families. Imagine what larger, wealthier churches could do.

One final thought about the problem of "paralysis by analysis." Many of us want to be sure, to study things a bit more, in order to take precisely the right action. Such an approach often results in inaction. We would be better served by the action/reflection model of Latin American Christians. Act, then reflect; if necessary, modify your actions based on what you learn. Select one or two of these community investment options and try investing there. Start discussions about community investing and SRI in your communities and churches. Don't delay and don't over-analyze your options before you act!

Andy Loving is an Investment Advisor Representative of First Affirmative Financial Network (FAFN), LLC. Just Money Advisors is not a subsidiary or affiliate of FAFN. FAFN is an independent Registered Investment Advisor. (SEC File # 801-56587).

Used by permission of the author, Andy Loving.

Making Trade Fair for Africa

by Sarah Tarver-Wahlquist

Sarah Tarver-Wahlquist serves as an Associate Editor of *Co-Op America Quarterly.*

Chee Yoke Ling, a Malaysian lawyer and activist, once likened free-trade to a 100-meter dash between Olympic gold medalist Carl Lewis and a peasant African farmer. It's clear before the bark of the starting gun who is going to win.

The fair trade movement seeks to redress some of the inequities built into such a system. Fair trade appeals to consumers' values and asks them to pay a relatively small price premium in order for those values to be expressed in everyday shopping decisions. Purchasing fair trade products ensures that producers are paid a fair price for those products. The relatively minor price premium translates into schools, improved health care, nutrition and more within the producers' communities.

The following story begins by describing the positive impact fair trade coffee has had on Rwanda. Author Tarver-Wahlquist then goes on to describe how fair trade works, the kind of difference it can make in small growers' lives, and provides suggestions on how to support fair trade in your own life.

Rwanda, a small country in East Africa, is well known in the West for its civil war of the 1990s, which culminated in the genocide of 1994, in which approximately 800,000 Tutsis and moderate Hutus were murdered. Tens of thousands fled Rwanda to neighboring countries, and the economy of Rwanda all but collapsed. More than ten years later, many refugees have returned home and are trying to rebuild a country torn apart by violence and poverty. Thousands of them—including the members of the Dukunde Kawa coffee cooperative—are finding success through the Fair Trade system.

The civil war, along with the crash in coffee prices worldwide, reduced the country's exportation of its main crop, coffee, by over 60 percent. And it's Fair Trade, a system that brings transparency and economic sustainability to trading relationships, that's resurrecting Rwanda's status as a major player in the coffee industry. In the last several years, with help from Fair Trade buyers and the US Agency for International Development (USAID), Rwandan coffee farmers have increased the quality of their coffee, so it is now some of the most sought-after in the specialty coffee industry.

The country's burgeoning specialty coffee industry is also healing both economic and social wounds left from the 1994 genocide. Hutus and Tutsis—the two groups pitted against one another in the genocide—are working side by side in coffee cooperatives, like the Cooperative Pour la Promotion des Activites-Café (COOPAC), a Fair Trade co-op in northwest Rwanda. COOPAC has doubled its coffee production each year since its inception in 2001. In its first year, members of COOPAC elected to use their Fair Trade premium to build a school for their community, and since then they have built health clinics and improved infrastructure by building roads and bridges. COOPAC also distributes livestock to members of the cooperative, and is beginning a microfinance program.

"Fair Trade is having a huge impact on the coffee industry in Rwanda," says Jennifer Bielman, senior program manager for Global Producer Services at TransFair USA. "We see it empowering farmers to [the point where they can] bargain with conventional buyers," rather than accepting rock-bottom prices.

Positive stories like this one are being told all across the African continent. The fair wages and stable trade relationships of Fair Trade allow producers to send their children to school, build needed water wells and other facilities, and even build health centers to provide an entire community with vital health care. This arrangement is made possible by consumers who commit to purchasing Fair Trade goods whenever possible, be it Fair Trade Certified coffee, tea, chocolate, or other foods, or fairly traded crafts.

The role that Fair Trade is playing in the social and economic recovery of Rwanda shows us that consumer choices have a significant impact on people in Africa. We have ample evidence that trade relationships that respect workers also empower communities to develop and grow in sustainable ways. By addressing development through trade, rather than simply through charitable aid, consumers put the power and direction of development in the hands that need it—people on the ground, in producer communities.

The Fair Trade Solution

Hilary French writes in her book *Costly Tradeoffs: Reconciling Trade and the Environment*: "Trade is neither inherently good nor bad. But how it is conducted is a matter of great concern—and an unprecedented opportunity. Trade can either contribute to the process of sustainable development or undermine it."

Fair Trade creates opportunities for farmers and artisans left most vulnerable in conventional free trade, where they may work under sweatshop-like conditions for below-subsistence wages. It guarantees a stable, premium wage for farmers; ensures that workers labor under fair, safe, cooperative conditions; promotes environmentally sustainable practices; and it provides transparency and accountability on the part of those who market the products.

With Fair Trade Certified commodities, like coffee and chocolate, producers are guaranteed a "floor price" for their crop that is designed to cover the costs of production and remains constant even as the market price drops. In addition, Fair Trade farmers are also paid a Fair Trade premium, which is designated for use in social and economic development.

For uncertified products, like crafts, a Fair Trade price is considered a living wage for the producer's work in a local context.

In addition to a fair wage, Fair Trade buyers often pre-finance producers, paying for a portion of the order in advance. This system gives producers capital with which to purchase supplies or invest in their business.

"Producers typically lack access to capital and may borrow money at a high interest rate in order to begin production," says Carmen K. Iezzi of the Fair Trade Federation. "Since, in conventional trade, they are only paid after delivery, a significant portion of their income goes to repaying debts. It creates a vicious cycle."

The benefits of Fair Trade have wide-ranging repercussions beyond the producers themselves. Using income earned through Fair Trade partnerships, producers build schools, health clinics, water wells, and more for their communities. Kuapa Kokoo, a cooperative of 35,000 cocoa farmers in Ghana, has put its Fair Trade premiums to use by building four school buildings, 27 corn mills, one bridge, and 174 water wells, to name just a few. These advances are crucial to the social and economic development in the farmers' communities, and set off a chain of events that better the lives of the farmers and all of those connected to them. Take, for example, the building of a new water well.

"For these families, a water well means even more than clean drinking water, says Erin Gorman, CEO of Divine Chocolate USA, a Fair Trade chocolate company partially owned by Kuapa Kokoo. "In Ghanaian culture, it is usually the work of the women and girls to retrieve water. In many cases, water can be half-a-day's walk away, which rules out the possibility of girls going to school. But when they're able to build a well closer to their village, all of a sudden there's more time in the day, and families are able to send their daughters to school."

Tremendous Potential for Africa

The Fair Trade model is having encouraging results throughout Africa. Exports of Fair Trade Certified coffee from Africa increased by 400 percent between 2002 and 2006, and the numbers continue to rise. Over 47,000 farmers in Africa grew the Fair Trade Certified coffee that was imported to the US in 2005; that coffee helped to support over 235,000 people in East Africa (based on an average family of five people) that year.

"Fair Trade works because it is a holistic approach," says Iezzi. "It's an approach that addresses all aspects of development—wages, trade relationships, and the environment—in one transaction."

"The potential for Fair Trade to positively impact Africa is tremendous," adds TransFair USA's Bielman. "The Fair Trade movement represents a group of people who are ahead of the curve, who realize that if you don't figure out ways to make farms more efficient and less impactful on the environment, and you don't figure out how to get incomes up so kids can go to school, it's an endgame. Fair Trade creates a paradigm shift, a new business model, that makes social and economic development possible."

The dramatic success of Fair Trade cooperatives in Africa in the last five years invites us to think about how many more people in Africa can benefit from Fair Trade if consumer demand increases. Right now, Fair Trade Certified coffee imported from Africa makes up five percent of Fair Trade coffee in the U.S., just .12 percent of the total U.S. coffee market. If consumer demand increased enough that African Fair Trade coffee made up just one percent more of the total US market, it would be an increase of 751 percent, supporting an additional 309,000 farmers (1.5 million people, including families) and creating an extra $5.6 million of income for farmers.

There is room for demand to grow, according to Bielman. "We work hard to really reach out to producers to get them certified early, to make sure that as demand grows, there's enough supply," she says. Even with the growing demand for Fair Trade Certified coffee, most cooperatives in Africa sell only a portion of their coffee at Fair Trade prices.

Likewise, US importation of Fair Trade Certified cocoa increased by 84 percent last year, but much of this cocoa came from Latin America. Kuapa Kokoo's 35,000 farmers in Ghana export only a small part of their harvest at Fair Trade prices, and Fair Trade is just beginning to make its way into the Cote d'Ivoire, which exports 70 percent of the world's cocoa.

Fair Trade retailers of handicrafts are increasing their sourcing from Africa and continuing to work with artisans on design and marketing to better meet the needs of the growing market for Fair Trade goods. In 2006, Ten Thousand Villages, the largest retailer of Fair Trade handcrafts and household items in the US, purchased 25 percent more goods from Africa than the year before. Both Ten Thousand Villages and SERRV International, which also sells a wide variety of Fair Trade goods, made producers in Africa a priority in 2006, and expect to see their sourcing from Africa increase in the coming years.

Supporting Africa Through Fair Trade

Whether they work in commodities or crafts, everyone in the Fair Trade world agrees: all of the successes of the Fair Trade movement are dependent on consumer demand for Fair Trade goods. "The single most important thing we need," says Gorman, "is for consumers to request Fair Trade."

Cael Chappel of Baskets of Africa agrees: "To ensure long-term, reliable relationships with producers, we need a viable market with consumers in the West."

Public awareness of Fair Trade is rising every year, but Fair Trade still only represents a tiny portion of the overall marketplace. For demand to grow, consumers must increase that demand.

"It really is about making a purchase and voting with that dollar," says Iezzi. "When you support Fair Trade, you're doing more than giving someone a job, you're supporting an entire community, as well as raising the issue that we should care about where things come from and who made them."

In the United Kingdom, public awareness about Fair Trade has reached a tipping point of 50 percent, and according to Oxfam, Fair Trade sales in the UK increased by 40 percent last year. Fair Trade goods are available in virtually every UK supermarket including products not yet available in the US, such as Fair Trade Certified fruit and wine from Africa. With increased consumer demand in the US and increased public awareness about the importance of fair prices and working conditions for producers, the Fair Trade market in the US will grow, benefiting producers in Africa and throughout the developing world.

Here are four simple steps you can take to help build the Fair Trade economy, so that farmers and artisans in Africa and around the world can continue to support their families and add to the social and economic development of their communities:

1. **Buy Fair Trade products whenever possible.** Always look for Fair Trade Certified commodities. Coffee, chocolate, tea, and sugar are all grown in Africa and sold in US stores. When buying crafts, clothes, or gifts, look for Fair Trade options by searching for members of the Fair Trade federation (*www.fairtradefederation.org*).

2. **Adopt-A-Supermarket** through Co-op America's Fair Trade Supermarket campaign. We'll send you resources so that you can adopt a local supermarket and encourage it to carry Fair Trade products. To join, visit our Web site, *www.fairtradeaction.org*

3. **Get your workplace, place of worship, school, or community group** involved in Fair Trade by signing up for Co-op America's Fair Trade Alliance, a community of people and organizations who have made a commitment to support Fair Trade by making it part of their daily use and events. To sign up, visit our Web site, *www.fairtradeaction.org*

4. **Educate your friends, family, and coworkers about Fair Trade.** Don't be shy! Fair Trade is empowering communities throughout Africa, and your support makes a difference. Host a house party where people learn about Fair Trade and can purchase Fair Trade products, or use the next holiday or birthday as a way to introduce someone to Fair Trade.

For ideas on throwing a Fair Trade house party, see our Sept./Oct. 2004 *Real Money* article at *www.coopamerica.org/pubs/realmoney/articles/ftparty.cfm*

From "Co-op America Quarterly," Number 71, Winter, 2007, 22-23, 25 and 27. Reprinted with permission from Co-op America, a nonprofit membership organization working to harness economic power—the strength of consumers, investors, businesses, and the marketplace—to create a socially just and environmentally sustainable society. To become a member and receive a copy of the National Green Pages™, call 800/58-GREEN or visit *www.coopamerica.org*

Investing in Fair Trade

By requesting and buying Fair Trade products, consumers help cooperatives in Africa and around the world become more sustainable. If you are a socially responsible investor, you may also want to consider directing some of your investments to help grow the Fair Trade movement. Here are some resources for investing in Fair Trade in Africa.

SERRV INTERNATIONAL—As part of the Fair Trade system, producers are often paid partial advances for their work, giving them the stable and steady income they need to work productively and avoid borrowing money at high interest rates. As one of the first Fair Trade organizations in the world, SERRV International has been working with farmers and artisans for nearly 60 years, and it provides investors with the opportunity to help support Fair Trade, through its SERRV International Loan Fund.

With a minimum investment of $1,000, investors help provide partial advance payments to farmers and artisans in Africa and around the developing world. The Fund pays competitive interest rates and is offered via formal prospectus by contacting SERRV. It is currently available in 27 states; contact SERRV to learn if the Fund is available in your state: 888-243-4423, or *loanfund@serrv.org*

OIKOCREDIT specializes in microcredit, allowing individuals and small businesses to obtain the capital they need to grow and thrive. About half of Oikocredit's borrowers are cooperatives, many of which are Fair Trade. Investors can make an investment of $1,000 or more in Oikocredit through the Calvert Foundation's Community Investment Notes. The minimum investment is $1,000, with a 0-2 percent interest rate for one- and three-year investments, and 1-3 percent interest for a five-, seven-, and ten-year investment. Contact: 202-265-0607, *www.oikocredit.org/sa/us*

EQUAL EXCHANGE is a worker-owned Fair Trade company selling Fair Trade Certified coffee, tea, sugar, cocoa, and chocolate from Africa, South America, and Asia. Wainwright Bank, a socially responsible bank in Boston, now offers a CD (certificate of deposit) for investors interested in helping Equal Exchange continue to grow.

Investments, which begin at $1,000 are pooled together and made available to Equal Exchange as a low-cost loan. Equal Exchange in turn uses the funds to increase their work with Fair Trade cooperatives. According to Equal Exchange, an investment of $2,000 allows Equal Exchange to buy the entire coffee harvest from a five-acre family farm... Contact: 971-404-5143, *www.equalexchange.com/eecd*

When Women Decide to Be Unstoppable

by Susan Wilkes and Jim Klobuchar

Jim Klobuchar and Susan Cornell Wilkes are a husband and wife writing team, passionate about increasing public awareness concerning the effectiveness of microcredit lending.

Jim wrote a popular column for the *Minneapolis Star Tribune* for 30 years. He has twice been nominated for a Pulitzer Prize in journalism and in 1984 was chosen the nation's outstanding columnist by the Society of American Newspaper Columnists. He now writes periodically for the *Christian Science Monitor*. He is also a noted adventurer, having climbed in the Himalayas, Andes and Alps and now leads treks in the Himalayas and South America as the head of an adventure travel organization. He is the author of 20 books.

Susan has worked with foundations and nonprofits in the United States and abroad in a thirty-year career as a leader and innovator. During her extensive experience with corporate, community, private and family foundations, she founded or led numerous nonprofit organizations, model programs and private/public sector collaborations. She has served on over 20 local and national Boards of Directors, and traveled and worked in 31 countries.

The authors of the following essay report that "in little more than 30 years after the microcredit idea began taking hold, nearly 40 million small entrepreneurs in poor countries around the world are bringing better lives to their families." Microcredit organizations provide small loans (as little as $35) to those most often denied access to such capital. These loans have been paid back, with interest, at the astonishing rate of over 95% in most countries. The following stories describe how women are often the most successful micro-entrepreneurs. As mothers, they are also the ones who provide primary care for children and are most concerned with improving their access to health and education.

Microcredit is not a "silver bullet" or panacea. It is, however, one of the more effective tools for improving the lives of the very poor. And, those of us with even modest resources can support microcredit organizations with relatively small donations that make a significant difference in the lives of others.

∞

The sight of women being forced to dress in their uniform of submission, the head-to-toe burqa decreed by the Taliban in Afghanistan, left millions of television watchers appalled. This, after all, was the twenty-first century.

But while they were being offended and angered, the American television audiences might well have asked themselves a question. When was it that women in America, that most enlightened of democracies, received the most fundamental of all rights of citizenship—the right to vote?

And the answer, of course, is well into the twentieth century. The struggle of women to gain the same rights, power, and basic dignity as men is as old as civilization itself. That struggle for equality clearly has made significant headway for women in the prosperous West in the last 100 years. It has made those advances in the courtroom, the legislative hearing rooms, the bedroom and the corporate boardrooms. But the condition of women in most of the world—the Middle East, Africa, great sweeps of Asia, and in Latin America—is almost as benighted today as it was in the age of the cave dwellers.

If a social evangelist had a choice of picking one tool, one movement with the goal of emancipating the poorest women on earth, the microcredit phenomenon wins without serious competition. And why are the poorest so important? Because women at the lowest end of the world's economic and social spectrum are the most repressed, the truly voiceless, the truly powerless. They are also the most numerous, into the hundreds of millions, and they cut across almost all of the ethnic, religious, and cultural roadmaps. And because they are the mothers of the poor, they are the only true salvation of the multitudes of children who are doomed without hope unless their families can produce enough income to protect their health, to feed them adequately, and to give them a fighting chance to learn in school.

Microcredit has opened that door for millions of women and therefore for their families. And why is that good news for America and the rest of the developed world?

It means suffering, ignorance, and hunger around the world have been reduced. For anybody of conscience and the normal compassion, that might be enough. But it means more. It means we have cut into that enormous gulf between those who live comfortably and in relative luxury and those who have to claw and grasp and hunt for scraps just to stay alive. It means that relieving poverty, at least in modest increments, makes this a better and safer world. It is a safer world because poverty ignored eventually will explode into violence and even into genocide. And if it does, it's small consolation to tell ourselves, "we're not to blame. We worked hard and deserve the life we have." We undoubtedly do. But the experience of microcredit, which is fundamentally supported and expanded by the industrial West, tells us how far enlightened (and not necessarily charitable) Samaritanism can go in liberating the disadvantaged. Remember, those are loans, not gifts.

Shift the television camera now from Afghanistan to East Africa. The Maasai culture in Africa, like the Maasai warrior of decades ago and the herdsman of today, is lean and hard. The Maasai adolescents still undergo excruciating circumcision rites, both boys and girls. The surmounting code for the males is to be fearless. Facing a lion, they are. Facing their women, they have been historically brutal.

They have abused and suppressed their women for centuries. It is part of traditional behavior. But today across Africa, the rank sexism of those cultures is changing, visibly and in some places dramatically, as it is in many of the world's developing countries that were once called primitive.

Sometimes it helps to put a face to a landmark change in how a once-abused people are treated. In the African savannah where the Maasai live, the face is that of a buoyant and hefty Maasai woman named Sinyati Lebene, a 61-year-old mother of six with songs on her lips, a bountiful torso, and eyes that dance like fireflies. For a collar she wears a bright beaded shanga, the familiar Maasai necklace that Sinyati displays both as an ornament and kind of billboard for her business. For years she has been wife number one of a Maasai cattle owner whose menage grew to four wives. At one time, he would beat her routinely when she asked him for money. He doesn't anymore. She earns her own money and makes most of the decisions that affect her life.

...women at the lowest end of the world's economic and social spectrum are the most repressed, the truly voiceless, the truly powerless....And because they are the mothers of the poor, they are the only true salvation of multitudes of children...

"It was never that way before," she said, "It started to change when I joined the other women. They told me about credit. They said I could repay the money I borrowed. It was the biggest thing I've done in my life."

Hers was a declaration that might serve as the mantra for millions of women around the world. Their lives changed when the doors swung open for them at the neighborhood bank. It was not the conventional bank as westerners understand banks. What opened to women was the wonder of simple credit—a wonder because until 25 or 30 years ago, poor women approaching a bank cashier's window in Tanzania or Bolivia or India would have been rousted off the premises by uniformed guards. They were lucky to escape arrest as vagrants. Poor people, especially poor women, had no collateral. With no banking history, with little or no education, with practically nothing to their names, they were an impossible credit risk.

Muhammad Yunus didn't think so. Yunus is the economist whose education spans both Asia and America and who, in the 1970s, introduced the principle of microcredit in his native Bangladesh. Because the poor had nothing to guarantee repayment, Yunus and pioneers like him created a way. The borrowers, 90 percent of them women, formed a credit group, a partnership of the poor. Together they could put up enough money to bail out any member who fell short in his or her payments. The $50 to $100 loans they took would come due in four to six months at something like 1 percent a week in interest. They also had to put down 5 percent in savings. For them it was a load. But the moral power of the group made it manageable. The seed money didn't blow in from the snows of Kilimanjaro. It came from nonprofits and foreign governments that funded the Maasai women's group originally. The equation is this: donors initially provide the pool for loans and operations, but the microcredit institution itself, made up of all its members, will some day be big enough and disciplined enough to make it without donors. It will have to be. Microcredit makes poor people bankable, and their bank—the source of their loans—can't be subsidized indefinitely.

This is how the poor are digging themselves out of the dumping grounds of society around much of the world. And yet the visitor to Africa is mildly astonished to hear a Sinyati Lebene, the rollicking Maasai grandmother, embracing a technical, impersonal buzz word like "microcredit" as though it were a spiritual epiphany in her life.

But it has been something close to that for Sinyati and for millions of other women who now find themselves empowered in ways they would not have foreseen only a few years ago. To understand why microcredit has been so crucial for impoverished and struggling women of the world, it might be instructive to take the visions of independence held by American women and compare them with those of women in the poor countries. American women demanded and fought for open doors that would give them access to broader options and choices in their lives, to equality in the workplace, control over their bodies, and greater access to the hierarchies of power. Much of this came down to access to money and mobility. Much of it has been achieved.

In the poor countries, it came down to liberation from the psychological prisons of male domination and of the actual peonage of women. The world's money brokers often sneer at the poor as dumb and lazy people without a clue about how to make it in the world. The truth is that most of the world's poor people *aren't* dumb or lazy or without dreams or creativity. They are simply poor, most of them born that way. And when the opportunities of microcredit began to open, the lenders quickly saw that the most reliable borrowers were likely to be women. Why? When women turned those small loans into more dresses or soap to sell or used it to build larger handicraft kiosks, the first beneficiaries of that new money invariably would be their children's health and education. There is no greater incentive for a woman. So they were almost a cinch to repay the loan.

It has worked out that way in millions of families.

The head of one of the world's major players among microfinance institutions is Nancy Barry, a mover and something of an all-purpose dynamo in the field of emancipating the poor. In 1989 she left a position with the World Bank, where she was responsible for 40 percent of that institution's entire portfolio, to become president of Women's World Banking (WWB). Somebody asked her why she would step away from so prestigious a role to run a non-government agency with four employees.

She replied, "I believed then and I believe now that the biggest changes in uplifting the poor and especially poor women are going to happen through smaller institutions. We can be an aggressive and creative company. In fact, we have to be. The key is in working with affiliates that have developed strong and reliable leadership in the poor countries. Look, to make headway, these women have to be as hard as nails. There's the story about a high official of the central bank who went out to meet hundreds of angry women in one of the Far East countries. They wanted better access. They waved fingers at him and demanded to know whether he helped his wife in the kitchen."

The guy was overmatched, clearly. He left the scene in disarray but with some fresh ideas about how to provide credit for angry women. It is a matter of record that the leader of the women who confronted the big shot banker eventually organized a cooperative of more than 100,000 basically illiterate women whose leaders insisted on an inviolable creed: "Make sure they repay the loans."

"If commercial banks had that philosophy," Nancy Barry said, "there'd be a lot less trouble in banking today."

"What's emerged in the years since Yunus got microcredit rolling is that women in the poor countries have become an undeniable force. They are not helpless. They are powerful. Out of the Bangladesh model and its later variations came successful banking systems and how to work with the poor. Nobody has to look at microfinance for poor women as some kind of charming, cute poodle of world corporate life. The truth is that it works better than corporate finance. It works in good times, but particularly in bad times. It builds itself on the shoulders of people like the woman in the Dominican Republic who started out as a garment factory worker when she was 13. She dreamed then of some day having a white wedding gown. So she took out a micro loan. She started out with one sewing machine, and in a few years she was running a factory that subcontracted to self-employed women. And later she stood up at a microcredit conference and shouted, 'If I can do it, anybody can.' Women cheered."

Before microfinance, families didn't think seriously about educating girls. But because women now are serious about that, and because they're always serious about the health of their children, they're repaying those loans...

But she brought down the house when she raised her arm and shouted again, "If women don't do it (help other women), *nobody* will."

Are there risks that go beyond meeting the loan, beyond potential resentful glares both from males and from village women willing to accept traditional roles for women?

There are. A woman who is a member of a WWB affiliate in Colombia reported to a hushed audience not long ago, "Drug gangs murdered 23 of our clients in their place of business."

Her organization is still operating.

Barry was asked another question: "In the historic, if uneven, advance of women (remembering the scenes of hooded women still current in 2002) how important is microcredit?"

She said, "It's not a panacea. It doesn't change the world overnight. But this, to me, is the most important lever. It's more important than the vote. What must come first is empowerment, financially and socially. It can give women, and by extension their families, control over their lives, or certainly that possibility. That gives women a fundamentally different attitude toward the future. It brings not only dignity, but hope, and now an even stronger motivation. The reasons it's working that way are clear. Before microfinance, families didn't think seriously about educating girls. But because women now are serious about that, and because they're always serious about the health of their children, they're repaying those loans, and the ranks of women now building their lives and their family's lives with microcredit keep growing."

It's not all fairy tale stuff. There's some evidence that maintaining a loan by working away from home allows some women less time with their children, to the detriment of the children. There's also evidence that some husbands will steal loan money or build resentments over the woman's changing role.

Yet this evidence seems strongly outweighed by the microcredit ledgers around the world revealing the millions of women who are recycling their loans and bringing more money into the family and therefore into their communities.

A fascinating part of this social evolution, still invisible to much of the gentrified world, is that it doesn't reveal itself to be a movement of some vast and hulking herd. The gift of microcredit is that it has allowed each woman the discovery of another self—her individualism. And from the ranks of the once-marginalized women of Africa have emerged managers and executives like Eva Mukasa, the general manager of the Uganda Women's Finance Trust Fund, an affiliate of Women's World Banking. Here is a breezy and confident executive with her hair smartly combed back, vaguely amused eyes when she is discussing big banking numbers, and an MBA in her portfolio. She has thousands of clients, some of them now capable of managing loans of more than $1,000. But it is the poorest of those clients who get her most earnest attention. She has seen poverty much of her life. She has the brains, the training, and the spine to bring poor women into her offices, which Ugandans now call "The Women's Bank." If they are first timers, they are frightened and overwhelmed. Eva tells them they can make it and shows them how. And most of them make it.

But if the clients of microcredit prize that emergence of their undiscovered identities, the other self of the Maasai woman in Tanzania, Sinyati Lebene, is a rollicking and impressive package. She speaks Maasai and Kiswahili, but it was a chore for the interpreter to get all of the syllables out, because Sinyate was sailing on a monologue of gratitude when we overtook her.

She was asked about those horror images of women in a polygamous Maasai household getting up before the sun, hauling water, building the fire, cooking in the smoke-filled huts, feeding, milking, and doing all of the drudgery.

She shrugged. "Sure. I get up early. It's the way we live. I get the water and milk the cows and make the meal and dress the children. I'm the number one wife. People say that must give some privileges. Not much. My husband's second wife died. One of my children was killed in an accident. I had six others, and I help take care of the eight children of the second wife. I don't know what privileges [they're talking about]. When a second wife comes in she gets some of the things the first wife owns, and maybe a cow or two.

"But when I found out about this credit group (Women Empowerment and Development Agency Company, WEDAC), I finally saw a way I could do some of the things I wanted to do. I could be my own person.

"I've had five loans in five years," she said. "Do you want to know something?"

I said I wouldn't tell a soul.

"I love my life. Nobody knew how this was going to work because in the Maasai, the men are in control. But the elders had these meetings and they said, okay, go ahead and see what happens."

What happened was that Martha Umbulla, who is the godmother of WEDAC, started rounding up her troops in a four-wheel drive commissioned by the McKnight Foundation in Minnesota. Her clients lived miles apart, in boma settlements or in villages. Martha wheeled around the Maasai savannah, dodging a lion here and there, to make sure she got maximum attendance at the meetings. Weekly meetings are critical for village banking groups because the borrowers get training there in bookkeeping, make their payments, and apply for new loans. There's one more critical component in those meetings. Bishop Thomas Laizer of the Evangelical Lutheran Church in Arusha talks about it with emotion.

"It's important that these women have a forum," he said. "Look, I grew up in a Maasai house. The word of the tribal leaders was final. Women weren't heard from. There's no question that Maasai women have suffered historically. I'm on the board of WEDAC because I believe in what it can do in building the lives of women and expanding the lives of their children and their communities. This is not just about loans and credit. This is about life. The women are a tremendous asset that has been ignored. These were people who have had to walk eight miles every day to get water and walk back again. And now with the money they make in these small enterprises, they can help build a system where water is delivered to their houses, and they can pay for it. In this forum they can talk to other women about health, about emotional problems, about choices. They can make decisions individually and as a group. They can listen to health experts telling them how to protect themselves from HIV infection, and they can hear this same expert tell them they have a right to say 'no.'"

But is this last an illusion?

"He's right," Martha Umbulla said. "For the first time in their lives, these women are experiencing the right to make decisions on their own because now they have their own assets and they don't have to depend solely on male decisions. They now bring up family planning. They've learned about group support. And they know how to handle interest and savings."

And how does all that translate for the effervescent Sinyati Lebene? "I started by making collars with beads and selling them, then I went to buying and selling food. I still do a big business making *loshoro*. Hey, do you know what that is? You boil maize overnight and cool it the next day and mix it with sour milk. It's like mush, like yogurt, and everybody loves it. You ought to try it."

Right.

She's fundamentally unstoppable, Sinyati. In later years she moved into livestock, buying a few cows and goats and fattening them, reselling at a 30 percent profit. With four other women she went into a partnership to buy seed and share the profits from the plots of ground that each of them owned. One of those women was her husband's third wife. Another was the daughter of the fourth wife.

> ...these women are experiencing the right to make decisions on their own because now they have their own assets and they don't have to depend solely on male decisions.

It's a different kind of society, this.

"People ask, are you jealous of the other wives?" Sinyati said. "With me, no. The others share in some of the things I bring home. Life has changed. I said my husband doesn't beat me anymore. That's the way life was then. I started doing my own work and making my own money. He thought that was all right. He doesn't take any of my money, although some Maasai men do. My husband doesn't care now when I come home, because he knows I've got my own things to do. When my oldest boy was killed in the accident, I couldn't pay my loan on time because the time was so bad for me. My husband sold one of his cows to pay it for me. This might sound different to you, but he's a good man and I love him. And I love my life now. I never thought I'd say that."

She grabbed the arms of her two friends in the small meeting hall and sang her way out into the yard, making up the words of her chants as she sang.

The women in the life of Wanjiku Kironyo of Nairobi, Kenya, are not so joyful. Wanjiku is a sociology professor who was appalled to learn about the lives of young women in the slums of Nairobi. Many of them are girls from the farm country who give their early years to cooking and caring for males in the family. In their cultures, most of these girls can't inherit land. When they reach the teen years, they're no longer welcome at home. Without schooling or skills, with no life left for them in their villages, they will head for a city like Nairobi, trying to survive.

A girl may find work as a housemaid in a rich home. More often than not, Wan-jiku found, the girl is used sexually by the man of the house, gets pregnant and is tossed out. She becomes a bargirl and the contract is clear: she's expected to boost sales by offering her body to customers.

She becomes pregnant again and loses her job. She now has two children and no income. What's left is prostitution or selling alcohol illegally. The police arrest her. She does six months in prison because there is no one to make bail for her. She has nothing to pawn. She returns to the street and finds herself back in jail. The cycle goes on. This is a life in ruin, but more than one life. There are the children, adrift. And what about the hundreds of women trying to escape abusive marriages, unable to go home because their families have paid a dowry to the husband? Their cycles are the same as those of the farm girls.

Multiply their lives by thousands, because many of these women have up to 8 or 12 children. It gets worse and uglier. Sometimes a 14-year-old girl is having her first child while her mother is having her seventh. If the child has a mental disorder with which the mother cannot cope, the child will slowly starve to death.

Wanjiku responded by organizing the Maji Mazuri Center in Nairobi, to which she now devotes a major part of her professional life. It has been a wrenching but vital rescue mission for scores of these battered and luckless women. What's saving them is not only the professional care of trained health workers but the redemptive power of microcredit. In groups of 18 to 20 the women receive small loans from the center, set up tiny businesses and repay their loans at a nearby post bank. "They learn," Wanjiku said, "to sell vegetables instead of their bodies. They learn that there are people they can trust, people who care for them. They become role models for their daughters. They learn about family planning and how to work together and how to pool their resources. They talk openly about AIDS and learn how to prevent it." And what started them back into the clean air of personal dignity was trust in somebody who cared, and knowing that they themselves could now be trusted.

The money they borrow and repay may be trivial by western standards. But it is the world and new life for women once outcast and abandoned.

Retirement, Money and the Reign of God

by Andy R. Loving, CFP®, AIF®

Retirement, money and the Reign of God—bet you haven't read about that combination lately. I hope this essay gets you thinking about it, and I hope we see more written about it. As a financial planner and disciple, I have been forced to grapple with these subjects through my retirement planning work with clients over the past fifteen years.

Most relatively affluent North Americans will at some point "retire." I count myself in that group. But what is the purpose of retirement in our society? Should retirement for a Christian be approached and lived out differently than for other relatively affluent North Americans? Many articles in this book share the perspective that standing with and acting to support the poor and oppressed is at the heart of what it means to participate in the Reign of God.

I think our gut instinct tells us that retirement for Christians who share this perspective should be different, but we are not sure exactly what that "difference" might look like. And it certainly will look different from one Christian to the next.

Reminding ourselves that retirement, as known today, is only a couple generations old is a good place to begin. Social Security, instituted in the 1930s, and the longer life expectancies of the latter twentieth century, mark the beginning of retirement as we know it. We should not consider its current practice as a norm that cannot be questioned. That is especially true for Christians struggling with our affluence in light of the growing economic gap between rich and poor.

Retirement without working is a sign of extreme privilege. Longer average retirements require larger sums of money. Being able to live on savings, pensions and Social Security for as many as 20 or 30 years is unprecedented in modern history. But achieving that state of privilege is a major focus throughout our work life. "How much will I need?" or "When can I retire?" is one of the most frequent questions new clients ask.

We worry about retiring but most of us feel we have a right to retire. We deserve it. We earned it. It is a part of the American Dream. We do not see it as a privilege of the few, but as a right for the masses. And while its attainment may be possible for a majority of North Americans, it is still a reality only for the privileged of our world. Retirement without working is indeed a sign of extreme privilege.

Maybe we should begin questioning the assumption that "retirement is a right," and ask, "When *should* I aim to retire, not when *can* I retire?" Our culture says we should retire as young as possible—as soon as we can. The younger one retires from working for pay, the more successful that person has been. I have had financial planning clients express a sense of failure because they are not sure when or if they will be able to retire. But to retire young requires the accumulation of significant assets, which requires saving a significant portion of our life's earnings for retirement. In other cases, it might mean that most of an inheritance will have to go towards retirement. Can we as Christians do that when we consider the world's needs? I argue that we should begin with the assumption that we will work for pay as long as is reasonably possible. This assumption contrasts with our culture's assumption that we will stop working for pay as soon as possible.

Of course, many circumstances affect when we retire. A therapist will probably have a better chance to work into their 70s than a construction worker or a plumber. Other people may have health problems that dictate retirement. Some people retire early in order to do justice work or work that heals our Earth. But the reality is that if I can and do work later (even part-time) instead of retiring early, I will have to save much less money. And I will have much more to share with a hurting world.

We worry about retiring but most of us feel we have a right to retire....Maybe we should begin questioning the assumption that "retirement is a right..."

Besides retiring early, what other values or characteristics are part of the classic American retirement? In my experience as a financial planner, travel and leisure are highly prized goals of retirement. After retiring from a stressful job, these are understandable goals. But they can be an example of conspicuous consumption as surely as big houses, big cars and fancy clothes are.

Our culture entices us to believe that continuous leisure and recreational travel are keys to an enjoyable and well-earned retirement. The retirement culture and industry tells us, "You earned your money and saved. If you can afford it, you should do it." But the Reign of God calls us to consider what is "enough."

Questions about "enough" earlier in life may have focused on the size of our house, the kind of car we drove, or the college we could afford for our children. In retirement, the focus of consumption often changes to leisure and travel, but the need to listen to the spirit inherent in the vision of the Reign of God is not diminished. While we cannot control some of the costs of retirement, like healthcare, we can significantly control other costs, such as housing. How willing are we to downsize our house and free up assets that can be used for retirement or the poor? Many of us, as we approach retirement, live in much bigger houses than we need. The kids are grown up and gone. But ties to a neighborhood, sentimentality and memories often make it hard to move. Staying in a house can be another act of perpetuating our privilege, our affluence. The answers are not clear cut, but struggling with how to live as affluent Christians in a world of need must not be avoided.

Another part of retirement planning that begs for reflection is to whom we will leave assets at our death? Most of my clients will leave everything to their children, grandchildren and extended family. Some wish they could leave money to organizations that represent their gospel values, but sincere love for their children and extended family and fear of the unknown future most often result in every-thing going to the kids. Could it be, however, that the financial and other invest-ments we have made in our children—raising them, educating them and caring for them—are enough? Do the needs of the children of the world, the "big" family of God, have some claim on the financial assets God has entrusted to us as stewards at the end of our lives? Even if we would then leave less to the children of our per-sonal extended family—our "small" family of God? I cannot answer that question for anyone else, but I believe we have to begin asking that if the Reign of God is as important to us as many of us say it is.

Perhaps there is a "middle way" in this situation. What if, first of all, we invested at least some of our financial assets in community investments—financial institu-tions that serve poor people and poor communities? Second, we would leave verbal or written instructions that these investments continue to be used in poor commu-nities even after our deaths. But we would also leave instructions to children and family that if a "significant need" (defined as narrowly or broadly as we desired) would arise, the money could be used with our blessing. A "significant need" could be an especially large healthcare or educational cost. The purchase of a second home, however, might not be seen as a "significant need." Definitions and details would differ from family to family and situation to situation.

The original investment would remain in institutions that serve the poor, though the actual institution might change. Subsequent generations could add to the pot of community investments, creating a family legacy for the poor that would still remain available to family members if significant needs should arise.

In the end, decisions prior to and during retirement for those who hope for the coming Reign of God cannot be handed over without question to our affluent cul-ture's financial services industry. We have to begin the process of reflecting criti-cally, theologically and biblically on retirement, money and the Reign of God.

Andy Loving is an Investment Advisor Representative of First Affirmative Financial Network (FAFN), LLC. Just Money Advisors is not a subsidiary or affiliate of FAFN. FAFN is an independent Registered Investment Advisor. (SEC File # 801-56587).

Used by permission of the author, Andy Loving.

Moving toward Jubilee
on a Grand Scale

Christians have a long history of trying
to squeeze Jesus out of public life and
reduce him to a private little savior. But
to do this is to ignore what the Bible really
says. Jesus talks a great deal about the kingdom of God—and what he means by that is
a public life reorganized toward neighborliness.

—*Walter Brueggemann*

The biblical authors never gave an abstract
definition of justice but keep pointing to the poor,
the oppressed, and the vulnerable as those whom God
is especially concerned to protect and restore. Justice,
we find, means standing with the lowest neighbor,
rejecting the worship of wealth or power, and creating
structures supportive of all…

—From *Reformed Faith and Economics*,
edited by Robert Stivers

Introduction—X

Money and Faith frequently refers to Walter Brueggemann's description of Jubilee, or more specifically, Jubilee Justice: "finding out what belongs to whom and giving it back." The process of doing so is not only a practice for the individual; it is also a practice for entire societies. Indeed it could be argued that Yahweh, when establishing the people of Israel, was especially interested that Israel practice the Jubilee in order to create a model *society*. Neighboring nations would observe this new nation and discover how to establish a more just society.

In order to give back "what belongs to whom," individuals and the society in which they live need to collaborate. Money and Faith alternately highlights both the individual and society. The previous two sections—on Sabbath and tithing, and investments and retirement—focus more on the individual. The following essays turn their attention to the larger societal context.

That's a good thing because this book raises difficult questions on a large scale. So it's important to raise possible solutions to those larger scale questions or challenges. For example, Money and Faith's middle four sections (the "prophetic" sections) discuss corporate power, negative externalities associated with the global economy, sustainability and much more. (Large scale indeed!) How could a society and its economic practices actually become more equitable, sustainable? In other words, what are some of the ways an entire society might practice the Jubilee?

The following essays highlight a few possibilities. Brown suggests green taxes and Barnes promotes establishing a "commons sector."

Reinventing the Commons

by Peter Barnes

> Peter Barnes is cofounder and former president of Working Assets Long Distance. Author of *Who Owns the Sky?* and *Pawns: The Plight of the Citizen-Soldier*, Peter founded the writers' retreat The Mesa Refuge in Point Reyes, California. The refuge "invites people to think and write about the edges between human activity—capitalism in particular—and the natural world we are obliged to preserve." I benefited greatly from two weeks at the refuge in April, 2007.

Barnes here imagines a solution to many of the challenges *Money and Faith* highlights, such as externalities and nature's "free" services. He reminds us that we all inherit the great gift of the commons at birth. This shared inheritance includes air, water, culture, language and so on. As we have seen, much of the common wealth is not valued economically. Barnes argues we need to create a "commons sector" in order to balance the corporate sector.

This book has described large-scale, societal and economic challenges. Barnes' ideas are intriguing because, when implemented, they carry the possibility of meeting those large-scale challenges.

Barnes' essay refers to *thneeds*. Theodore Geisel—better known as Dr. Seuss—coined the term in his book *The Lorax*. A *thneed* is a thing we want but don't really need. In the book, an entrepreneurial chap (the Once-ler) makes *thneeds* by cutting down the truffula trees. The Lorax, who speaks for the trees, protests. The Once-ler responds: "I'm being quite useful. This thing is a Thneed. A Thneeds a Fine-Something-That-All-People-Need!"

Imagination is more important than knowledge.

—Albert Einstein, 1929

...I've argued that Capitalism 2.0—or surplus capitalism—has three tragic flaws: it devours nature, widens inequality, and fails to make us happier in the end. It behaves this way because it's programmed to do so. It *must* make thneeds, reward property owners disproportionately, and distract us from truer paths to happiness because its algorithms direct it to do so. Neither enlightened managers nor the occasional zealous regulator can make it behave much differently.

In this part of the book I advance a solution. The essence of it is to fix capitalism's operating system by adding a commons sector to balance the corporate sector. The new sector would supply virtuous feedback loops and proxies for unrepresented stakeholders: future generations, pollutees, and nonhuman species. And would offset the corporate sector's *negative* externalities with *positive* externalities of comparable magnitude. If the corporate sector devours nature, the commons sector would protect it. If the corporate sector widens inequality, the commons sector would reduce it. If the corporate sector turns us into self-obsessed consumers, the commons sector would reconnect us to nature, community, and culture. All this would happen automatically once the commons sector is set up. The result would be a balanced economy that gives us the best of both sectors and the worst of neither.

To be sure, building an economic sector from scratch is a formidable task. Fortunately, the commons sector *needn't* be built from scratch; it has an enormous potential asset base just waiting to be claimed. That asset base is the commons itself, the gifts of nature and society we inherit and create together. As we'll see, these gifts are worth more than all private assets combined. It's the job of the commons sector to organize and protect these gifts, and by so doing, to save capitalism from itself.

Our Common Wealth

Everyone knows what *private* wealth is, even if they don't have much of it. It's the property we inherit or accumulate individually, including fractional claims on corporations and mutual funds. In the United States in 2005, this private wealth (minus mortgages and other liabilities) totaled $48.5 trillion. As previously noted, the top 5 percent of Americans owns more of this treasure than the bottom 95 percent.

But there's another trove of wealth that's not so well-known: our *common* wealth. Each of us is the joint recipient of a vast inheritance. This shared inheritance includes air and water, habitats and ecosystems, languages and cultures, science and technologies, social and political systems, and quite a bit more.

Common wealth is like the dark matter of the economic universe—it's everywhere, but we don't see it. One reason we don't see it is that much of it is, literally, invisible. Who can spot the air, an aquifer, or the social trust that underlies financial markets? The more relevant reason is our own blindness: the only economic matter we notice is the kind that glistens with dollar signs. We ignore common wealth because it lacks price tags and property rights.

If the corporate sector devours nature, the commons sector would protect it. If the corporate sector widens inequality, the commons sector would reduce it. If the corporate sector turns us into self-obsessed consumers, the commons sector would reconnect us to nature, community, and culture.

I first began to appreciate common wealth when Working Assets launched its socially screened money market fund. My job was to write advertisements that spurred people to send us large sums of money. Our promise was that we'd make this money grow, without investing in really bad companies, and send it back—including the growth, but minus our management fee—any time the investor requested. It struck me as quite remarkable that people who didn't know us from a hole in the wall would send us substantial portions of their savings. Why, I wondered, did they trust us?

The answer, of course, was that they didn't trust *us*, they trusted *the system* in which we operated. They trusted that we'd prudently manage their savings not because we'd *personally* earned their confidence, but because they knew that if we didn't, the Securities and Exchange Commission or some district attorney would bust us. Beyond that, they trusted that the corporations we invested in were honest in computing their incomes and reliable in meeting their obligations. That trust, and the larger system it's based on, were built over generations, and we had nothing to do with it. In short, although Working Assets provided a service people willingly paid for, we also profited from a larger system we'd simply inherited.

I got another whiff of common wealth when Working Assets considered going public—that is, selling stock to strangers through an initial public offering. Our investment banker informed us that, simply by going public, we'd increase the value of our stock by 30 percent. He called this magic a *liquidity premium*. What he meant was that stock that can be sold in a market of millions is worth more than stock that has almost no market at all. This extra value would come not from anything *we* did, but from the socially created bonus of liquidity. We'd be reaping what others sowed. (In the end, we didn't go public because we didn't want to be subjected to Wall Street's calculus.)

Trust and liquidity, I eventually realized, are just two small rivulets in an enormous river of common wealth that encompasses nature, community, and culture. Nature's gifts are all those wondrous things, living and nonliving, that we inherit from the creation. Community includes the myriad threads, tangible and intangible, that connect us to other humans efficiently. Culture embodies our vast store of science, inventions, and art.

Despite its invisibility, the value of our common wealth is immense.

Despite its invisibility, the value of our common wealth is immense. How much, roughly, is it worth? It's easy to put a dollar value on private assets; they're traded regularly, so their exchange value—if not their intrinsic value—is readily knowable. This isn't the case with common wealth. Many shared inheritances are valuable beyond measure. Others are potentially quantifiable, but there's no current market for them.

Fortunately, economists are a clever lot, and they've developed methodologies to estimate the value of things that aren't traded. Using such methodologies, it's possible to get an order of magnitude for the value of common wealth. The conclusion that emerges from numerous studies is that even though much common wealth can't be valued monetarily, the parts that can be valued are worth more than all private assets combined (see figure 5.1).

It's worth noting that figure 5.1 understates the gap between common and private wealth. That's partly because it omits much common wealth that can't be quantified, and partly because a portion of the value attributed to private wealth is in fact an appropriation of common wealth. If this mislabeled portion is subtracted from private wealth and added to common wealth, the gap between the two widens further.

Figure 5.1 **Approximate Value of Common, Private, and State Assets, 2001 ($ Trillions)**[1]

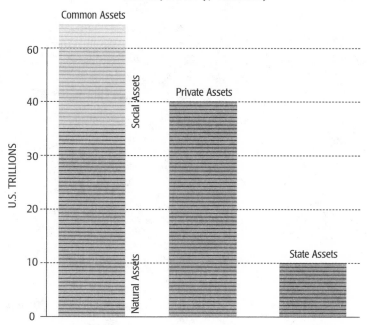

Reflects only quantifiable asssets. Source: Friends of the Commons, *State of the Commons 2003-04.* http://friendsofthecommons.org/understanding/worth.html. Reprinted with permission.

An example may help explain this. Suppose you buy a house for $300,000, and without improving it, sell it a few years later for $400,000. You pay off the mortgage and walk away with a pile of cash. Your private wealth increases. But think about what *caused* the house to rise in value. It wasn't anything you did. Rather, it was the fact that your neighborhood became more popular. That, in turn, resulted from population shifts, a new highway perhaps, an improved school, or the beautification efforts of neighbors. In other words, your increased wealth is a capture of socially created value. It shows up as private wealth but is really a gift of society.

These numbers, crude as they are, tell us something important. Despite our obsession with private wealth, most of what we cherish, we share. To believe otherwise is to imagine a flower's beauty owes nothing to nutrients in the soil, energy from the sun, or the activity of bees.

It's time to notice our shared gifts. Not only that, it's time to name them, protect them, and organize them. The practical question is *how?*

Common Property Is Property Too

In Dr. Seuss's *The Lorax*, the eponymous character speaks for the trees, while his antagonist, the Once-ler, speaks for industry, jobs, and growth. Though both

How Much Do We Own?

Natural Assets

In 2002 economists Robert Costanza and Paul Sutton estimated the contribution of ecosystem services to the U.S. economy at $2 trillion.[2] Ecosystem services represent the benefits humans derive from natural ecosystems, including food from wild plants and animals, climate regulation, waste assimilation, fresh water replenishment, soil formation, nutrient cycling, flood control, pollination, raw materials, and more. Using data from many previous studies, as well as satellite photography, Costanza and Sutton estimated values for ecosystems per unit of *biome* (an acre of rain forest, or grasslands, or desert, for example). They then multiplied by the total area of each biome and summed over all services and biomes.

If $2 trillion represents the yearly contribution of nature to the U.S. economy, what's the underlying value of America's natural assets? One way to answer this is to treat yearly ecosystem services as "earnings" produced by "stocks" of natural assets. These earnings can then be multiplied by the average price/earnings ratio of publicly traded stocks over the last fifty years (16.5/1) to arrive at an estimated natural asset value of $33 trillion.

This figure is, if anything, an underestimate, because it ignores a singular aspect of nature: its irreplaceability. If Corporation X were to go out of business, its useful contributions to society would quickly be supplied by another corporation. If a natural ecosystem were to disappear, however, it could not so easily be replaced. Thus, an *irreplaceability premium* of indeterminate magnitude should be added to the $33 trillion.

Social Assets

The value of community and cultural assets has been less studied than that of natural assets. However, we can get an order of magnitude by considering a few examples.

The Internet has contributed significantly to the U.S. economy since the 1990s. It has spawned many new companies (America Online, Amazon.com, Ebay, to name a few), boosted sales and efficiency of existing companies, and stimulated educational, cultural, and informational exchange. How much is all that worth?

There's no right answer to this question. However, a study by Cisco Systems and the University of Texas found that the Internet generated $830 billion in revenue in 2000.[3] Assuming the asset value of the Internet is 16.5 times the yearly revenue it generates, we arrive at an estimated value of $13 trillion.

Another valuable social asset is the complex system of stock exchanges, laws, and communications media that makes it possible for Americans to sell stock easily. Assuming that this socially created "liquidity premium" accounts for 30 percent of stock market capitalization, its value in 2006 was roughly $5 trillion. If that much equity were put in a mutual fund whose shares belonged to all Americans, the average household would be $45,000 richer.

Not-for-profit cultural activities also pump billions of dollars into the U.S. economy. A 2002 study by Americans for the Arts found that non-profit art and cultural activities generate $134 billion in economic value every year, including $89 billion in household income and $24 billion in tax revenues.[4] Using the 16.5 multiplier suggests that America's cultural assets are worth in excess of $2 trillion.

These three examples alone add up to about $20 trillion. The long list of other social assets—including scientific and technical knowledge, our legal and political systems, our universities, libraries, accounting procedures, and transportation infrastructure—suggest that the total value of our social assets is comparable in magnitude to that of our natural assets.

characters use clever language, it's not an even match. The Once-ler has property rights, while the Lorax has only words. By the end of the story, the Once-ler has cut down all the truffula trees; the Lorax's protests are eloquent but futile. The obvious moral is: trees need property rights too.

And why not? Property rights are useful human inventions. They're legally en-forceable agreements through which society grants specific privileges to owners. Among these are rights to use, exclude, sell, rent, lend, trade, or bequeath a particu-lar asset. These assorted privileges can be bundled or unbundled almost any which way.

It's largely through property rights that economies are shaped. Feudal economies were based on estates passed from lords to their eldest sons, alongside commons that sustained the commoners. Commoners were required, in one way or another, to labor for the lords, while the lords lived off that labor and the bounty of the land. The whole edifice was anchored by the so-called divine right of kings.

Similarly, capitalism is shaped by the property rights we create and honor today. Its greatest invention has been the web of property rights we call the *joint stock cor-poration*. This fictitious entity enjoys perpetual life, limited liability, and—like the feudal estate of yesteryear—almost total sovereignty. Its beneficial ownership has been fractionalized into tradeable shares, which themselves are a species of property.

There's nothing about property rights, however, that requires them to be concen-trated in profit-maximizing hands. You could, for example, set up a trust to own a forest, or certain forest rights, on behalf of future generations. These property rights would talk as loudly as shares of Pacific Lumber stock, but their purpose would be very different: to preserve the forest rather than to exploit it. If the Lorax had owned some of these rights, Dr. Seuss's tale (and Pacific Lumber's) would have ended more happily.

Imagine a whole set of property rights like this. Let's call them generically, *common property rights*. If such property rights didn't exist, there'd be a strong case for inventing them. Fortunately, they do exist in a variety of forms—for example, land or easements held in perpetual trust, as by the Nature Conservancy, and corporate assets managed on behalf of a broad community, as by the Alaska Permanent Fund.

Some forms of common property include individual shares—again, the Alaska Permanent Fund is an example. These individual shares, however, differ from shares in private corporations. They're not securities you can trade in a market; rather, they depend on your membership in the community. If you emigrate or die, you lose your share. Conversely, when you're born into the community, your share is a birthright.

I recognize that, for some, turning common wealth into *any* kind of property is a sacrilege. As Chief Seattle of the Suquamish tribe put it, "How can you buy or sell the sky, the warmth of the land?" I empathize deeply with this sentiment. However, I've come to believe that it's *more* disrespectful of the sky to pollute it without limit or payment than to turn it into common property held in trust for future generations. Hence, I favor *propertization*, but not privatization.

Organizing Principles of the Commons Sector

Property rights, especially the common kind, require competent institutions to manage them. What we need today, then, along with more common property, is a set of institutions, distinct from corporations and government, whose unique and explicit mission is to manage common property.

I say *set* of institutions because there will and should be variety. The commons sector should not be a monoculture like the corporate sector. Each institution should be appropriate to its particular asset and locale.

Some of the variety will depend on whether the underlying asset is limited or inexhaustible. Typically, gifts of nature have limited capacities; the air can safely absorb only so much carbon dioxide, the oceans only so many drift nets. Institutions that manage natural assets must therefore be capable of limiting use. By contrast, ideas and cultural creations have endless potential for elaboration and reuse. In these commons, managing institutions should maximize public access and minimize private tollbooths.

Despite their variations, commons sector institutions would share a set of organizing principles. Here are the main ones.

Leave Enough and As Good in Common

As Locke argued, it's okay to privatize *parts* of the commons as long as "enough and as good"[5] is left for everyone forever. *Enough* in the case of an ecosystem means enough to keep it alive and healthy. That much, or more, should be part of the commons, even if parts of the ecosystem are private. In the case of culture and science, *enough* means enough to assure a vibrant public domain. Exclusive licenses, such as patents and copyrights, should be kept to a minimum.

Put Future Generations First

Corporations put the interests of stockholders first, while government puts the interests of campaign donors and living voters first. No one at the moment puts future generations first. That's Job Number One for the commons sector.

In practice, this means trustees of common property should be legally accountable to future generations. They should also be bound by the *precautionary principle*: when in doubt, err on the side of safety. And when faced with a conflict between short-term gain and long-term preservation, they should be required to choose the latter.

The More the Merrier

Whereas private property is inherently *exclusive*, common property strives to be *inclusive*. It always wants *more* co-owners or participants, consistent with preservation of the asset.

This organizing principle applies most clearly to commons like culture and the Internet, where physical limits are absent and increasing use unleashes synergies galore. It also applies to social compacts like Social Security and Medicare, which require universal participation. In these compacts, financial mechanisms express our solidarity with other members of our national community. They're efficient and fair because they include everybody. Were they to operate under profit-maximizing principles, they'd inevitably exclude the poor (who couldn't afford to participate) and anyone deemed by private insurers to be too risky.

One Person, One Share

Modern democratic government is grounded on the principle of one person, one vote. In the same way, the modern commons sector would be grounded on the principle of one person, one share.

In the case of scarce natural assets, it will be necessary to distinguish between usage rights and income rights. It's impossible for everyone to *use* a limited commons equally, but everyone should receive equal shares of the *income* derived from selling limited usage rights.

Include Some Liquidity

Currently, private property owners enjoy a near-monopoly on the privilege of receiving property income. But as the Alaska Permanent Fund shows, it's possible for common property co-owners to receive income too.

Income sharing would end private property's monopoly not only on liquidity, but also on attention. People would *notice* common property if they got income from it.

They'd care about it, think about it, and talk about it. Concern for invisible commons would soar.

Common property liquidity has to be designed carefully, though. Since common property rights are birthrights, they shouldn't be tradeable the way corporate shares are. This means commons owners wouldn't reap capital gains. Instead, they'd retain their shared income stakes throughout their lives, and through such stakes, share in rent, royalties, interest, and dividends.

A Glimpse Ahead

Unlike a computer operating system, Capitalism 3.0 won't come on a disk. It can't be downloaded, either. It must be built in the real world, asset by asset and commons by commons. The process is summed up in figure 5.2...

Figure 5.2 **From Here to Capitalism 3.0**

I: Capitalism 2.0

Private corporations devour un-organized commons with help from the state. The playing field is heavily tilted.

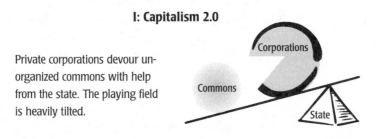

II: Reinventing the Commons

The state assigns rights to commons institutions, just as it has to corporations.

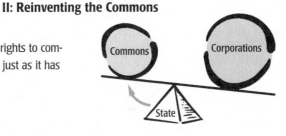

III: Capitalism 3.0

Private corporations and organized commons enhance and constrain each other. The state maintains a level playing field.

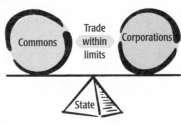

Under Capitalism 2.0, private corporations devour unorganized commons with help from the state. The playing field is heavily tilted. During the transition phase, the state assigns rights to commons institutions, just as it does to corporations. The playing field begins to level off. Finally, under Capitalism 3.0, private corporations and organized commons enhance and constrain each other. The state maintains a level playing field.

1. Private wealth: *Statistical Abstract of the United States, 2006* (Washington, D.C.: U.S. Census Bureau, 2006), Table 703. *www.census.gov/prod/2005pubs/06statab/income.pdf*

2. Ecosystem services: Robert Costanza and Paul Sutton, "Global Estimates of Market and Non-Market Values Derived from Nighttime Satellite Imagery, Land Cover, and Ecosystem Service Valuation," *Ecological Economics*, June 2002, 509-527. *www.uvm.edu/giee/research/publications/Sutton_and_Costanza.pdf*

3. Internet income: Measuring the Internet Economy (Austin: Cisco Systems and the University of Texas, Jan. 2001). *www.momentumresearchgroup.com/downloads/reports/internet-indicators-2001.pdf*

4. Internet not-for-profit income: *Arts and Economic Prosperity: The Economic Impact of Nonprofit Arts Organizations and Their Audiences* (Washington, D.C.: Americans for the Arts, 2002). *http://pubs.artsusa.org/library/ARTS095/html*

5. "enough and as good": Locke, *Second Treatise*.

Tools for Restructuring the Economy

by Lester Brown

The Washington Post called Lester Brown "one of the world's most influential thinkers." *The Telegraph of Calcutta* refers to him as "the guru of the environmental movement." In 1986, the Library of Congress requested his personal papers noting that his writings "have already strongly affected thinking about problems of world population and resources."

Founder of the Worldwatch Institute, Brown is one of the world's most widely published authors. His books have appeared in some 40 languages. In May 2001, he founded the Earth Policy Institute to provide a vision and a road map for achieving an environmentally sustainable economy. He is the recipient of many awards, including 23 honorary degrees, a MacArthur Fellowship and the 1987 United Nations' Environment Prize. (Excerpted from Earth Policy Institute, see *www.earth-policy.org*)

∞

[Earlier], I cited Oystein Dahle's warning that the failure of prices to tell the ecological truth could undermine capitalism, just as the failure of prices to tell the economic truth undermined socialism. The Chinese recognized this risk of prices not telling the ecological truth when they banned tree cutting in the Yangtze river basin following the near-record flooding in 1998. They said that a tree standing was worth three times as much as a tree cut. If they had included not only the flood control value of trees but also the value in recycling rainfall to the country's interior, a tree standing might easily be worth six times as much as a tree cut.[1]

The use of a highly valued resource such as a tree for a lowly valued purpose such as lumber imposes an economic cost on society. Similarly, since the price of a gallon of gasoline does not include the cost of climate change, it too imposes a cost on society. If losses such as these, now occurring on an ever larger scale, keep accumulating, the resulting economic stresses could bankrupt some countries.

The key to sustaining economic progress is getting prices to tell the ecological truth. Ecologists and economists—working together—can calculate the ecological costs of various economic activities. These costs can then be incorporated into the market price of a product or service in the form of a tax. Additional taxes on goods and services can be offset by a reduction in income taxes. The issue in "tax shifting," as the Europeans call it, is not the level of taxes but what they tax.

> Reestablishing a stable, sustainable relationship between the global economy and the earth's ecosystem depends on restructuring the economy at a pace that historically has occurred only in wartime.

There are several policy instruments that can be used to restructure the economy, including fiscal policy, government regulation, eco-labeling, and tradable permits. But restructuring the tax system is the key to eliminating the crippling economic distortions. Tax policy is particularly effective because it is systemic in nature. If taxes raise the price of fossil fuels to reflect the full cost of their use, this will permeate the economy, affecting all energy-related economic decisions.

Today's fiscal systems, a combination of subsidies and taxes, reflect the goals of another era—a time when it was in the interest of countries to exploit their natural resources as rapidly and competitively as possible. That age has ended. Now natural capital is the scarce resource. The goal is to restructure the fiscal system so that the prices reflect the truth, protecting the economy's natural supports.

It is not easy to grasp the scale and urgency of the needed restructuring. Reestablishing a stable, sustainable relationship between the global economy and the earth's ecosystem depends on restructuring the economy at a pace that historically has occurred only in wartime. When national security is threatened, governments take extreme measures, such as drafting able-bodied men into the armed forces, commandeering natural resources, and sometimes even taking over strategic industries. Although it may not yet be obvious to everyone, we may well be facing a threat that is comparable in scale and urgency to a world war.

The Fiscal Steering Wheel

Fiscal policy is an ideal policy instrument for building an eco-economy because both taxes and subsides are widely used and work through the market. By relying primarily on these two tools to build an eco-economy, we capitalize on the market's strengths, including its inherent efficiency in allocating resources. The challenge is to use taxes and subsidies to help the market reflect not only the direct costs and benefits of economic activities but the indirect ones as well. If we use fiscal policy to encourage environmentally constructive activities and to discourage destructive ones, we can steer the economy in a sustainable direction.

Some environmental goals—such as limiting the catch in a fishery or properly disposing of nuclear waste—can be achieved only by government regulation. Edwin Clark, former senior economist with the White House Council on Environmental Quality, observes that some of the other tools discussed here, such as tradable permits, "require establishing complex regulatory frameworks, defining the permits, establishing the rules for trades, and preventing people from acting without permits." In some cases, it is simply more efficient to ban environmentally destructive activities than to try to tax them out of existence. While the advantage has shifted toward the use of tax policy in achieving environmental goals, there is still a role for regulation to play.[2]

A major weakness of the market is that while nature's goods—lumber, fish, or grain—move through the market, many of nature's services do not. Since there is no bill rendered for pollinating crops, controlling floods, or protecting soil from erosion, these services are often thought of as free. And because they have no apparent market value, they are often not protected. Fiscal policy can be used to compensate for this shortfall as well.

A market that tells the ecological truth will incorporate the value of ecosystem services. For example, if we buy furniture from a forest products corporation that engages in clearcutting, we pay the costs of logging and converting the logs into furniture, but not the costs of the flooding downstream. If we restructure the tax system and raise taxes on clearcutting timber so that its price reflects the cost to society of the resultant flooding, this method of harvesting timber likely would be eliminated.

Taxes designed to incorporate in their prices the environmental costs of producing goods or providing services enable the market to send the right signal. They discourage such activities as coal burning, the use of throwaway beverage containers, or cyanide gold mining. Subsidies can be used to encourage such activities as planting trees, using water more efficiently, and harnessing wind energy. Environmental taxes and subsidies also can be used to represent the interests of future generations in situations where traditional economics simply discounts the future.

The advantage of using fiscal policy to incorporate the indirect environmental cost is that economic decisions at all levels—from those made by political leaders and corporate planners to those made by individual consumers—are guided by the market. It has a pervasive influence. If it tells the ecological truth, it minimizes the information that individual decision makers need to make an environmentally responsible decision.

Tax Shifting

Tax shifting involves changing the composition of taxes but not the level. It means reducing income taxes and offsetting them with taxes on environmentally destructive activities such as carbon emissions, the generation of toxic waste, the use of virgin raw materials, the use of nonrefillable beverage containers, mercury emissions, the generation of garbage, the use of pesticides, and the use of throw-away products. This is by no means a comprehensive list, but it does include the more important activities that should be discouraged by taxing. There is wide agreement among environmental scientists on the kinds of activities that need to be taxed more. The question now is how to generate public support for the whole-sale tax shifting that is needed.

In this area, Europe is well ahead of the United States, largely because of the pioneering efforts of Ernst von Weizsacker, formerly head of the Wuppertal Institute and now a member of the German Bundestag. He not only pioneered this concept, but has provided ongoing intellectual leadership on the issue.[3]

The way tax shifting works can be seen in the table compiled by Worldwatch researcher David Roodman. (See Table 11-1.) It looks at Europe, where most of the shifting has occurred, and gives a sense of how nine countries have reduced taxes on personal income or wages while increasing them on environmentally destructive activities. Sweden was the first country to begin this process, with a program to lower taxes on personal income while raising them on carbon and sulfur emissions to discourage the burning of fossil fuels, particularly those with high sulfur content. For several years, only the smaller countries of Europe, such as Denmark, the Netherlands, and Sweden, followed this path. But during the late 1990s, France, Germany, Italy, and the United Kingdom joined in.

Tax shifting has appeal in Europe in part because it creates jobs, an item of concern in a region plagued with high unemployment. Shifting from the use of virgin raw materials to recycled materials, for example, not only reduces environmental disruption, it also increases employment since recycling is more labor-intensive. This was one of the reasons Germany adopted a four-year plan of gradually reducing taxes on incomes while increasing those on energy use in 1999. When completed, this will shift 2.1 percent of total revenue generated; with an annual revenue budget of nearly $1 trillion, it would shift $20 billion a year. Denmark leads the way in the amount of taxes being shifted, with a total of 3 percent moved thus far by measures adopted in 1994 and 1996. The Danish government taxes the

Table 11-1. Shifting Taxes from Income to Environmentally Destructive Activities

Country, First Year in Effect	Taxes Cut on	Taxes Raised on	Revenue Shifted* (percent)
Sweden, 1991	personal income	carbon and sulfur emissions	1.9
Denmark, 1994	personal income	motor fuel, coal, electricity, and water sales; waste incineration and landfilling; motor vehicle ownership	2.5
Spain, 1995	wages	motor fuel sales	0.2
Denmark, 1996	wages, agricultural property	carbon emissions from industry; pesticide, chlorinated solvent, and battery sales	0.5
Netherlands, 1996	personal income and wages	natural gas and electricity sales	0.8
United Kingdom, 1996	wages	landfilling	0.1
Finland, 1996	personal income and wages	energy sales, landfilling	0.5
Germany, 1999	wages	energy sales	2.1
Italy, 1999	wages	fossil fuel sales	0.2
Netherlands, 1999	personal income	energy sales, landfilling, household water sales	0.9
France, 2000	wages	solid waste; air and water pollution	0.1

*Expressed relative to tax revenue raised by all levels of government.
Source: Adapted from David Malin Roodman, "Environmental Tax Shifts Multiplying," in Lester R Brown et al., *Vital Signs 2000* (New York: W.W. Norton & Company, 2000), 138-39.

use of motor fuels, the burning of coal, the use of electricity, landfilling, and ownership of motor vehicles. The tax on the purchase of a new car in Denmark is typically higher than the price of the vehicle itself.[4]

The Netherlands, a country with an advanced industrial economy concentrated in a small land area, uses taxes to curb the release of heavy metals, including cadmium, copper, lead, mercury, and zinc. Between 1976 and the mid-1990s, the industrial discharge of these various elements fell 86-97 percent each. The Dutch firms that developed the pollution control equipment used to achieve these reductions gained an edge on firms in other countries, greatly expanding their export sales and earnings.[5]

The environmentally destructive activities now taxed in Europe include carbon emissions, sulfur emissions, coal mining, landfilling, electricity sales, and vehicle ownership. Countries elsewhere might tax other activities to reflect their particular circumstances. Among these might be taxes on excessive water use, the conversion of cropland to nonfarm uses, tree cutting, pesticide use, and the use of cyanide in gold mining. Over time, taxes on environmentally destructive activities could increase substantially, perhaps one day accounting for the lion's share of tax collection.

Governments typically take care to ensure that environmental taxes are not socially regressive. David Roodman describes how Portugal has avoided this with its tax on water, an increasingly scarce resource in this semiarid country. The town of Setubal provides households with 25 cubic meters of water per month that is tax-free. It then "terraces" additional water taxes, raising the tax through three successively higher levels of consumption.[6]

The concept of taxing environmentally destructive activities received a major boost in the United States in November 1998 when the U.S. tobacco industry agreed to reimburse state governments $251 billion for past Medicare costs of treating smoking-related illnesses. This was, in effect, a retroactive tax on the billions of packs of cigarettes sold in the United States during the preceding decades. It was a staggering sum of money—nearly $1,000 for every American. This was a tax on cigarette smoke, a pollutant that is so destructive to human health that it may cause more damage than all other pollutants combined.[7]

This "tax" that the industry is paying on past damage associated with smoking will be funded by raising the price of cigarettes. Between January 1998 and April 2001, the average U.S. wholesale price of cigarettes climbed from $1.33 per pack to $2.21, a 66-percent increase in two years. It is expected to climb further, helping to discourage cigarette smoking.[8]

Another value of environmental taxes is that they communicate information. When a government taxes a product because it is environmentally destructive, it tells the consumer that it is concerned about this. And restructuring the tax system has a systemic effect, steering millions of consumer decisions in an environmentally sustainable direction every day—ranging from how to get to work to what to order for lunch.

Tax shifting to achieve environmental goals has broad support. Polls taken in the late 1990s in both the United States and Europe show overwhelming support for the concept once it is explained. On both sides of the Atlantic, support of the electorate is 70 percent or greater. Tax shifting is also an attractive economic tool because it can be used to achieve so many environmental goals. Once it is used in one context, it can easily be applied in others.[9]

If the world is to restructure the economy before environmental destruction leads to economic decline, tax restructuring almost certainly will be at the center of the effort. No other set of policies can bring about the systemic changes needed quickly enough. In an article in *Fortune* magazine that argued for a 10-percent reduction in U.S. income taxes and a 50¢-per-gallon hike in the tax on gasoline, Harvard economist N. Gregory Mankiw summarized his thinking as follows: "Cutting income taxes while increasing gasoline taxes would lead to more rapid economic growth, less traffic congestion, safer roads, and reduced risk of global warming—all without jeopardizing long-term fiscal solvency. This may be the closest thing to a free lunch that economics has to offer."[10]

[Editor's note: Another powerful tool for "restructuring the economy" is subsidy shifting. Due to space constraints we did not include Brown's section on subsidies. Similar to taxes, subsidies encourage certain behavior and discourage others. If a government, for example, subsidizes the use of irrigation water, farmers do not have much incentive to curtail water use. On the other hand, when governments phase in price increases for irrigation water, farmers respond by figuring out how to use less. This same principle can be applied to most any commodity.]

1. Parallel of ecological and economic truths from Oystein Dable, discussion with author at Worldwatch Briefing, Aspen, CO, 22 July 2001: Erik Eckholm, "Chinese Leaders Vow to Mend Ecological Ways," *New York Times*, 30 August 1998; Erik Eckholm, "China Admits Ecological Sins Played Role in Flood Disaster," *New York Times*, 26 August 1998; Erik Eckholm, "Stunned by floods, China Chastens Logging Curbs," *New York Times*, 27 February 1998.

2. Edwin Clark, letter to author, 25 July 2001.

3. Ernst U. von Weizsacker and Jochen Jesinghaus, *Ecological Tax Reform* (London: Zed Books, 1992).

4. David Malin Roodman, "Environmental Tax Shifts Multiplying," in Lester R. Brown et al., *Vital Signs 2000* (New York: W.W. Norton & Company, 2000), 138-139; German annual budget from U. S. Central Intelligence Agency, *World Fact Book*, www.cia.gov/cia/publications/factbook viewed 1 August 2001; vehicle tax in Denmark is 180 percent, as reported by Marjorie Miller, "British Car Buyers Taken for a Ride," *Los Angeles Times*, 23 July 1999.

5. David Malin Roodman, *Getting the Signals Right: Tax Reform to Protect the Environment and the Economy*, Worldwatch Paper 134 (Washington, D.C.: Worldwatch Institute, May 1997), 11.

6. David Malin Roodman, *The Natural Wealth of Nations* (New York: W. W. Norton & Company, 1998), 189.

7. U.S. Department of Agriculture (USDA), Economic Research Service (ERS), "Cigarette Price Increase Follows Tobacco Pact," *Agricultural Outlook*, January-February 1999.

8. USDA, ERS, Tobacco Situation and Outlook, September 2000, 8; USDA, ERS, *Tobacco Situation and Outlook*, April 2001, 5.

9. Roodman, op. Cit. Note 6, 243.

10. N. Gregory Mankiw, "Gas Tax Now!" *Fortune*, 24 May 1999, 60-64.

Lester R. Brown, *Eco-Economy: Building an Economy for the Earth* (New York: W.W. Norton, 2001).

Epilogue

Lasting change happens when people see for themselves that a different way of life is more fulfilling than their present one.

—*Eknath Easwaran*

The power of God is present at all places, even in the tiniest tree leaf.

—*Martin Luther*

*I*ntroduction—XI

Money and Faith: The Search for Enough. With a title like that, one thing seems clear (enough, anyway!): there is no neat way to tidy up, conclude or resolve all of this book's explorations.

Along the way we've rested, pausing to consider our money autobiographies, the role faith plays in our relationship with money, and whether or not economic wealth makes us a happier people. We've even dared venture into relatively untraveled territory and asked if more really is better, considered the biblical tradition of Jubilee, and stared, if only briefly, at the often daunting subject of economics. Finally, in light of all this exploration, we've asked the question which all of us answer daily with our lives—how shall we then live?

A question which, like many of *Money and Faith's* themes, remains with us all of our days. So the journey will continue.

At this point take a brief look at the "Welcome" on page 12. In that piece I share a number of the motivations behind this book. I conclude now with essays that leave us with images and feelings of what the world might be like when the motivations birthing this book have, to an extent, disappeared.

In "Radical Acceptance," I reflect on the story of Jesus' temptations in the wilderness—how Christ's response to the Tempter reveals Jesus' acceptance of his own identity. To me, his responses embody a spirituality and faith that can lead to greater freedom in our relationship with money and our lives in general.

In "And All the Trees of the Fields Will Clap Their Hands," I experience a connectedness, a truth that Paul proclaims in Ephesians 4: "...we are all members of one body." In terms of the themes in this book, our challenge is to use money and create economies that honor and enrich our connectedness.

 Radical Acceptance

by Michael Schut

Henri Nouwen writes:

> During our short lives the question that guides much of our behavior is: 'Who are we?' Although we may seldom pose that question in a formal way, we live it very concretely in our day-to-day decisions.
>
> The three answers that we generally live—not necessarily give—are: 'We are what we do, we are what others say about us, and we are what we have,' or in other words: 'We are our success, we are our popularity, we are our power.'...Jesus came to announce to us that an identity based on success, popularity, and power is a false identity—an illusion! Loudly and clearly he says: 'You are not what the world makes you; but you are children of God.'[1]

"Sounds to me like you're talking about conversion," the man in the back of the room offered. I was leading a workshop on economic growth and sustainability, not on conversion, but I think he was right, because raising questions about economic growth and our "right to consume" challenges a number of our culture's more ingrained idolatries, like "efficiency," or the tendency to equate our self-worth with the size of our bank account.

Anything that challenges such idols requires us to swim upstream. The strength to do so often comes from a change of heart, from some sort of conversion, a fact recognized by the man attending that workshop.

Conversion

The word conversion carries a bit of baggage, associated as it is with fear-based preaching, tent revivals and sin. But we need this word—at least if we agree that we're off base a bit, broken and in need of healing.

Often I think we associate sin with a list of do's and don'ts—the best known being the Ten Commandments. So, if we think we are following those, it's possible we might start to feel that we've got a handle on this sin thing.

But Jesus seems to think there is something deeper, more profound, than whether or not we are following a list. In the Gospel story of the rich young man (Mark 10:17-31), Jesus is asked, "What must I do to inherit eternal life?" He initially responds by pointing to the list when he says, "You know the commandments..." Jesus supports the importance of the young man's claim that he has kept "all these...since I was a boy." But then Jesus looks at the young man, loves him, and moves beyond the list. He sees that in spite of the young man's efforts to obey those commandments something within still holds him back; his sin is more profound than whether or not he has successfully followed the list, the letter of the law.

The apostle Paul seems to concur with Jesus when he writes that we are actually "slaves to sin." (Romans 6) Strong language, certainly implying an understanding of sin as much more than whether or not we are behaving well, or following some list. If indeed we are enslaved to sin, what is the essence of that enslavement?

Jesus in the Wilderness

Let's consider Jesus' temptations in the wilderness to help answer that question.[2]

> Then Jesus was led by the Spirit into the desert to be tempted by the devil. After fasting forty days and forty nights, he was hungry. The tempter came to him and said, 'If you are the Son of God, tell these stones to become bread.'
>
> Jesus answered, 'It is written: Man does not live on bread alone, but on every word that comes from the mouth of God.'
>
> Then the devil took him to the holy city and had him stand on the highest point of the temple. 'If you are the Son of God,' he said, 'throw yourself down. For it is written:
> He will command his angels concerning you,
>   and they will lift you up in their hands,
> so that you will not strike your foot against a stone.'
>
> Jesus answered him, 'It is also written: Do not put the Lord your God to the test.'
>
> Again, the devil took him to a very high mountain and showed him all the kingdoms of the world and their splendor. 'All this I will give you,' he said, 'if you will bow down and worship me.'
>
> Jesus said to him, 'Away from me, Satan! For it is written: Worship the Lord your God, and serve him only.'
>
> Then the devil left him, and angels came and attended him.
>
> —Matthew 4:1-11

In Jesus' responses to the three temptations we find a profound insight into understanding the essence of our enslavement.

The first word from the devil's mouth is small but powerful: "If." If you are the Son of God. The devil immediately challenges, or at least questions, Jesus' identity, his sense of self. In the passage immediately preceding this one, Matthew describes

the baptism of Jesus when God says, "You are my son, whom I love..." His beloved-
ness is given and his identity as God's son secure. The timing is fascinating. The
devil challenges Jesus' identity immediately following God's profound affirmation
of it. The devil is, in a sense, saying, "Oh yea? If you are God's beloved son, prove
it to me." The "if" serves to raise doubt in Jesus' mind about his self-identity.

So, first, prove you're the son of God by turning these stones into bread. That
would have been pretty impressive! We might characterize this first temptation,
then, like this: prove who you are by your abilities.

How about the second temptation? Here the devil again challenges Jesus' identity. *If* you are the Son of God, throw yourself down off the temple—surely God
would save *you*. In being rescued by God, Jesus would prove his self-worth because
God deemed it necessary to respond dramatically. The temptation here, then, is to
prove who you are by how others react and respond to you.

The third temptation is more straightforward: not so much a questioning of
Jesus' identity as an appeal to greed. In offering Jesus all the kingdoms of the world,
the devil offers unlimited power, prestige and wealth. The third temptation is to
prove who you are by possessions and power.

Self-Justification and Madison Avenue

First, prove who you are by your abilities.

Second, prove who you are by how others react and respond to you.

Third, prove who you are by your possessions and your positions of power.

At their core, each of these is essentially a temptation to "justify our selves." In
this reading of Jesus' temptations, the essence of our enslavement to sin emanates
from our efforts at self-justification.

Rather than believing that we are who we are by the grace of God, that we are
God's beloved, we become caught in the need to justify our selves. Once we do, we
have to prove ourselves all over again. It's the proverbial "rat race."

Notice how Madison Avenue knows so well that we face these temptations.
Every advertisement in every magazine or TV commercial somehow says "you are
not okay as you are—buy this, look like this, be like this." The way we can "buy
this, look like this, be like this," is through acquiring, saving, investing, and—especially—spending plenty of money.

Money is a primary tool through which we meet the demands of insatiability.
Much of our drive to succeed financially connects to our perceived need to prove
ourselves—to our parents, our business partners, our peers and on and on.

Caught in this race to self-justify, our lives become filled with more activities
and stuff than we could ever possibly need, *and* our planet groans from the weight.
In rejecting these temptations, Jesus shows another way, based not on self-justification, but on living deeply the truth that we are who we are by God's grace. Jesus'
response to the tempter in the wilderness reveals a path where we are set free from
the need to prove or justify ourselves. In experiencing conversion at that depth, we
can move toward a life that is both more satisfying and more compassionate.

My Own Temptations

I first heard this interpretation of this text from the Rev. Dale Jamtgaard at the Lutheran retreat center Holden Village. Like Dale, I was at Holden as a volunteer teacher. I left Dale's session smiling, kind of skipping inside. These temptations seemed so universal, so reflective of human nature. And to be set free from them...well, that is phenomenal news.

Imagine that freedom really sinking in.

Taken by Dale's thoughts, I summarized them during my next teaching session. I shared with those gathered that I am most susceptible to the need to prove who I am by how others respond to me and to some extent by my abilities. (I've never made enough money to find out if I'd like to prove who I am by my possessions!)

I suggested to the class that if I taught out of the need to prove myself by how they responded to me, that I would most likely do whatever it took to make sure they responded positively. I might somehow manipulate the group to get what I wanted, or feel a need to be particularly funny or relevant or smart. That psychic space is not exactly a place of freedom. If on the other hand I live out of, and rest in, a sense of being "the beloved," my identity and worth firmly root themselves in that lasting reality. That feels free.

Living in that freedom does not mean I no longer use my abilities to, in this example, teach. But when I feel called to some other profession, or lose my ability to teach, I don't at the same time lose the very thing I needed to prove my identity.

What about You?

Consider the three temptations and their common essence of self-justification. In which do you most see yourself? Are you caught in efforts to prove yourself through your abilities, by how others respond to you, by your possessions and power?

Do you find yourself sometimes living free of the need to justify yourself? If so, what difference does that make?

1. Henri Nouwen, *Here and Now: Living in the Spirit* (New York: Crossroads Publishing, 1994), 134-135.

2. Thanks to the Rev. Dale Jamtgaard, a retired Lutheran pastor from Portland, for these thoughts on Jesus' temptations.

"...*And All the Trees of the Field Will Clap Their Hands*"

by Michael Schut

"Earth seems to be a reality that is developing with the simple aim of celebrating the joy of existence."

—Thomas Berry and Brian Swimme, *The Universe Story*

In the prologue to *The Universe Story*, Berry and Swimme suggest that human activities in the twentieth century have ended the sixty-seven million year venture called the Cenozoic era. Our future will be:

> ...worked out in the tensions between those committed to the Technozoic, a future of increased exploration of Earth as resource, all for the benefit of humans, and those committed to the Ecozoic, a new mode of human-Earth relations, one where the well-being of the entire Earth community is the primary concern.

I want to share a story, one which for me hints at this new mode of "human-Earth relations" to which Berry refers. My hope is that in the telling of this story your memory and senses might recall a moment in your life when you too felt you were living closer to the Ecozoic era than the Technozoic, closer to health and relationship than exploitation and disconnection.

I spent the summer and early fall of 1992 leading wilderness backpacking and rock climbing trips for Sierra Treks. After co-leading trips in the Northern Cascade's Glacier Peak Wilderness Area and Yosemite's backcountry, I had the job of supplying a group with food and gear halfway through their ten-day backpacking trip. I was to meet this Fuller Seminary student-group fifteen miles in on the fourth night of their trip.

I awoke early the morning of the third day of their trip, packed the faded yellow Chevy Suburban with a hundred and eighty pounds of food and gear, and hooked up the horse trailer. The evening before had been spent in the pasture, cornering our pack animals, Alex and Ama; I now led these long-haired, often stubborn llamas into the trailer's adjacent stalls. State highway gave way to backcountry gravel roads as I drove carefully to the trail head. Unloading Alex and Ama, cinching, adjusting, tightening their packs, loading ninety pounds onto each of them, and hoisting my own pack, we set off on the trail.

The mid-September day was crisp, dry and clear, comfortable for shorts and a tee-shirt. The trail took us first through a broad, mid-elevation valley grazed by a local rancher's livestock. The valley floor heaved, narrowed, and steepened and grass gave way to pine forest, white rock walls and talus slopes. Quaking, golden aspen leaves held my eye and the sun's light. In late afternoon the llamas and I descended and crossed a dry creek bed, scrambled up the opposite bank, and found a spacious flat bench to bed down on.

I fed and tethered the llamas close by, then cooked my own gourmet pasta dinner. The day's last challenge remained: to find enough strong tree limbs into which I could hoist a hundred and fifty pounds of food. That done, I rolled out my bag and climbed in, absolutely at peace, comfortably nestled between earth, rock, tree and star.

The next morning I awoke, lowered the thankfully undisturbed food bags, ate a quick breakfast, once again became a "beast of burden" along with Alex and Ama, and continued on the trail. We passed from the Hoover Wilderness area into Yosemite's backcountry. By late afternoon we found the group camped on an island of grass, rock and tree in the middle of Rainbow Canyon.

After spending a few days rock climbing and summiting Tower Peak with the group, I donned my pack, loaded Alex and Ama, and set off for the trailhead. Again the day was bright, warm and invigorating. The air, though, snapped with coolness and the promise of winter.

It was toward the end of this fifteen-mile hike that a transformative moment of intense clarity graced my life. In a way it is so simple and brief a moment that it is hard to describe. I was simply descending out of the high country and approaching the valley below. We had just passed through a grey and white boulder-strewn talus field and then a thick willow stand. From behind, late afternoon sun rays streamed to earth.

A large grove of young aspen trees grandly and quietly presented themselves ahead of us. Perhaps one thousand aspens were gathered there, close ranked, crowding the hard-packed trail; none of them measuring more than two to three inches in diameter, perhaps ten to fifteen feet tall. Touched by a light breeze, each leaf reflected back hues of silver, of gold. As I entered that chorus of aspen tree and color, I left behind all self-consciousness, all worry, all distraction. The leaving of such cares was itself unconscious as I felt transfixed in this presence, overtaken by beauty and a sudden unveiling of the unending dance and song of creation!

I felt like royalty. It was almost as if that grove of aspens had parted, just then, allowing me to pass on the narrow trail. But there was no sense of separation, no hierarchy between me and the quaking aspen. The newness and joy, the peace and "kingliness" seemed a gift bestowed simply and directly to me from that golden grove. It seemed that their "golden-leafed" garments swayed silently in the breeze as their smooth, silver, slender trunks bowed in respect, recognition and celebration of relationship. I smiled on the outside and bowed on the inside, seeing more clearly than ever before their absolute beauty and rooted freedom in being who they were created to be. We acknowledged each other. I felt we were dancing, laughing and celebrating.

Looking back on that hike, I wonder if for that brief moment I was given the grace to see, feel and join creation's song of praise. Perhaps I experienced a taste of Isaiah's proclamation: "You will go out in joy and be led forth in peace; the mountains and hills will burst into song before you, and all the trees of the field will clap their hands." (Isaiah 55:12)

The experience was a moment of surprise, a moment of self-forgetfulness, placing my life and concerns in a much larger perspective. For me, to be open to such times, whether in community or solitude, whether in the city or wilderness, is to be open to awe and amazement; my response, finally, ultimately, is joy, humility and gratitude.

Earth is "a reality that is developing with the simple aim of celebrating the joy of existence," Thomas Berry suggests. This experience with the aspens is one of my more poignant moments of participation in that celebration. My mind frequently travels back to that hike and the moments of timeless grace: grace because I did not seek out such an experience; it was all a gift, timeless as only self-forgetfulness and intense relationship can be.

From *Earth Letter*, May 1996. Copyright 1996 Earth Ministry. Used by permission of Earth Ministry, Seattle, WA.

Money & Faith
Study Guide

by Michael Schut

ℋow to Use this Material

Welcome to this community-building study guide. We are excited to offer this course and glad for your interest in it. Its format and ethos are like the study guides in both *Simpler Living, Compassionate Life: A Christian Perspective*, and *Food and Faith: Justice, Joy and Daily Bread*.[1]

This curriculum is designed to be flexible and user-friendly. Participants share the leadership role of facilitator. You are encouraged to propose and discuss your own "burning questions" if those provided do not speak to you. Sessions can take place over an adult/college-age Sunday morning class or a longer gathering at someone's home, and so on.

While going through all twelve sessions is, of course, the most comprehensive option, some congregational and/or small group situations may not allow time for this. **On page 231 find suggested optional course lengths of 6, 8 or 10 weeks.** Another option is to spread the course out, meeting six times in the fall and six in the spring; or meet monthly rather than weekly. One group reading *Simpler Living, Compassionate Life* spent one week on each and every essay!

Before Meeting One

Read this ("How to Use This Material") as well as the readings for that session. (See page 234 under "Read Before Meeting One.")

Course Goals

Your own goals and hopes will surely vary. These are the goals that inspired the writing of this course:

- To build a sense of community and support within the group and make connections between your faith and your relationship with and use of money
- To demystify money, laugh at ourselves and the green stuff a little bit
- To seek to understand, emotionally and intellectually, that abundance for all creation is a hallmark of God's kin-dom
- To explore and try on faith-based traditions and practices, such as Sabbath and redistributive justice
- To challenge cultural assumptions, such as more is better and economic growth is an unquestioned good
- To consider corporate power and ways it can be redirected in order to contribute to greater equity and ecological sustainability
- To highlight practical steps and policies individuals, families, congregations, even societies, can implement to hasten such equity and sustainability
- To listen to perspectives and voices not often heard in everyday life
- To have fun, to feel freer and become more trusting

Course Organization

Facilitator: The role of course facilitator rotates each week; this should contribute to a shared sense of ownership, responsibility and community among participants. **However, the facilitator's role is important and the role should be taken seriously. Good leadership contributes a good deal to your group process.** Not everyone in your group needs to serve as facilitator, particularly those who feel especially uncomfortable doing so. See page 234 for an overview of the facilitator's role.

Meeting One's facilitator will most likely be the person who initially called your group together.

Setting and Timing: We want to emphasize, first of all, that *Money and Faith* is meant to be flexible, and can be used in a variety of settings.

* *Congregations*: The material is well-suited for a college-age or adult education class. Unlike many curricula, which specifically state how many minutes should be spent on each section, we chose to allow the group to make such decisions based upon the flow of the discussion and interest of the group. However, each meeting's facilitator should have a good overview of the topics and questions emphasized in each session.

* *Homes*: Probably the ideal setting is to gather in group members' homes with enough time (about 1-1/2 to 2 hours) to experience and go through the material at a relaxed pace. Such settings allow for more thoughtful exploration and help establish a sense of community. You could also then choose to share a dessert or potluck dinner as well.

* *College or University Classes*: *Money and Faith* would serve well in higher education settings as a reader or a textbook.

For those using the course in a 50-60 minute time slot, each meeting includes questions in bold. We suggest you discuss those first, then come back to others as time allows. Feel free to modify meetings as you see fit.

Group Size: Ideal group size is between six and eight participants. If your group is larger, remain together for the opening prayer/meditation as well as the closing. We encourage you to consider breaking up into groups of six to eight for the discussion periods. Many larger groups choose to stay together, however, which is fine.

Book Sharing: Of course, it's simplest if everyone has a copy of *Money and Faith*. On the other hand, and in the spirit of this book, if sharing works out well, great. Of course the facilitator needs a copy the week prior to that person's meeting.

Journal: The study guide provides some space to take notes and jot down feelings, ideas and impressions. You may wish to bring an additional journal or notebook. Those notes will become a valuable resource, charting your thoughts and feelings over time.

A Note on the Readings: Money and Faith's study guide seeks to help form a learning community. This community will hear from a variety of "voices." Some of those will be your own and those of your fellow group members. Others will come from the readings. Try not to treat these readings as especially authoritative. Think of them as the stories and ideas of other group members not able to join your discussion in person.

Not all of the perspectives will be meaningful or useful to everyone. Focus on what you do find meaningful. The object is not that everyone emerges from this experience thinking, doing and believing the same things. Rather, in an open sharing of ideas and experiences, each individual's own exploration of the issues will be enhanced and supported.

Length of Readings: Each meeting's discussions emanate primarily from a set of readings: approximately 60-90 minutes of reading each week. Since much of the learning and discussion comes from your perceptions and thoughts on these readings, you are *strongly* encouraged to complete these beforehand.

Supplies Needed: Bring your copy of *Money and Faith*, a pen or pencil, and, if you wish, a journal or notebook.

Guidelines for Participation

This course values your perspectives and life experiences. We encourage you to interact with each other and the materials honestly. Be open about your questions, misgivings and hopes. Author Cecile Andrews suggests a number of guidelines for creating a community-oriented group. Here are a few of her ideas[2]:

- Respond as equals. In this course we act on the idea that we are all equal.
- Be authentic. We spend a lot of our lives trying to look successful. No one gets to know us. In this group, try not to pretend. Describe what you really think or feel.
- Focus on the heart. Some conversations come just from the head. When you communicate from the heart you bring in the whole of yourself: emotions, imagination, spiritual insight and thoughts.
- View conversations as barn-raising instead of battle.
- Question conventional wisdom and seek out alternative explanations and views.
- Disagree respectfully. When you risk sharing how you feel or what you believe, disagreements naturally arise. Attacking people's ideas or treating them disrespectfully or dismissively will not help create an open and trusting group.
- Discover wisdom through stories. Throughout human history people have learned through story telling. Everyone can tell his or her story and there's no right or wrong interpretation. Ultimately, stories connect people; in listening to someone else's story, we often hear strains of our own.

Confidentiality

Finally, talking about money and faith, particularly in the kind of setting Cecile describes above, often leads to fairly profound and vulnerable places. Please treat as *confidential* what is shared during your time together.

Meeting Format

Each meeting has all or most of the following components:

- The facilitator should read the "Facilitator Overview" prior to the meeting. Any specific or unusual instructions for that meeting will appear in this section. Again, it is imperative that the meeting's facilitator comes well prepared.
- Participants should be familiar with the meeting's "Purpose" and "Overview." The facilitator should review both with the group at the beginning of each session.
- "Read Before Today's Gathering" lists that meeting's readings. Read these prior to getting together.
- The "Opening Meditation and Prayer" provides for a brief centering time. Feel free to bring in prayers of your own or pray spontaneously. Some meditations will be short; others include a reading and question for reflection.
- The "Check-In" is a *brief* (one-minute) report back to the group about the "Action Step" you took during the week. Though not everyone will necessarily have time to share you will learn from each other during these brief reports.
- Some meetings include a "Group Reading" to be read within the meeting.
- Each meeting's "Group Discussion" (or "Small Group/Pair Discussion") is based on that week's readings.
- Most meetings suggest a meaningful and "doable" (or so we trust) "Action Step."
- End with the "Closing Prayer" or one of your own choosing.

One Final Important Note

Use this study guide as a resource to engage with the ideas presented, not as a "course" to be "mastered." Your creative adaptation to meet your own needs is encouraged. You may not have time to answer every question, or feel drawn to discuss only a few of the questions, or have questions of your own. You may want to spend two weeks on certain meetings. Please modify as you see fit.

Course Overview

Below find summaries of each meeting, followed by shorter alternatives to the full twelve-session course. As you read the meeting summaries, you may find a theme or length that would work well for your group.

The Personal: Money's Place in Our Lives

No matter the size of your bank account, the number of storage sheds you rent, the size of your home, or the depth of faith you profess, you may live and feel as if you don't have enough; on the other hand, you may live and feel an abiding sense of abundance. **Meeting One** introduces the themes of scarcity and abundance and how our own experiences with money inform the way we see the world.

Meeting Two delves more deeply into what Walter Brueggemann calls the conflict between our "attraction to the good news of God's abundance" and the "power of our belief in scarcity."

From there, **Meeting Three** humorously and rather unceremoniously takes money off its pedestal and considers the green stuff from a more removed vantage point.

Meeting Four explores the place of wealth in God's kin-dom, and introduces a practice that initially may seem completely incongruent: the sacramental use of money.

The Prophetic: Money, Sustainability and the Jubilee

As highlighted in *Money and Faith's* "Overview" (page 14), the book shifts somewhat from the personal to the prophetic at this point. **Meeting Five** challenges some of the very basic assumptions underlying our money-creating economy and asks whether or not economic growth actually makes us a happier people.

Meeting Six highlights characteristics of large corporations and describes how North Dakota wheat farmers stood up to one of them.

Meeting Seven invites into the conversation two perspectives on economic globalization from the Global South.

As described by Walter Brueggemann, Jubilee Justice means "finding out what belongs to whom and giving it back." **Meeting Eight** emphasizes the Jubilee as a central biblical theme.

The Purposeful (or Practical): How Shall We Then Live?

Though this question certainly runs through *Money and Faith*, these final four meetings address it more directly. **Meeting Nine** opens the door to two potentially spacious, liberating practices: Sabbath and tithing.

If Meeting Nine opens a door, **Meeting Ten** opens, at least for some of us, Pandora's box as it invites exploration of retirement and investments. No matter the amount of our investments, what is that money actually doing in the world? And just what is the purpose of retirement?

The question "How shall we then live?" needs to be applied not only to our own lives but also to how we structure our life together. If that structure currently leads to ecological degradation and economic inequity, what are some of the possible solutions to those big concerns? This is the question posed in **Meeting Eleven**.

Meeting Twelve provides time to discuss your response to *Money and Faith*. How might you feel called to respond? What has been most challenging, most freeing? The readings reflect on our spirituality and interconnectedness. The meeting concludes with a celebratory potluck.

If You Have Six, Eight or Ten Weeks...

Some congregations, organizations and small groups may not have time available for the full twelve-session study guide. Suggestions for six-, eight- or ten-session groupings follow. After that appear thematic suggestions as well.

Please note: in order to shorten the course, Meeting Twelve often gets left out. That final meeting provides time for reflecting on the course as a whole, time to share how you feel called to respond to *Money and Faith*, and so on. If you choose to go through a shortened version, you are encouraged to integrate portions of Meeting

Twelve into your last gathering. Or, meet one additional time in order to close with Meeting Twelve.

Six Sessions

Meeting One: Enough for All
Meeting Two: The Central Problem of Our Lives
Meeting Four: The Sacramental Use of Money
Meeting Five: Happiness, Externalities and Economic Growth
Meeting Eight: Jubilee Justice
Meeting Ten: Investments, Retirement and Jubilee

Eight Sessions

Meeting One: Enough for All
Meeting Two: The Central Problem of Our Lives
Meeting Four: The Sacramental Use of Money
Meeting Five: Happiness, Externalities and Economic Growth
Meeting Seven: Economic Globalization—Views from the South
Meeting Eight: Jubilee Justice
Meeting Ten: Investments, Retirement and Jubilee
Meeting Twelve: With Hands and Hearts Wide Open

Ten Sessions

Omit Meeting Three and Meeting Six.

If your group wishes to focus on a theme, see possible thematic groupings below. Feel free as well to design your own organizing theme.

Theme (six-week)—Scarcity and Abundance: Money and Our Personal Journeys

Meeting One: Enough for All
Meeting Two: The Central Problem of Our Lives
Meeting Four: The Sacramental Use of Money
Meeting Nine: Sabbath and Tithing—There Is Enough
Meeting Ten: Investments, Retirement and Jubilee
Meeting Twelve: With Hands and Hearts Wide Open

Theme (eight-week)—Money, Justice and Gratitude

Meeting One: Enough for All
Meeting Three: Money Off Its Pedestal
Meeting Five: Happiness, Externalities and Economic Growth
Meeting Seven: Economic Globalization—Views from the South
Meeting Eight: Jubilee Justice
Meeting Ten: Investments, Retirement and Jubilee
Meeting Eleven: Jubilee on a Grand Scale
Meeting Twelve: With Hands and Hearts Wide Open

Theme (eight-week)—How Shall We Then Live?
  Meeting One: Enough for All
  Meeting Two: The Central Problem of Our Lives
  Meeting Four: The Sacramental Use of Money
  Meeting Five: Happiness, Externalities and Economic Growth
  Meeting Eight: Jubilee Justice
  Meeting Nine: Sabbath and Tithing—There Is Enough
  Meeting Ten: Investments, Retirement and Jubilee
  Meeting Eleven: Jubilee on a Grand Scale

1. Michael Schut served as editor of both books. Published by Living the Good News (now owned by Church Publishing), both are available at your local bookstore or *www.livingthegoodnews.com* or *www.earthministry.org*).

2. These guidelines are taken from two sources: Cecile Andrews, *The Simplicity Circle: Learning Voluntary Simplicity Through a Learning for Life Study Circle*, 1994 and *The Circle of Simplicity: Return to the Good Life*, HarperCollins, 1997.

Meeting One: **Enough for All**

Purpose

To introduce the course as a whole and discuss course guidelines

To introduce yourself and begin to create a comfortable setting

To begin exploring notions of abundance, scarcity and God's economy

Facilitator Overview

This is an important meeting as you begin to set the tone for the course and begin to get to know one another. As today's facilitator, please:

1. Help create a welcoming space, and ensure all have access to *Money and Faith*.
2. Take responsibility for leading the meeting.
3. Pay attention to time; move the discussion along when necessary.
4. Ensure everyone has a chance to participate.
5. *Prepare for the gathering*: read the study guide and readings carefully; have a clear sense of the meeting's content and flow, and of how time might best be spent.
6. Read (with the group) the Purpose and Overview.
7. Make sure to read aloud—as highlighted below— the "Guidelines for Participation."
8. Leave enough time at the conclusion of the meeting to ensure everyone understands the Action Step: to write a money autobiography.
9. Designate next meeting's facilitator.

Introductions

Briefly introduce yourself. (Soon you will get a chance to say more!)

Opening Meditation

Read aloud to the group:

> "I have held many things in my hands, and I have lost them all; but whatever I have placed in God's hands, that I still possess."
>
> —*Martin Luther*

> "In the world, it is not what we take up, but what we give up that makes us rich."
>
> —*Henry Ward Beecher*

Ask:
In one sentence, what does the title of this book, *Money and Faith: The Search for Enough*, suggest to you? (Feel free to use the space below to jot down your answer.)

Opening Prayer

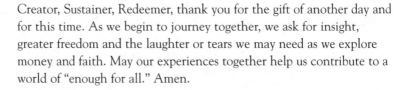

Creator, Sustainer, Redeemer, thank you for the gift of another day and for this time. As we begin to journey together, we ask for insight, greater freedom and the laughter or tears we may need as we explore money and faith. May our experiences together help us contribute to a world of "enough for all." Amen.

Further Introductions

(Please respect each other's time. If you are meeting during an adult/college-age Sunday morning class these introductions most likely need to be kept to one minute per person. If you have 1-1/2 to 2 hours, you of course have more leeway.)

Introduce yourselves:
- Your family background, geographical roots, profession.
- What particularly intrigues you about this book, or this course?
- What particular goals or expectations do you have for your time together?

Group Reading

Please read the following aloud: you may wish to take turns.

Welcome—so glad you have chosen to journey through this study guide. Perhaps you are excited, perhaps nervous, perhaps wondering why you're here in the first place, perhaps wondering if you can hang out with the others assembled here!

No matter how you are feeling, we hope this first meeting is fun and relaxed. Today focuses on stories, on sharing a little bit of your own sacred journey. So settle in, enjoy the attention of the group and the opportunity to talk about yourself.

This entire book and study guide is not meant *primarily* to dispense information. There *is* a good deal of information, a lot to learn. But the emphasis is to reflect on and incorporate that information into your own life story in such a way that the content begins to make a home within you and deepens the connections between daily life and faith.

Hopefully you have had time to read today's articles (listed above under "Read Before Meeting One"). "How to Use This Material," (see page 227) provides a course overview, establishes guidelines for interaction and covers logistical details.

The "Guidelines for Participation" are important; they help create an open and caring community. *Please read those together out loud* (see page 229); then resume below.

"How to Use this Material" (if you have not yet read this, please do so before your next gathering) highlights a number of this study guide's important characteristics which merit summary mention here:
• The role of course facilitator rotates each session.
• The course is designed to be flexible; you can meet during an adult education/college-age Sunday morning class or gather in someone's home and spend 1-1/2 to 2 hours together.
• Come prepared each week/gathering. Most all the study guide's questions emanate from each session's readings, so read them beforehand. Review each meeting's questions as well, in case there are others you wish to raise.

Group Discussion
Just to make sure everyone is clear about course organization, the facilitator's role and so on, take ten minutes or so to review the following questions, or others group members may have, about course guidelines and logistics:
• Are there any questions about course format, organization or leadership?
• Any questions or comments on the facilitator's role?
  Please note: Not everyone in the group needs to serve as facilitator, but the role is designed to be shared among the group.
• Any questions or comments regarding the "Guidelines for Participation"?
• Finally, please bring your copy of *Money and Faith*, a pen or pencil and, if you wish, a journal/notebook to each gathering.

What's to Come?
This study guide consists of twelve sessions. Your group may be going through only a portion of those. In either case, take a few minutes to orient yourselves by reviewing the study guide's outline as seen in the Table of Contents.

For the remainder of Meeting One, pair up (perhaps with someone you don't know very well) in order to give everyone more time to share. *Do leave time at the end to come back together to review the Action Step described below.*

Pair Discussion
(As mentioned in the Introduction, some groups take 1-1/2 to 2 hours for each gathering. Others only have 50-60 minutes. If your time is limited, please consider the bold questions below first.)

1. "Enough for All" suggests that while this book is about money, perhaps most fundamentally it is about how we experience and see the world. How would you describe how you see the world, specifically related to abundance and scarcity?

2. How does your answer to #1 manifest itself, particularly in your understanding of and relationship with God?

3. Can you recall a time when you experienced such a depth of abundance that you knew that that abundance was, and is, God's intention for all creation? What about that experience is most memorable?

4. "Enough for All" introduces the phrase "God's economy." How would you characterize or describe God's economy?

Group Discussion
Come back together for the Closing Prayer and Action Step. If you have time please share some of the significant themes emerging from your pair discussions.

Closing Prayer
(Every Sunday the worship service at Trinity United Methodist Church, in Seattle, prays the following in unison.)

"I pledge, O God, to discover how much is enough for me to be truly fulfilled, neither rich nor poor, and to consume only that.

"I pledge, O God, to be part of the discovery of how much would be enough for everyone—not only to survive but to thrive—and to find ways for them to have access to that.

"May this offering of restraint and justice teach me to live like Jesus, healing my life and the life of this world. Amen."

Closing and Action Step

Read the following together.

This week's Action Step is to write your *"money autobiography."* (See page 22 for a description and instructions.) Doing so often provides a particularly revealing window through which we can gain insight into who we are and what we value.

The basic idea is to write a three-page (or longer if you wish) autobiography dealing with the subject of your life as it relates to money. Writing about your life through the lens of money is often a powerful exercise, and will add significantly to the discussions in your upcoming gatherings.

What you do with your writings is up to each of you, and to your group. Reading them aloud to one another (in small groups of three or so, or to the whole group) is an option. So is keeping them private. Or ask everyone to read a certain portion of their written reflections. Or pair up and read your story to just one person, either during class-time or a get-together during the week over coffee. Whatever you decide, please remember to keep your commitment to confidentiality.

Finally, please note that this study guide *does not,* in the ensuing meetings, set aside time for sharing the money autobiographies. Ideally, it would. Providing adequate time to share them, however, would require two or three entire meetings.

If your group feels at all drawn to sharing your autobiographies, though, you are strongly encouraged to make time for that. You would deepen your ability to connect with and understand each other's comments and questions throughout the course, and you would enrich your experience of community and your ability to support one another as you explore the often challenging topic of money.

So, depending on how (or if) you choose to share your money autobiographies, you will most likely need to gather a couple additional times, or extend a number of the already scheduled gatherings.

Again, please see page 22 for directions on writing money autobiographies and enjoy!

Reminder

Designate next gathering's facilitator. Read selections prior to Meeting Two (see "Read Before Today's Gathering," page 239).

eeting Two: The Central Problem of Our Lives

Purpose

To continue to get to know one another

To explore what Brueggemann calls the "central problem of our lives": that "we are torn apart by the conflict between our attraction to the good news of God's abundance and the power of our belief in scarcity."

Read Before Today's Gathering

"Writing Your Money Autobiography" —p. 22

"The Liturgy of Abundance, the Myth of Scarcity," Walter Brueggemann —p. 25

"Scarcity: The Great Lie," Lynne Twist —p. 31

Facilitator Overview

The facilitator's role is important. The facilitator needs to:

1. Take responsibility for leading the meeting.
2. Pay attention to time; move the discussion along when necessary.
3. Ensure everyone has a chance to participate.
4. *Prepare for the gathering*: read the study guide and readings carefully; have a strong sense of the meeting's content and flow, and of how time might best be spent.
5. Help create a welcoming space.
6. Read (with the group) the Purpose and Overview.
7. Allow for time at the end of the meeting to go over the session's Action Step.
8. Designate next meeting's facilitator.

Overview

Money and Faith's "Welcome" (page 12) introduced the goal that this book be personal, prophetic, pastoral and purposeful. This meeting continues to emphasize the personal through exploring how each of us sees the world. The meeting also briefly expands beyond the personal to touch on the prophetic through initial reflection on the idea of an "economy of abundance."

Opening Meditation

In the "Introduction" to his autobiography, *The Sacred Journey*, author Frederick Buechner (pronounced *Beekner*) writes: "What I propose to do now is to try listening to my life as a whole for whatever of meaning, of holiness, of God there may be in it to hear. My assumption is that the story of any one of us is in some measure the story of us all."

Buechner believes that all good theology is autobiography. From that perspective, you were "doing theology" as you wrote your money autobiography.

As an opening meditation today, please share with the group one thing from your autobiography that seems significant to you: an insight, hope or desire, or something you have learned. After everyone has had opportunity to speak, continue with the opening prayer. (Begin with a few moments of silence; always feel free to pray in your own words as well, rather than reading the prayers provided.)

Opening Prayer

> Creator God, thank you for our stories, for the ways we learn through listening and for the times we catch glimpses of you within our lives.
>
> The apostle Paul says in Acts that we "live and move and have our being" in you; so every moment we bathe in your presence. Jesus said in the Gospel of John that he came "that they may have life, and life abundant;" help us see, trust in and share that abundance. You declared in Genesis that all your creation is "very good;" may we learn to honor that goodness every day.
>
> We pray with thanksgiving, amen.

A Note on the Money Autobiography

In today's Opening Meditation you had the opportunity to begin to share with one another based on writing your money autobiography. The rest of this study guide does not include time to read your reflections to one another. Meeting One's Action Step (page 238) suggested a number of ways you could choose to do so, however. If your group has chosen to share your money autobiographies, please return to this point in the study guide when you are finished.

Reminder: If your time is limited, please consider the bold questions below first.

Pair Discussion: Lynne Twist's Scarcity Myths
(Pair up, perhaps with someone you don't know very well.)

1. **Lynne Twist suggests three myths undergird the lie of scarcity: There's Not Enough; More Is Better; That's Just the Way It Is.**

   Are you aware of these myths operating in your life? If so how?

Is one of the three particularly powerful for you? Why?

How might your life be different without those myths holding such power?

Large Group Discussion: Brueggemann

2. What themes emerged from your pair discussions?

> **We must confess that the central problem of our lives is that we are torn apart by the conflict between our attraction to the good news of God's abundance and the power of our belief in scarcity.**
>
> —*Walter Brueggemann*

3. How would you describe the "central problem of our lives" (see Brueggemann quote) regarding money and faith?

4. Brueggemann writes, "The closer we stay to Jesus, the more we will bring a new economy of abundance to the world." Have you found that to be true in your own life? Why or how...or why not?

5. What would an economy of abundance, nurtured by closeness to Jesus, look like?

6. Brueggemann writes, "Christians have a long history of trying to squeeze Jesus out of public life and reduce him to a private little savior." He then suggests that the kingdom of God is a "public life reorganized toward neighborliness." What do you think he means by this or what do you take from his words?

Closing Prayer

Creator God, we have heard today that intimacy with Jesus leads to an economy of abundance. Many in our world and parts of our own hearts remain closed to such intimacy. Open us and our world to the power and compassion we see in Jesus.

- Your kingdom—an economy of abundance—come.
- Your will—to do justice, love mercy and walk humbly—be done.
- On Earth—on this awe-inspiring, beautiful home we share—as it is in heaven.

Amen.

Action Step

Here's a little mindfulness game to play: as you go through the upcoming week you will look at the world through your own particular lens. Become aware of a time when you are operating out of scarcity. Stop. See if you can switch your lens to one of abundance. What happens?

Or find a situation when someone else, or something in the media, trumpets scarcity as "that's just the way it is." Can you creatively discover another way to look at, and possibly act within, the situation?

Reminder

Designate next gathering's facilitator. Read selections prior to Meeting Three (see "Read Before Today's Gathering," page 243).

Meeting Three: Money Off Its Pedestal

Purpose

To explore money itself, gain some distance, provide new perspectives

To consider what money is, how it is created

To see money as a gift to be held lightly with an open hand, rather than clenched with a fist

Read Before Today's Gathering

"How Money Works," Dave Barry —p. 41

"What Is Money?" and "Origins of Money," David Boyle —p. 45

"Some Food We Could Not Eat," Lewis Hyde —p. 48

Facilitator Overview

1. Take responsibility for leading the meeting.
2. Pay attention to time; move the discussion along when necessary.
3. Ensure everyone has a chance to participate.
4. *Prepare for the gathering:* read the study guide and readings carefully; have a strong sense of the meeting's content and flow, and of how time might best be spent.
5. Help create a welcoming space.
6. Read (with the group) the Purpose and Overview.
7. Allow for time at the end of the meeting to go over the session's Action Step.
8. Designate next meeting's facilitator.

Overview

Hopefully you now know one another a bit better, have gained insight through writing your money autobiography and had time to consider your view of the world, particularly related to the themes of scarcity and abundance. This meeting begins to more closely consider money itself—one of the primary areas of life that comes to mind in relationship to abundance or scarcity. Through humor, history and cultural comparisons, the readings help provide perspective on what has become a conspicuous idol. We take money off its pedestal, if only for a time.

Opening Meditation

Read the following together.

> "Come, all you who are thirsty, come to the waters; and you who have no money, come, buy and eat! Come, buy wine and milk without money and without cost. Why spend money on

what is not bread, and your labor on what does not satisfy? Listen, listen to me and eat what is good, and your soul will delight in the richest of fare. Give ear and come to me; hear me, that your soul may live."

—Isa 55:1-3a

Gerald May's book *The Awakened Heart* includes the chapter "Entering the Emptiness." In it, May contends that all of us experience emptiness. Some of these experiences are universal—like "losing love, youth, or health, or feeling compassion for the pains of others"—while others are uniquely our own.

Most of us tend to shy away, if not flee, from emptiness. Yet May insists that missing "our emptiness is, finally, to miss our hope." I believe he writes that because it is our emptiness that nudges our hearts toward God. Our emptiness is an experience of space and longing for God.

But emptiness is not comfortable. Most of us more often than not would rather fill it than feel it. Today's reading by Lewis Hyde describes our proclivity to use money to secure consumer goods in an attempt to fill inner emptiness. But Hyde writes, "The consumer of commodities is invited to a meal without passion...that leads to neither satiation nor fire....He is hungry at the end of the meal, depressed and weary as we all feel when lust has dragged us from the house and led us to nothing."

The prophet Isaiah recognizes this tendency as well, asking, "Why spend money on what is not bread, and your labor on what does not satisfy?"

Both Hyde and Isaiah contend that there are options that offer our emptiness room to breathe—spiritual practices that do not demand that we immediately fill the emptiness.When we do not insist on immediately filling emptiness, we open ourselves to the possibility of receiving—for we have not rushed out to fill ourselves with that which does not satisfy.

Hands and hearts full of stuff are by definition not empty. To the empty-handed, to the one aware of emptiness, gifts can be given.

Opening Prayer

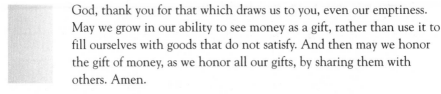

God, thank you for that which draws us to you, even our emptiness. May we grow in our ability to see money as a gift, rather than use it to fill ourselves with goods that do not satisfy. And then may we honor the gift of money, as we honor all our gifts, by sharing them with others. Amen.

Large Group Discussion: Demystifying Money

1. Dave Barry asks: "If our money really is just pieces of paper, backed by nothing, why is it valuable? Because we all believe it's valuable!" If money's value is indeed based on belief, how does that strike you or affect you?

2. David Boyle points out that most money is created "by the stroke of a pen," through debt creation by banking institutions. Were you aware of that on a visceral level? How does it strike you?

> Many native cultures measure wealth not by what one possesses, but by what one feels able to give away…. They give away the best of what they own, their finest. If we can afford to give away our best—if we can give away what we love most—then we must be very wealthy, indeed.
>
> —Wayne Muller

3. Boyle contends that money was not originally used to keep "each other down" and facilitate competition over scarce resources. Rather, money "was about mutual recognition and facilitating human relationships." How has that major shift in money's purpose colored your understanding and experience of life?

Small-Group Exercise: Life-Sentences
Gather in groups of two or three.

4. Meeting Two explored Lynne Twist's three myths that "define our relationship to money." Her book, *The Soul of Money,* also describes "life sentences" we struggle with in relationship to money. We embrace these sentences as truth, when in fact they are patterns of thinking, often unconscious. For example, I

> The modern banking system manufactures money out of nothing. The process is perhaps the most astounding piece of sleight of hand that was ever invented... Bankers own the earth; take it away from them, but leave them with the power to create credit, and with the stroke of a pen they will create enough money to buy it back again.
>
> —Lord J. Stamp

might believe "There will never be enough." Or you may take "I will always worry about money" as a given. Twists lists "Marry the money and love will come later" as a powerful sentence in her life.

Unexamined life sentences often become limiting factors in life. In the space below write some of your more powerful money-related life sentences.

5. Are you satisfied with those sentences? If not, how might you re-write them? Try writing out a few options in the space below.

Large Group Discussion: Lewis Hyde

6. What struck you most in Hyde's piece?

7. Boyle writes, "Most anthropologists agree that money started as a form of ritual gift." Hyde's piece highlights how, in many indigenous cultures, the gift was designed to "always move." So, money originated as a gift, that must in turn move, be given away. Describe an experience or situation when you interacted with or understood money in that way.

8. Hyde writes, "The consumer of commodities is invited to a meal without passion...that leads to neither satiation nor fire..." Isaiah similarly asks why "Spend money on what is not bread, and your labor on what does not satisfy?" Do you? When? Why?

Closing Prayer

Thank you for the gift of life, of food, of clean water; thank you for our friends and our families. Thank you for this time together and for the beauty and generosity of your creation. We ask for some levity, perspective, freedom, in relationship to money. May we gain deeper trust in you, may we experience contentment, may we have eyes to see all the gifts in our lives. Amen.

Action Steps

The "Purpose" section above asks "Can we see money, like life itself, as a gift meant to be held lightly with an open hand, not clenched as with a fist?" Have you recently thought of a group, a person, a cause, a friend, and felt a nudge to give them a gift—of money, time, or talent—but have not seen your way to do so yet? Make the gift this week and then note what the experience is like for you.

Another idea: take a look at those re-written "life sentences" above. How might you practice or embody one of those this next week? Then try it!

Reminder

Designate next gathering's facilitator. Read selections prior to Meeting Four (see "Read Before Today's Gathering," page 248).

Meeting Four: The Sacramental Use of Money

Purpose
To become more comfortable talking about money, wealth and equity

To explore the practice of redistributive justice

Read Before Today's Gathering
"Compassion," Henri Nouwen
—p. 59

"The Call of the Rich Man and the Kingdom of God in Mark," Ched Myers
—p. 66

Facilitator Overview
1. Take responsibility for leading the meeting.
2. Pay attention to time; move the discussion along when necessary.
3. Ensure everyone has a chance to participate.
4. *Prepare for the gathering*: read the study guide and readings carefully; have a strong sense of the meeting's content and flow, and of how time might best be spent.
5. Help create a welcoming space.
6. Read (with the group) the Purpose and Overview.
7. Allow for time at the end of the meeting to go over the session's Action Step.
8. Designate next meeting's facilitator.

Overview
As mentioned in Meeting Two, and introduced in *Money and Faith's* "Welcome" (page 12), I intend that this book be personal, prophetic, pastoral and purposeful (practical). This meeting and its readings suggest compassion, to "suffer with," offers the gift of joy, the challenge of "downward mobility" and declare that the redistribution of wealth is an important practice within the Christian faith. They are challenging readings that begin to take on the flavor of a prophetic word.

Opening Meditation
"Contrary to many legends, the saints are not spooky figures, morally superior, abstentious, pietistic. They are seldom remembered, much less haloed. In truth, all human beings are called to be saints, but that just means called to be fully human...The saints are simply those men and

women who relish the event of life as a gift and who realize that the only way to honor such a gift is to give it away."[1]

—*William Stringfellow*

Check-In

How was your experience making that gift you've been thinking about for a while now, or practicing your *re-written* money-related life sentences. (See last meeting's Action Steps.)

Opening Prayer

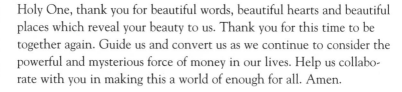

Holy One, thank you for beautiful words, beautiful hearts and beautiful places which reveal your beauty to us. Thank you for this time to be together again. Guide us and convert us as we continue to consider the powerful and mysterious force of money in our lives. Help us collaborate with you in making this a world of enough for all. Amen.

Large Group Discussion: Money as a Sacrament
(If you have limited time, start with the questions in bold.)

1. How did you react to today's readings? What emotions did you feel?

2. William Stringfellow writes ("Money," from *Dissenter in a Great Society*): "Freedom from idolatry of money, for a Christian, means that money becomes useful only as a sacrament—as a sign of the restoration of life wrought in this world by Christ." In his view the offertory or collection is a sacramental element of a worship service in that it represents "the oblation of the totality of life to God." Money becomes

> **Being faithful to God is always manifest practically in a transfigured distribution of resources.**
>
> —*Tom Beaudoin*

a "witness" to the offering of one's "decisions, actions and words to God." **What do you think of this idea of money as sacrament? Tell about an experience or time in your life when money was a sacrament to you.**

Pairs

Turn to your neighbor to discuss the following.

3. Brainstorm with your partner some practices that could help money become "useful as a sacrament"

   – for you;

   – for your family;

   – for your faith community.

Large Group Discussion: Redistributive Justice and Compassion
Share some of your best ideas from the pair discussions.

The final integration of counter-cultural personal life occurs when we deliberately enter the presence of persons for whom the consumer and commodity ideology is not a dream, but a nightmare.

—*Father John Kavanaugh*

4. Myers contends that redistributive justice is a primary practice for those following Jesus. Nouwen says that compassion calls us to "downward mobility."

How does this strike you? Do you agree? Why or why not?

How have you and your faith community sought to "redistribute wealth as reparation to the poor"?

5. Nouwen states that compassion is "central to all great religions." What has this call to compassion brought forth in you?

6. Ched Myers' exegesis of the "call of the rich man" in Mark 10 suggests the parable is not so much about the rich, but about the nature of God's kin-dom. The kin-dom is a place the rich cannot enter, at least not "with their wealth intact."

By the world's standards, most Americans are wealthy. What do you think about Myers' statement? How do you feel when you consider it?

7. Do you know people or families whose relationship with/use of money you respect? Tell about them.

Closing Prayer

Dear God, life itself is indeed a beautiful gift. May we be filled with wisdom and grace, for it is often difficult to trust you when money so often seems to provide what we need. Guide us down the road of "sainthood" where we might more and more resemble those who relish life as a gift and realize "that the only way to honor such a gift is to give it away." Help us see how money can be a sacrament, used as a sign of Christ's restoration of life in the world. With gratitude, amen.

Action Step

Go back to any of the three previous action steps; you could choose to continue practicing one of those. Or, perhaps that money autobiography is not quite done? Work on that.

Reminder

Designate next gathering's facilitator. Read selections prior to Meeting Five (see "Read Before Today's Gathering," page 252).

Meeting Five: **Happiness, Externalities and Economic Growth**

Purpose

To increase understanding of how today's dominant economy (the Big Human Economy) operates in order to begin seeing that economy in a new light

To transition from our personal relationship with money to consider the system that creates monetary wealth

Read Before Today's Gathering

"The Eight-Hundred Pound Gorilla," Michael Schut —p. 74

"Prelude to After Growth," Michael Schut —p. 82

"After Growth," Bill McKibben —p. 84

"The Ecological and Economic Model and Worldview," Sallie McFague —p. 96

Facilitator Overview

1. Take responsibility for leading the meeting.
2. Pay attention to time; move the discussion along when necessary.
3. Ensure everyone has a chance to participate.
4. *Prepare for the gathering*: read the study guide and readings carefully; have a strong sense of the meeting's content and flow, and of how time might best be spent.
5. Help create a welcoming space.
6. Read (with the group) the Purpose and Overview.
7. Allow for time at the end of the meeting to go over the session's Action Step.
8. Designate next meeting's facilitator.

Group Reading

Please read the following together.

Up until now, this book's journey has primarily focused on the more personal: How do you see? What's your relationship with money like? What role does money play in your life? You've had time to consider themes of scarcity and abundance, written your own "money autobiography" and read challenging pieces on faith and wealth. Hopefully, you have gained understanding and insight and perhaps started to integrate new faith-based practices into your own relationship with money.

Bring these learnings along with you now as the book's focus shifts! Too often books, teachers, our own thinking and ways of life, stop at the personal level: as if faith bore no impact whatsoever on public life, on the marketplace, on the kind of society we create.

Money and Faith now shifts to that larger arena. That shift could be described as moving from considering the idolatry of money on a personal scale to considering that idolatry on a societal, even global scale. Or: beyond our personal relationship with money, how does our faith call us to relate to that money-making system we call the economy?

> **The great obstacle is simply this: the conviction that we cannot change because we are dependent upon what is wrong. But that is the addict's excuse, and we know that it will not do.**
>
> —*Wendell Berry*

As I wrote in *Money and Faith*'s "Welcome" (page 12), this book seeks to be personal, prophetic, pastoral and purposeful (practical). At this point, the book and study guide shift from the personal to the more prophetic—in the sense that prophets often make us uncomfortable, ask us to see in a new way and consider previously unexamined realities.

In her essay "Scarcity: The Great Lie," Lynne Twist suggests that "that's just the way it is" is one of the myths undergirding the lie of scarcity. Today you're being asked to think about the global economy. When taking on anything so vast and complicated, it's crucial to remember that myth—to know that there are other options, should we as a society decide that the way things are now don't seem to work that well. That's *not* "just the way it is."

Opening Meditation

If you like, spend a few minutes together in silence, then read Isaiah 6:9-11.

> The Lord said, "Go and tell this people: 'Be ever hearing, but never understanding; be ever seeing, but never perceiving.' Make the heart of this people calloused; make their ears dull and close their eyes. Otherwise they might see with their eyes, hear with their ears, understand with their hearts and turn and be healed."
>
> Then I said, "For how long, oh Lord?" And God answered: "Until the cities lie ruined and without inhabitant, until the houses are left deserted and the fields ruined and ravaged..."

God's words through Isaiah crash through the undergrowth of the millennia, as solid, real and strong as granite. The dust settles. We are brought up short.

The Big Human Economy has blinded us, stopped up our ears, so that we hear but do not understand, see but do not perceive.

Opening Prayer

Creator God, bless us with eyes that see and ears that hear ever more clearly the kind of persons we are called to be. We pray for the vision to co-create the kind of world, the kind of economy, that would reflect your image more closely. In Jesus' name, amen.

Small-Group/Pair Discussion: Quality of Life

Let's start today in groups of two or three. Quietly consider and write down your answers to the following two questions. Then discuss those with your small group.

1. One of the surveys McKibben cited asked, "What single factor would most improve the quality of your life?" How would you answer that question?

2. McKibben reports that researchers have found: "Money consistently buys happiness right up to about $10,000 per capita income, and that after that the correlation disappears." No matter your income, does part of you feel and think that more money would make you happier? Why or why not?

Large Group Discussion: Faith and Economics

3. In one sentence, share what single factor would "most improve the quality of your life."

> Trickle down economics, which holds that so long as the economy as a whole grows everyone benefits, has been repeatedly shown to be wrong.
>
> —*Joseph Stiglitz,*
> *Nobel Prize Winning Economist*

4. The essay titled "The Eight-Hundred Pound Gorilla," highlighted the following characteristics of the Big Human Economy (essentially McFague's neo-classical economics):
   • Nature's "free" services
   • Externalities
   • Measuring growth via the Gross National Product (GNP).

Understanding each of these is important in terms of being able to see our economic system in new ways; take some time to discuss the essay.

Did anything particularly strike you about these three characteristics? How does, or might, your faith inform your perspectives on such issues?

5. McFague describes a vision of the good life based on "sustainability." How can your church community live more sustainably as a people called to "love your neighbor as yourself"?

6. What do you think of characterizing the Big Human Economy as a "violent economy"?

7. The Big Human Economy assumes the world to be a profane place. Would you agree; why or why not? Our faith traditions hold that the world is, rather, a sacred place. How do you begin to reconcile the contradictions?

8. Do you recall times when God's creation shone with a sense of the sacred? If you have time, some of you may wish to briefly share those stories.

Closing Prayer

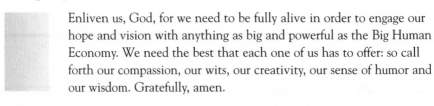

Enliven us, God, for we need to be fully alive in order to engage our hope and vision with anything as big and powerful as the Big Human Economy. We need the best that each one of us has to offer: so call forth our compassion, our wits, our creativity, our sense of humor and our wisdom. Gratefully, amen.

Action Step

"The Eight-Hundred Pound Gorilla" described externalities associated with our current economic system. Consider your daily or weekly routine. Identify at least one negative externality to which you contribute. Commit to reducing the amount of your contribution, starting with one day or one week, and see how it goes. Share your idea with the group.

Reminder

Designate next gathering's facilitator. Read selections prior to Meeting Six (see "Read Before Today's Gathering," page 257).

Meeting Six: Wheat Farmers and Corporate Power

Purpose

To understand some characteristics currently built into corporations

To consider how corporations can help create greater equity and ecological sustainability

Read Before Today's Gathering

"Corporate Personhood," Michael Schut —p. 104

"Command and Control," William Greider —p. 105

"Breadbasket of Democracy," Ted Nace —p. 117

Facilitator Overview

1. Take responsibility for leading the meeting.
2. Pay attention to time; move the discussion along when necessary.
3. Ensure everyone has a chance to participate.
4. *Prepare for the gathering*: read the study guide and readings carefully; have a strong sense of the meeting's content and flow, and of how time might best be spent.
5. Help create a welcoming space.
6. Read (with the group) the Purpose and Overview.
7. Allow for time at the end of the meeting to go over the session's Action Step.
8. Designate next meeting's facilitator.

Overview

Meeting Five took a broad look at economics and the system that creates monetary wealth. Today's gathering examines one part of that system—large corporations. The purpose is not to lay blame but, again, to help us see in a new way. Corporations are intricately connected to most of our lives. Many reading this book will own at least some stock; most of the products we buy come to us via corporate capacity.

Corporations have become a dominant presence in our lives, illustrated by the fact that most of us could identify at least 25-50 corporate logos. How many plant or animal species native to our region could we so name?

Looked at simply and somewhat objectively, however, corporations are legal entities, created through a series of choices. It follows then that they can be changed, through a series of different choices. As

Ted Nace says, "Because their [corporation's] powers are determined by laws, not by nature, it is possible to engineer them with all sorts of qualities....The key lesson is this: corporations are only as powerful as they are legally designed to be."

Check-In
Last session's Action Step asked you to reduce your contribution to a negative externality. How did that go? Was it relatively easy, a hassle, fun? What would it take for you to continue with that change?

Opening Prayer
You may want to begin with a time of centering silence and then pray together:

> "Two things I ask of you, O Lord;
>> do not refuse me before I die:
> Keep falsehood and lies far from me;
>> give me neither poverty nor riches,
>> but give me only my daily bread.
> Otherwise, I may have too much and disown you
>> and say "Who is the Lord?"
> Or I may become poor and steal,
>> and so dishonor the name of my God."
> Amen.
>> —Proverbs 30:7-9

Group Discussion: Corporations
1. How did you respond to today's readings; what struck you most?

2. Nace introduces the simple question, "What is an economy for?" Take a couple minutes to think about how you would answer that question. Write down a summary of your answer below; share those with one another.

3. My essay highlighted corporate personhood as a particularly powerful buttress of corporate power. Greider addressed further characteristics of modern-day corporate structure, including:
   • Limited liability
   • Majority (rather than unanimous) shareholder rule
   • Concentration of power and wealth.

Each of those structural realities came about through a series of choices and can be changed with a different set of choices. What do you think of Greider's critiques?

In basic character, the Corporation resembles a shrewd and muscular wild animal that sooner or later figures out how to break out of its cage. Instead of building new cages, we should investigate the DNA of these creatures.

—*William Greider*

4. Imagine you could significantly change one of the characteristics considered in the previous question. What would you choose to do and why? What would change as a result?

5. Nace briefly describes a township in Pennsylvania which declared that "corporate 'personhood' rights no longer would apply" there. Think of an issue in your life or your region. How would such an approach—asserting the rights of actual persons over the rights of corporate persons—in some way make life better for real people?

Closing Prayer

Creator, Sustainer, Redeemer,

As Creator you speak and bring forth life; as Sustainer you open your hand and nurture life; as Redeemer you reconcile and heal life.

As co-creators, created in your image, we too can nurture and heal life. We pray for humility and wisdom in the face of complicated issues raised by corporate power and pray that those structures may one day also be committed to nurturing and healing life. Amen.

Action Step

Much of our food supply is controlled by large corporations (like Monsanto, Cargill, ADM). In the United States, under that agribusiness system, the average morsel of food travels 1,500 miles to reach our plates. In buying locally grown food we support "agri-culture" (local farmers, rural communities) rather than "agri-business" and their corporate owners.

This week purchase some locally grown foods. Check out a local Farmers Market (visit *www.localharvest.org* to locate one near you); or, most grocery stores now carry some local items. If this Action Step is something you already do, check out the Center for a New American Dream at *www.newdream.org*; or visit Co-Op America's site at *www.responsibleshopper.org* Perhaps you'll find another commodity (besides food) you could purchase in such a way as to support more local, sustainable economies.

Other Resources
- Locate Community Supported Agriculture farms at *www.sare.org/csa/index.htm*
- Two great books describe eating locally for a year:
  - Barbara Kingsolver and her family eat locally in Virginia. Her book is *Animal, Vegetable, Miracle.*
  - Bill McKibben's *Deep Economy* describes his year eating locally in Vermont.

Reminder
Designate next gathering's facilitator. Read selections prior to Meeting Seven (see "Read Before Today's Gathering," page 261).

Meeting Seven: Economic Globalization— Views from the South

Purpose
To invite into this conversation a former Haitian president and a Brazilian theologian in order to listen to the voices of those often relegated to the sidelines

Read Before Today's Gathering
"Globalization: A Choice between Death and Death," Jean-Bertrand Aristide —p. 130

"Liberation Theology and Ecology," Leonardo Boff —p. 134

Facilitator Overview
1. Take responsibility for leading the meeting.
2. Pay attention to time; move the discussion along when necessary.
3. Ensure everyone has a chance to participate.
4. *Prepare for the gathering*: read the study guide and readings carefully; have a strong sense of the meeting's content and flow, and of how time might best be spent.
5. Help create a welcoming space.
6. Read (with the group) the Purpose and Overview.
7. Allow for time at the end of the meeting to go over the session's Action Step.
8. Designate next meeting's facilitator.

Overview
Following on Meeting Six's conversation about corporate power, this meeting explores globalization from the perspective of writers from other cultures. Rooted in the prophetic tradition where those with power are confronted by the lives and circumstances of those on the outside, we are invited to see with new eyes.

Opening Meditation
On a certain Sabbath years ago, Jesus visited the synagogue in Nazareth. He read from the prophet Isaiah:

> "The spirit of the Lord is on me, because God has anointed me to preach good news to the poor. God has sent me to proclaim freedom for the prisoners and recovery of sight for the blind, to release the oppressed, to proclaim the year of the Lord's favor."
>
> —Luke 4:18-19

Isaiah himself writes:

> Is not this the kind of fasting I have chosen:
>> to loose the chains of injustice
>> and untie the cords of the yoke,
>> to set the oppressed free
>> and break every yoke?

> Is it not to share your food with the hungry
>> and to provide the poor wanderer with shelter—
>> when you see the naked, to clothe him,
>> and not to turn away from your own flesh and blood?

> —Isaiah 58:6-7

Opening Prayer

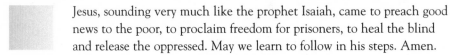

Jesus, sounding very much like the prophet Isaiah, came to preach good news to the poor, to proclaim freedom for prisoners, to heal the blind and release the oppressed. May we learn to follow in his steps. Amen.

Group Discussion: Liberation Theology and Economics
(For those with limited time, begin with those questions in bold.)

1. What in today's readings prompted your strongest reaction; what most struck you?

2. **At the beginning of this study guide, scarcity and abundance were significant themes. Consider the Haitian peasants whom we read about. Based on the readings:**

   What in their lives seemed abundant? What was scarce?

   How does that compare with the abundance and scarcity you experience in your life?

3. What were some of the negative externalities experienced by many Haitians as a result of free-trade policies?

4. How is economic globalization similar to the colonization indigenous peoples have experienced over the last 500 years? How is it different?

Pair/Small-Group Discussions: Option for the Poor (Join one or two others with whom you've not yet spent much time.)

5. Leonardo Boff wrote about the Catholic social teaching of the "preferential option for the poor." He says that to "opt for the poor entails a practice."

   In what ways (practices) does your church opt for the poor?

> The spoil of the poor is in your houses; what do you mean by crushing my people, by grinding the face of the poor?
>
> —Isaiah 3:14

In what ways do you opt for the poor?

How do you see, or when do you experience, yourself as poor?

Large Group

Briefly share highlights or themes from your pair/small group conversations.

Closing Prayer

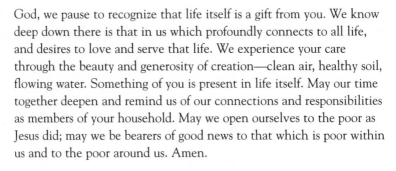

God, we pause to recognize that life itself is a gift from you. We know deep down there is that in us which profoundly connects to all life, and desires to love and serve that life. We experience your care through the beauty and generosity of creation—clean air, healthy soil, flowing water. Something of you is present in life itself. May our time together deepen and remind us of our connections and responsibilities as members of your household. May we open ourselves to the poor as Jesus did; may we be bearers of good news to that which is poor within us and to the poor around us. Amen.

Action Step

Aristide's essay reflects on his country's experience with "free trade." The "fair trade" movement grew up in response to free trade policies. (Meeting Ten includes a reading and further consideration of fair trade.) Essentially, fairly traded products seek to ensure that growers and producers receive a living wage. Many fair trade products are also grown or produced sustainably.

This week seek out a fairly traded product. Coffee and tea are often available. If not, ask your grocer to stock fair trade items. If some of your purchases are already fairly traded, see if you can find a new (to you) fair trade product.

Many churches serve fair trade coffee. If yours does not, find out what it would take to introduce fair trade to your entire congregation.

Resources to Get You Started
- TransFair USA: *www.transfairusa.org*
- Equal Exchange: *www.equalexchange.org*

Reminder

Designate next gathering's facilitator. Read selections prior to Meeting Eight (see "Read Before Today's Gathering," page 265).

Meeting Eight: **Jubilee Justice**

Purpose
To consider the biblical theme and practice of Jubilee

Read Before Today's Gathering
"Jubilee Justice," Maria Harris
—p. 140

"On Being a Jubilee Church," Rich Lang
—p. 149

Facilitator Overview
1. Take responsibility for leading the meeting.
2. Pay attention to time; move the discussion along when necessary.
3. Ensure everyone has a chance to participate.
4. *Prepare for the gathering*: read the study guide and readings carefully; have a strong sense of the meeting's content and flow, and of how time might best be spent.
5. Help create a welcoming space.
6. Read (with the group) the Purpose and Overview.
7. Allow for time at the end of the meeting to go over the session's Action Step.
8. Designate next meeting's facilitator.

Overview
Some suggest that the Jubilee is a central tenet of both the Old and New Testaments. Jubilee justice, as described by Walter Brueggemann, means "finding out what belongs to whom and giving it back." Doing so would certainly be good news to the Haitian peasants we read about in Meeting Seven. Brueggemann's pithy statement also bears considerable resemblance to the way Jesus described his mission in Luke 4 to preach good news to the poor, to release the oppressed, to set the prisoner free…as we read in Meeting Seven's Opening Meditation.

This meeting is the last of four under the "prophetic banner." Meetings One through Four sought to essentially highlight more personal themes while Meetings Nine through Twelve seek to move into the more practical/purposeful. (Not that the three—the personal, prophetic and purposeful—can be neatly divided and separated.)

Opening Meditation/Prayer

Litany of Jubilee

Facilitator: Because Earth belongs to God and its fruits are "free," the people should justly distribute those fruits rather than hoard them.

Group: Teach us Brother Jesus to practice Jubilee.

Facilitator: The word "Sabbath" appears in the story of manna in the wilderness (Exodus 16:15-26). This story was more than a lesson about God's sustaining love. It also served as a reminder that the purpose of economic organization is to guarantee enough for everyone, not surplus accumulation by the few.

Group: Teach us Brother Jesus to practice Jubilee.

Facilitator: Our attempts to control the forces of production are to be regularly interrupted by prescribed Sabbath Rest for both the land and human labor (Exodus 31:12-17; Deuteronomy 15:1-7). We are to rest one day a week and let the land rest every seventh year just as God rested.

Group: Teach us Brother Jesus to practice Jubilee.

Facilitator: The "Sabbath Rest" cycle culminated in a "Jubilee" every 50th year (Leviticus 25). In agrarian societies (like Biblical Israel and most Third World countries today), the cycle of poverty begins when a family has to sell off its land in order to pay off a debt. It reaches its conclusion when landless peasants can sell only their bodies, becoming bond-slaves. The Jubilee was given to prevent this from happening.

Group: Teach us Brother Jesus to practice Jubilee.

Facilitator: What this meant was that every 50th year the land that had been sold was returned to the family that originally owned it (Leviticus 25:13, 25-28). All financial debts were cancelled; all debt written off. All slaves were freed (Leviticus 25:35-55; Deuteronomy 15:1-18). The rationale for this unilateral restructuring of the economy was to remind Israel that the land belongs to God (Leviticus 25:23) and that they were an Exodus people who must never return to a system of Empire and slavery (Leviticus 25:42).

Group: Teach us Brother Jesus to love mercy, do justice and walk humbly with our God. In this way we become a Jubilee people. Amen.[1]

Check-In

Briefly, what was your experience in trying to buy fair trade products?

Pair Discussion: Jubilee
1. Harris presents five guidelines of economic justice:
   a. There are limits to growth.
   b. There are limits to earning.
   c. There are limits to accumulation.
   d. There are no limits to all people having the right to certain benefits.
   e. There are no limits to human resistance...and there are no limits to human imagination.

   Consider the limits to earning and accumulation. What do you think of those limits? How might you make those practical in your own life; how might they be made manifest in the wider society?

2. Harris briefly describes people she has met whose practice of Jubilee left a strong impression on her. Have you met others who similarly affected you? How did they practice Jubilee?

> If we are going to dismiss the Jubilee because Israel practiced it only inconsistently, we should also ignore the Sermon on the Mount because Christians have rarely embodied Jesus' instruction to love our enemies.
>
> —Ched Myers

Large Group Discussion
3. What from your pair discussions would you like to share with the whole group?

4. How do you practice Jubilee in your own life?

5. Pastor Rich Lang's sermon celebrates his congregation's choice to become a Jubilee Congregation. He believes the "...foundation of Jubilee spirituality, a Jubilee politics of justice, is the bonding of a people." How do you understand this and would you agree?

6. **How does your church practice the Jubilee? How else might your church practice the Jubilee?**

7. **Harris suggests that mourning is a common reaction to the practice of Jubilee justice ("Find out what belongs to whom and give it back..."). For what do you need to mourn, either personally, socially, or ecologically, as you seek to contribute to Jubilee justice? Why?**

Closing Prayer

Creator, Sustainer, Redeemer, we confess that sharing does not always come easily. We acknowledge that most of us live on land stolen from indigenous tribes. We know that this country's original wealth flowered on the backs of stolen slave labor. We have not practiced Jubilee.

We also confess with the Psalmist that "The Earth is the Lord's and all that is therein;" we know that all we have comes from you—and so we open our hands. Help us loosen our grasp. Help us become a Jubilee people. Amen.

Action Step

This week read over your money autobiography. (If you have not finished yet, do that first!) In your story, where do you see yourself seeking to practice Jubilee?

Reminder

Choose a facilitator and read the selections for Meeting Nine (page 269).

1. Rich Lang, Pastor of Seattle's Trinity United Methodist.

Meeting Nine: Sabbath and Tithing— There Is Enough

Purpose

To invite rest and Sabbath into our lives

To challenge the cultural framework "time is money"

To explore the practice of tithing

Read Before Today's Gathering

"It is Good," Wayne Muller —p. 154

"The Gift Must Always Move," Ched Myers —p. 158

"The Ultimate Question: Where Is My Security?" K. Killian Noe —p. 164

Facilitator Overview

1. Take responsibility for leading the meeting.
2. Pay attention to time; move the discussion along when necessary.
3. Ensure everyone has a chance to participate.
4. *Prepare for the gathering*: read the study guide and readings carefully; have a strong sense of the meeting's content and flow, and of how time might best be spent.
5. Help create a welcoming space.
6. Read (with the group) the Purpose and Overview.
7. Allow for time at the end of the meeting to go over the session's Action Step.
8. Designate next meeting's facilitator.

Overview

As mentioned in the previous meeting, Meetings Nine through Twelve emphasize purposeful/practical steps we can take. In light of our own relationship with money and in response to the prophetic voices raised in this study guide, how shall we then live?

Today's meeting highlights Sabbath and tithing, two well-known Christian practices. Sabbath connects to our relationship with time; tithing connects to our relationship with money. Time and money are two of the areas in which many of us experience a sense of scarcity. I have found that both Sabbath and tithing, though, actually offer a sense of abundance of both time and money. As I place money in the offering plate or send a check to a great organization, I find, at least some of the time, that that action builds a sense of sufficiency within me. I want to open my hand and give back that which was really never mine in the first place.

It's quite the same with Sabbath keeping, a tough practice for me. When I do receive Sabbath rest as a gift, however, I find it the perfect antidote to time-famine, the feeling that there is never enough time.

So both, really, are ways of practicing and embodying abundance. Both usher me closer to a world of sufficiency and trust.

Opening Meditation

Please read the following from Matthew 6:25-34:

> "Therefore I tell you, do not worry about your life, what you will eat or drink; or about your body, what you will wear. Is not life more important than food, and the body more important than clothes? Look at the birds of the air; they do not sow or reap or store away in barns, and yet [God] feeds them. Are you not much more valuable than they? Who of you by worrying can add a single hour to his life?

> "And why do you worry about clothes? See how the lilies of the field grow. They do not labor or spin. Yet I tell you that not even Solomon in all his splendor was dressed like one of these. If that is how God clothes the grass of the field, which is here today and tomorrow is thrown into the fire, will God not much more clothe you, O you of little faith? So do not worry, saying, 'What shall we eat?' or 'What shall we drink?' or 'What shall we wear?' For the pagans run after all these things, and [God] knows that you need them. But seek first God's kingdom and God's righteousness, and all these things will be given to you as well. Therefore do not worry about tomorrow, for tomorrow will worry about itself. Each day has enough trouble of its own."

Spend a few minutes in silence, letting go of your worries.

Opening Prayer

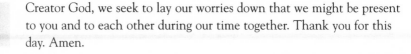

Creator God, we seek to lay our worries down that we might be present to you and to each other during our time together. Thank you for this day. Amen.

Group Reading

(We suggest members take turns reading.)

Time equals money. There may be no more insidious or destructive tenet in modern life. Some of us say it as if it's a given, an assumption we all share. Others of us use the phrase half-jokingly or sarcastically, but then realize we are doing the math in our heads.

Time equals money and many of us end up feeling like we don't have enough of either. When we equate the very gift of life to money, we end up commodifying all of life, and see the world through the mind-bending prism of the dollar sign.

"Show me your checkbook and I will tell you what you believe."

—*Anonymous*

I remember when gas stations first installed credit card pay stations at each pump (why, by the way, do we have to "Remove Card Quickly"?). I was pretty turned off. This "technological advance" meant one less face-to-face, human interaction in my day. I did not want my life to become so convenient, so efficient, that it no longer held such interactions.

Here was one more opportunity to live as a consumer, where every economic transaction is reduced to the most basic elements: my choice, my credit card, a computer, and bits of information communicated digitally to my bank. Or, here was an opportunity to live as a person in a community, where economic transactions acknowledge our relationship with others. Perhaps as I walk into the gas station I hold the door open for someone and greet them. Perhaps I have the opportunity to wait in a short line, practice patience, and remind myself that a good life is not measured by its productivity or speed. Perhaps as I approach the cashier, I notice that she looks haggard. It's late and I wonder if this is a second job. In small ways I seek to be kind to her, smile, make eye contact, and thank her for her help.

Now, I often use the "pay outside with credit card" option. I don't feel bad about that. But I do ask myself why. Why am I in a hurry? What on earth did I do, how did I ever get "enough" done, when my only option was "pay inside with cash"? Why do I more often choose convenience over interaction? Am I operating out of the "time is money" framework?

As a commodity, time becomes something that must be managed and not wasted. Activities are measured by their time-efficiency....We are so trapped in an endless spiral to purchase more devices, lured by the promise that they will save us time, that we have lost the ability to...luxuriate in the present.

—*Richard Gaillardetz*

On another level, beyond my own life, why do the companies who own the stations invest in the pay-at-the-pump option? Simply put, because they are operating out of the "time equals money" worldview. The less time we take at the pump, the sooner the next customer can purchase their gas, the more gas is sold, the more money made. And, as more of us choose to pay outside, the company needs to employ fewer cashiers.

Large Group Discussion: Sabbath and Tithing

1. The "Time Is Money" worldview is essentially diametrically opposed to a rich practice of Sabbath. What Sabbath practices have you found especially meaningful—as an individual, as a family, or within your congregation?

> If we refuse rest until we are finished, we will never rest until we die. Sabbath dissolves the artificial urgency of our days, because it liberates us from the need to be finished.
>
> —*Wayne Muller*

2. Myers connects Sabbath with economics in his essay. How have you seen or experienced Sabbath as an economic practice?

3. Noe connects tithing with the call to engage in acts of justice. How have you connected tithing with justice?

4. Muller ties our willingness to rest with our beliefs about the nature of life: "At rest, we come face-to-face with the essence of life." Would you agree? How have you experienced Sabbath rest? How does it bring you in touch with the very nature of life?

5. What has been your experience with tithing, or giving money away in general?

6. How do you respond to Noe's extension of tithing to "proportionate giving"?

7. If talking about tithing feels uncomfortable, how about sharing your 1040s (a practice I know at least one church has tried)? What might be gained through revealing at least a bit more about our finances to one another?

8. Many today feel their lives are burdened with too much activity and/or too much stuff. How might you, as a group, or as a congregation, support one another in "dis-encumbering" your lives?

Closing Prayer

 Loving God, spark our thinking, enliven our hopes, and enter our world in ever-surprising and life-giving ways. Thank you that, contrary to popular culture, and often popular belief, time is not money and we need not rush around as if there's never enough of either. For rest in that grace, we pray. Amen.

Action Step

Connecting Sabbath with economics, as Myers discusses, is a potentially liberating and revolutionary practice. This week, find a way to practice Sabbath specifically connected to economics. Those of you who have a difficult time not working (at your job) on the Sabbath, rest from your work. Or, you, and maybe your family too, could agree for one day each week to not spend money. Put the checkbook, cash and credit cards to rest. Don't participate in the monetary economy, but choose rather to enrich the gift economy within your circle of friends and family.

Reminder

Designate next gathering's facilitator. Read selections prior to Meeting Ten (see "Read Before Today's Gathering," page 274).

Meeting Ten:

Investments, Retirement and Jubilee

Purpose
To consider what our money is actually doing when it is invested, when it is spent

To ask how the Jubilee might be reflected in those practical, everyday choices

Read Before Today's Gathering
"Investing, the Poor and Social Change," Andy Loving
　　—p. 173

"Making Trade Fair for Africa," Sarah Tarver-Wahlquist
　　—p. 180

"When Women Decide to Be Unstoppable," Susan Wilkes and Jim Klobuchar
　　—p. 186

"Retirement, Money and the Reign of God," Andy Loving
　　—p. 195

Facilitator Overview
1. Take responsibility for leading the meeting.
2. Pay attention to time; move the discussion along when necessary.
3. Ensure everyone has a chance to participate.
4. *Prepare for the gathering*: read the study guide and readings carefully; have a strong sense of the meeting's content and flow, and of how time might best be spent.
5. Help create a welcoming space.
6. Read (with the group) the Purpose and Overview.
7. Allow for time at the end of the meeting to go over the session's Action Step.
8. Designate next meeting's facilitator.

Overview
If Jubilee is a central biblical tenet, how might individuals and congregations reflect the Jubilee, specifically related to spending and investing money? What purposeful actions can we take that begin to move us in the direction of, as Walter Brueggemann describes it, "finding out what belongs to whom and giving it back"? Andy Loving describes practical ways our own personal and congregational investments can express values of compassion, solidarity and creation-care. In describing the fair trade movement, "Making Trade Fair for Africa" reveals how buying fair trade is an investment many of us can make on a regular basis, as is supporting microfinance institutions and efforts.

Opening Meditation
Read the Psalm together.

The Lord is my shepherd; I shall not want. He maketh me to lie down in green pastures: he leadeth me beside the still waters.

He restoreth my soul: he leadeth me in the paths of righteousness for his name's sake. Yea, though I walk through the valley of the shadow of death, I will fear no evil: for thou art with me; thy rod and thy staff they comfort me.

Thou preparest a table before me in the presence of mine enemies: thou anointest my head with oil; my cup runneth over. Surely goodness and mercy shall follow me all the days of my life: and I will dwell in the house of the Lord for ever.

—Psalm 23 (*King James Version*)

Opening Prayer

 Loving God, the Psalmist seems to have found that place within where he did not "want." May each of us grow to discover those places and may we learn to spend more and more time there. Amen.

Check-In

Last week's Action Step challenged you to practice Sabbath connected specifically to economics. What did you come up with? How did that go?

Small-Group Discussion

(Discuss the following questions in groups of three or four; come back together for the Group Discussion below. Reminder: for those groups with less time, consider the questions in bold first.)

1. What in Andy Loving's essay struck you?

2. What sort of feelings, questions, concerns or hopes surface when you think about retirement?

3. What is retirement for anyway?

Large Group Discussion

Begin by reading the prayer below, the one that concluded Meeting One (from Trinity United Methodist Church in Seattle).

"I pledge, O God, to discover how much is enough for me to be truly fulfilled, neither rich nor poor, and to consume only that.

"I pledge, O God, to be part of the discovery of how much would be enough for everyone—not only to survive but to thrive—and to find ways for them to have access to that.

"May this offering of restraint and justice teach me to live like Jesus, healing my life and the life of this world. Amen."

4. What is your response to this prayer?

I know what it is to have little, and I know what it is to have plenty. In any and all circumstances I have learned the secret of being well-fed and of going hungry, of having plenty and of being in need. I can do all things through him who strengthens me.

—Philippians:11b-13

5. How could a congregation support its members as they grapple with questions of retirement?

6. What sort of connections do you see between your faith and the ideas in today's readings? Discuss your answers.

7. Today's readings highlighted socially responsible investing, fair trade and microfinance. How else, where else, do you spend or invest money in ways you feel move toward Jubilee?

8. If you belong to or attend a congregation:

    a. Are you aware of its investment goals and/or portfolio? (If not, perhaps a few of you would be interested in looking into that.)

    b. Growing numbers of congregations now purchase fair trade items, especially coffee. Meeting Seven's Action Step encouraged you to find out if your congregation does. If not, are any interested in getting that started? Perhaps at first once a month?

Closing Prayer

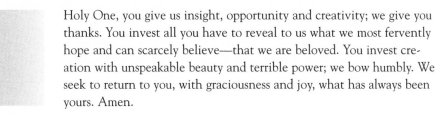

Holy One, you give us insight, opportunity and creativity; we give you thanks. You invest all you have to reveal to us what we most fervently hope and can scarcely believe—that we are beloved. You invest creation with unspeakable beauty and terrible power; we bow humbly. We seek to return to you, with graciousness and joy, what has always been yours. Amen.

Action Step

If you have investments, research where those funds are invested. Would you consider moving funds into screened investments or Community Development Financial Institutions? Or perhaps future funds could be placed in such investment vehicles. Ask someone to keep you accountable for doing so.

Or, find out where your congregation invests its money. How do those investments seek to reflect your congregation's values? How might they do so?

Reminder

Designate next gathering's facilitator. Read selections prior to Meeting Eleven (see "Read Before Today's Gathering," page 278).

Meeting Eleven: **Jubilee on a Grand Scale**

Purpose
This book has not shied away from "big concerns" (inequity, the global economy, ecological concerns) so this meeting emphasizes "big solutions"

Read Before Today's Gathering
"Tools for Restructuring the Economy," Lester Brown
—p. 199

"Re-Inventing the Commons," Peter Barnes —p. 209

Facilitator Overview
1. Take responsibility for leading the meeting.
2. Pay attention to time; move the discussion along when necessary.
3. Ensure everyone has a chance to participate.
4. *Prepare for the gathering*: read the study guide and readings carefully; have a strong sense of the meeting's content and flow, and of how time might best be spent.
5. Help create a welcoming space.
6. Read (with the group) the Purpose and Overview.
7. Allow for time at the end of the meeting to go over the session's Action Step.
8. Designate next meeting's facilitator.

Overview
Because this book highlights concerns about money and the economy on a global scale, it seems important that it also highlight some of the possible solutions to those concerns. The ideas presented by both Lester Brown and Peter Barnes describe powerful policies and prophetic possibilities about how national- and even global-scale investments can be made in the name of both greater equity and ecological sustainability. Brown's piece discusses tax shifts, and Barnes describes his vision of a "commons sector."

Opening Meditation
Begin with silence and then read the following excerpt from Psalm 104.

> [10] God makes springs pour water into the ravines;
>   it flows between the mountains.
> [11] They give water to all the beasts of the field;
>   the wild donkeys quench their thirst.

^{12} The birds of the air nest by the waters;
    they sing among the branches.
^{13} God waters the mountains from God's upper chambers;
    the earth is satisfied by the fruit of God's work.

Opening Prayer

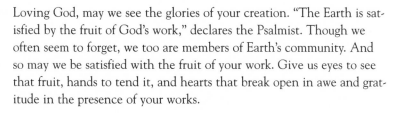

Loving God, may we see the glories of your creation. "The Earth is satisfied by the fruit of God's work," declares the Psalmist. Though we often seem to forget, we too are members of Earth's community. And so may we be satisfied with the fruit of your work. Give us eyes to see that fruit, hands to tend it, and hearts that break open in awe and gratitude in the presence of your works.

As always, we thank you for the time we give to one another each time we gather, for what we learn and experience. May we grow in our awareness of your presence and goodness. Amen.

Check-In

What did you find out about your investments? How about your church's investments? What was the experience like for you?

Large Group Discussion: The Commons

1. **In what ways do you see your faith connecting to the ideas emphasized in today's readings?**

2. **How did Barnes' promotion of a third sector, the commons sector, strike you?**

3. Give an example of some aspect of our *common wealth* of which you are particularly aware. How have you benefited?

4. **Do you think the scale of Barnes' ideas potentially match the scale of the challenges inherent in creating a more equitable and sustainable economy? Why or why not?**

Pair Discussions

5. Lester Brown writes that the scale and urgency needed to reestablish a "stable, sustainable relationship between the global economy and the earth's ecosystem" is one that has only previously occurred during wartime. Discuss together: are we actually in a "war" when it comes to this unsustainable place where we find ourselves?

6. If our society is to move toward a Jubilee economy, one more sustainable and equitable, how do you perceive the kinds of change that will be required? As a sacrifice? As a way of living that is actually more satisfying? Some combination of these?

Large Group Discussion

Time permitting, share with one another your "pair discussion" reflections.

Closing Prayer

Loving God, our economic system is so vast and "making a difference" often seems out of reach. Grant us grace and perseverance as we seek to live the Jubilee on a scale that protects creation's common wealth. May our eyes see the shared wealth present all around us. Amen.

Action Step

Before your next gathering, take some time to be still and ask yourself, "What is God calling me to next in relationship to *Money and Faith*?" What are you feeling excited, or perhaps convicted, about?

Two Suggestions

• First, consider celebrating your final gathering with a potluck, or shared dessert. If you do, make plans for that.
• Second, some groups choose to continue gathering, beyond the twelve meetings. Meeting Twelve raises that possibility and suggests a variety of potential directions/resources. During this next week, before you re-convene, you may want to consider whether or not you would like to continue meeting.

Reminder

Choose a facilitator and read the selections for Meeting Twelve.

Meeting Twelve: With Hands and Hearts Wide Open

Purpose
To reflect on this course and possible directions/responses to which you feel called

To thank one another for this time together

Read Before Today's Gathering
"Radical Acceptance," Michael Schut —p. 218

"...and All the Trees of the Field Will Clap Their Hands," Michael Schut —p. 222

Facilitator Overview
1. Take responsibility for leading the meeting.
2. Pay attention to time; move the discussion along when necessary.
3. Ensure everyone has a chance to participate.
4. *Prepare for the gathering*: read the study guide and readings carefully; have a strong sense of the meeting's content and flow, and of how time might best be spent.
5. Help create a welcoming space.
6. Help plan/host the potluck or dessert, if your group decides to celebrate that way.

Opening Meditation
While ministering here on Earth, Jesus sought to open eyes and ears at every turn. He said it's more blessed to give than to receive. He invited the powerful to become like a little child. He pointed those worrying about food and clothing to the lilies and sparrows and said seek first God's kin-dom. He embarrassed the self-righteous by honoring the widow's mite and the one who prayed behind closed doors. He depicted God as one who forgave the lost and reckless son by sprinting to him with open arms and throwing a party worthy of one once thought dead. He spoke of a rich farmer trusting in his bulging granaries, whose life was to end the next day.

He gifted the blind man with his sight.

Once those eyes and ears were opened, it's almost as if with bated breath he says, "Can you see now; can you hear? Forgiveness is yours, abundance is yours, you are loved, follow me, create this world anew, and hasten the arrival of God's kin-dom here on Earth."

It's that kind of invitation Jesus continues to offer all of us. May we be open to seeing, hearing and following.

Opening Prayer

God of heaven and Earth, life is a tricky balance. Money is tricky stuff. It's as if every cell in our bodies carries two cores.

Within the first, our hands and hearts hold fast, gripped by a primal fear—of want, of hunger, of scarcity.

Within that first core nests a still deeper one. And there, our hearts and hands are flung wide open, embracing beauty, so full they could not possibly begin to constrict in a white-knuckled fist of fear.

Be present with us when we hold fast. Move us, with a shove if need be, to that deeper place where all we have is a gift, ready to be given away.

In Christ's name, amen.

Group Reading

(We suggest members take turns reading.)

First of all, you are to be commended for simply gathering together, for your willingness to even broach the rather taboo subject of money. Your presence and time is in and of itself a gift to one another.

Today is the last scheduled gathering. Your group, though, may wish to continue meeting. On page 286 please find a number of other recommended resources. You could also spend more time on topics or themes raised by this book that were not yet addressed during your time together. *Money and Faith* covers plenty of territory. This study guide provided a map through portions of that territory; plenty of unexplored ground remains.

> **Hell is the state in which we are barred from receiving what we truly need because of the value we give to what we merely want. It is a condition of ultimate deprivation, that is, poverty.**
>
> —*Jacob Needleman*

Another possibility: if you have not shared your money autobiographies with one another, you could choose to do so at this juncture.

If only some members of your group wish to continue gathering, that subset of people could do so.

In any case, you know one another better now than when you began. Whether or not you meet together formally from here on out, hopefully the support and care you have offered one another will remain.

Large Group Discussion

1. Meeting Eleven's Action Step asked you to be still and consider, "What is God calling me to next in relationship to *Money and Faith*?" Share your response to that question with one another.

> I have held many things in my hands, and I have lost them all; but whatever I have placed in God's hands, that I still possess.
>
> —*Martin Luther*

2. How might others in this group support you?

3. Take a moment to consider the three temptations from my essay and their shared essence of self-justification. In which do you most see yourself? Do you find yourself caught in the need to prove who you are:

   – through your abilities;

   – by how others respond to you;

   – by your possessions and positions of power?

   How so?

4. How do these three temptations connect to or impact your relationship with money?

5. What in this book has most challenged you?

> So do not worry, saying, 'What shall we eat?' or 'What shall we drink?' or 'What shall we wear?'...But seek first God's kingdom and God's righteousness, and all these things will be given to you as well.
>
> —Matthew 6:31 and 33

6. What has been the most helpful, perhaps freeing?

7. In terms of your experience during this class, for what are you most grateful?

8. What will stay with you? What's most memorable?

Closing Prayer

Creator God, at the last of our gatherings we give thanks. Thank you that you can carry, hold, even wait out, wherever we find ourselves at any given time: whether generous, or fearful, or trusting, or grasping with all our might. May this time we have shared help us journey closer to living in trust. Meet us in our need. May we see the gifts that are ours to give. With hands and hearts open, amen.

Celebration: Closing Potluck

Thank you for your participation! God go with you.

Appendix A: *About Earth Ministry*

Founded in 1992, Earth Ministry is a national leader in the movement to connect faith and care for creation. Our work engages individuals and congregations in knowing God more fully through deepening relationships with all of God's creation. Through this experience our personal lives and our culture will be transformed.

Christianity has much to offer in helping our culture live respectfully in balance with all creation. Our faith also calls us to understand the convergence of social and environmental justice issues and to take faithful action to live out our values in our homes, congregations, workplaces and democratic processes. Earth Ministry's mission is to inspire and mobilize the Christian community to play a leadership role in building a just and sustainable future.

Programs, Resources and Opportunities for Involvement

Earth Ministry provides programs and resources to help individuals, congregations, clergy and denominations connect their faith with caring for creation.

National Resources

The anthology of essays and study guide *Simpler Living, Compassionate Life: A Christian Perspective* was awarded the 2000 Second Place Book Award for spirituality by the Catholic Press Association.

The anthology/study guide *Food & Faith: Justice, Joy and Daily Bread*, focuses on bringing about a healthier and more equitable world through the food we eat.

The *Greening Congregations Handbook* is a comprehensive and inspiring "toolbox" full of articles, stories, ideas and resources for cultivating creation awareness and care within a congregation.

Earth Letter, our acclaimed newsletter of Christian ecological spirituality for daily life, is published quarterly and is a benefit of membership in Earth Ministry.

Earth Ministry publications may be ordered via our online store at *www.earthministry.org* Everyone is welcome to sign up for our email newsletters.

Northwest Resources

In addition to national resources, people who live in the Northwest can take advantage of area gatherings, lectures, restoration events, field trips and advocacy efforts. Our *Colleague Support Program* helps to strengthen the work of our volunteers who foster creation awareness and care in their congregations. *Washington Interfaith Power & Light* is a project of Earth Ministry and organizes a religious response to the threat of global warming. For more information on these and other programs, or to order any of the above resources, please contact us:

Earth Ministry
6512 23rd Ave NW, Suite 317   Email: *emoffice@earthministry.org*
Seattle, WA 98117   Web site: *www.earthministry.org*
(206) 632-2426   Blog: *www.earthministry.blogspot.com*

Appendix B: *Resources—Read, Study and Act*

Books

My top six books for further *Money and Faith* related study are:

Boyle, David. *The Little Money Book*. Bristol, England: Alistair Sawday Publishing Company, 2003.

Cobb, John B., Jr. *Sustainability, Economics, Ecology and Justice*. Maryknoll, New York: Orbis Books, 1992.

McFague, Sallie. *Life Abundant: Rethinking Theology and Economy for a Planet in Peril*. Minneapolis: Fortress Press, 2001.

McKibben, Bill. *Deep Economy: The Wealth of Communities and the Durable Future*. New York: Times Books, Henry Holt and Company, 2007.

Myers, Ched. *The Biblical Vision of Sabbath Economics*. Washington, DC: Tell the Word, Church of the Savior, 2001.

Twist, Lynne. *The Soul of Money: Transforming Your Relationship with Life and Money*. New York: W.W. Norton, 2003.

Ecumenical Faith-Based Organizations

Bartimaeus Cooperative Ministries (*www.bcm-net.org*, 805-649-1327) has developed a Sevenfold Covenant that "focuses on issues of investment, debt, giving, work and Sabbath, consumption, solidarity and the environment."

Ministry of Money (*www.ministryofmoney.org*, 202-737-7692) provides opportunities to explore our relationship to money from a faith perspective.

Oikocredit (*www.oikocredit.org*) is an ecumenical organization based in the Netherlands. The organization challenges churches and individuals to "share their resources through *socially responsible* investments and by empowering disadvantaged people with credit."

Complementary Currencies

Complementary currencies are used around the world. Whether complicated and extensive or simple and neighborly, these currencies all represent a different kind of money. They have helped create successful peer-to-peer tutoring programs in inner-city schools, increased community involvement and re-woven patterns of reciprocity and generosity. Operating outside the monetary system, these unique currencies may well play an important part in establishing sustainable economies. Find out more from the following resources:

- Edgar Cahn's book *No More Throw-Away People*. A pioneer in this field, find out more about Cahn's work at *www.timebanks.org*
- Visit *www.complementarycurrency.org* for a wealth of references and resources.
- Europe has established many Local Exchange Trading Systems (LETS): *www.gmlets.u-net.com*

- Ithaca (New York) Hours are probably the most well-known complementary currency in the United States: *www.ithacahours.com*
- Find many links here: *www.ecobusinesslinks.com/local_currencies.htm*

Economics and Consumerism

Co-op America (*www.coopamerica.org*, 800-584-7336) harnesses "economic power…to create a socially just and environmentally sustainable society."

The Center for a New American Dream's (*www.newdream.org*, 877-68-DREAM) mission is "to help Americans consume responsibly to protect the environment, enhance quality of life and promote social justice."

Redefining Progress (*www.rprogress.org*, 510-444-3041) is a leading public policy think tank committed to ensuring "a sustainable and equitable world for future generations."

The Simple Living Network (*www.SimpleLiving.net*).

The International Forum on Globalization is an alliance of leading activists, scholars, economists and writers formed to stimulate new thinking, activity and education in response to economic globalization: *www.ifg.org*

Fair Trade

Fairly traded products seek to ensure that producers of that product receive a living wage. Many fair trade products are also grown or produced sustainably. Meetings Seven (page 261) and Ten (page 274) in the study guide, as well as Sarah Tarver-Wahlquist's essay (page 180), highlight the concept and practice of fair trade.

Coffee and tea are two commonly available fair trade products. Many churches serve fair trade coffee and tea. Resources to get you started:

- TransFair USA: *www.transfairusa.org*, 510-663-5260
- Equal Exchange: *www.equalexchange.org*, 774-776-7400 features an Interfaith Program. See *www.equalexchange.com/interfaith-program*
- The Fair Trade Federation: *www.fairtradefederation.org*, 202-636-3547

Socially Responsible Investments (SRI)

Andy Loving's essay introduced SRIs. Listing the following is not meant as an endorsement, but referencing some of the most well-known SRI investment companies is important as a starting point for further research.

- Calvert—*www.calvert.com*
- Domini—*www.domini.com*
- Parnassus—*www.parnassus.com*
- Oikocredit—*www.oikocredit.org* (See previous page.)

The following magazine includes a focus on SRIs:

- *Green Money Journal*—*www.greenmoneyjournal.com*

Videos

Countering Pharaoh's Production-Consumption Society Today features Walter Brueggemann. Ideal for Advent and Lent, *Countering Pharaoh* can be conducted over four or five sessions. The program includes over an hour of video on DVD and a CD-Rom with printable written materials. See the Living the Questions series: *http://www.livingthequestions.com/xcart/home.php?cat=161*

The Story of Stuff is a short, easy to understand and entertaining on-line video. Check it out at *http://www.storyofstuff.com*

The Global Banquet: The Politics of Food, one of the best videos on globalization, sustainability and the food industry, is divided into two 25 minute segments. Produced by Maryknoll World Productions, *www.maryknoll.org*

Who's Counting? Marilyn Waring on Sex, Lies and Global Economics, produced by Bullfrog Films (94 minutes long) features Marilyn Waring, former member of New Zealand's parliament: *www.bullfrogfilms.com*

Bibliography

The following bibliography is not meant to be comprehensive, but rather reflective of the books used in editing and writing *Money and Faith*.

Christian Perspectives and Theology

Bass, Dorothy, Ed. *Practicing Our Faith: A Way of Life for a Searching People*. San Francisco: Jossey-Bass, 1997.

Beaudoin, Tom. *Consuming Faith: Integrating Who We Are with What We Buy*. Lanham, Maryland: Sheed and Ward, 2003.

Boff, Leonardo. *Cry of the Earth, Cry of the Poor*. Maryknoll, New York: Orbis Books, 1997.

Clapp, Rodney, Ed. *The Consuming Passion: Christianity and the Consumer Culture*. Downers Grove, Illinois: Inter Varsity Press, 1998.

Cobb, John B., Jr. *Sustainability, Economics, Ecology, and Justice*. Maryknoll, New York: Orbis Books, 1992.

Duchrow, Ulrich. *Alternatives to Global Capitalism: Drawn from Biblical History, Designed for Political Action*. The Netherlands: International Books, 1995.

Foster, Richard J. *Money, Sex and Power: The Challenge of the Disciplined Life*. San Francisco: Harper & Row, 1988.

Gaillardetz, Richard. *Transforming Our Days: Spirituality, Community, and Liturgy in a Technological Culture*. New York: Crossroad Publishing Company, 2000.

Harris, Maria. *Proclaim Jubilee: A Spirituality for the Twenty-First Century*. Louisville, KY: Westminster John Knox Press, 1996.

Haughey, John C., S.J. *The Holy Use of Money*. Garden City, New York: Doubleday and Company, 1986.

_____. *Virtue and Affluence: The Challenge of Wealth*. Kansas City, Missouri: Sheed and Ward, 1997.

Kavanaugh, John F. *Following Christ in a Consumer Society*. Maryknoll, New York: Orbis Books, 1981, 1991, 2006.

Kinsler, Ross and Gloria. *The Biblical Jubilee and the Struggle for Life*. Maryknoll, New York: Orbis Books, 1999.

Leddy, Mary Jo. *Radical Gratitude*. Maryknoll, New York: Orbis Books, 2002.

Long, Stephen D. *Divine Economy: Theology and the Market*. New York: Routledge, 2000.

Lowery, Richard. *Sabbath and Jubilee*. St. Louis, Missouri: Chalice Press, 2000.

McFague, Sallie. *Life Abundant: Rethinking Theology and Economy for a Planet in Peril*. Minneapolis, Minnesota: Fortress Press, 2001.

Meeks, M. Douglas. *God the Economist: The Doctrine of God and Political Economy.* Minneapolis, Minnesota: Augsburg Fortress Press, 1989.

Muller, Wayne. *Sabbath: Restoring the Sacred Rhythm of Rest.* New York: Bantam Books, 1999.

Myers, Ched. *The Biblical Vision of Sabbath Economics.* Washington, DC: Tell the Word, Church of the Savior, 2001.

Nouwen, Henri. *Here and Now: Living in the Spirit.* New York: Crossroad Publishing, 1994.

Rasmussen, Larry. *Earth Community, Earth Ethics.* Maryknoll, New York: Orbis Books, 1996.

Schut, Michael, Ed. *Simpler Living, Compassionate Life: A Christian Perspective.* Denver, Colorado: Living the Good News, 1999.

_____. *Food and Faith: Justice, Joy, and Daily Bread.* Denver, Colorado: Living the Good News, 2002.

Schweiker, William and Charles Mathewes, Eds. *Having: Property and Possession in Religious and Social Life.* Grand Rapids, Michigan: William Eerdmans Publishing Company, 2004.

Tanner, Kathryn. *Economy of Grace.* Minneapolis: Augsburg Fortress Press, 2005.

Wright, Mary and Chuck Collins. *The Moral Measure of the Economy.* Maryknoll, New York: Orbis Books, 2007.

Wuthnow, Robert. *Poor Richard's Principle: Recovering the American Dream through the Moral Dimension of Work, Business, and Money.* Princeton, New Jersey: Princeton University Press, 1996.

_____. *Rethinking Materialism: Perspectives on the Spiritual Dimension of Economic Behavior.* Grand Rapids, Michigan: William B. Eerdmans, 1995.

The Corporation

Anderson, Ray. *Mid-Course Correction: Towards a Sustainable Enterprise, the Interface Model.* Atlanta, Georgia: Peregrinzilla Press, 1998.

Hartmann, Thomas. *Unequal Protection: The Rise of Corporate Dominance and the Theft of Human Rights.* New York: Rodale Press, 2002.

Korten, David. *The Post-Corporate World: Life after Capitalism.* San Francisco: Berrett-Koehler Publishers, 1999.

_____. *When Corporations Rule the World.* San Francisco: Berrett-Koehler Publishers, 1995.

Economics: The Big Picture

Alperovitz, Gar. *America Beyond Capitalism: Reclaiming our Wealth, our Liberty, and our Democracy*. Hoboken, New Jersey: John Wiley and Sons, 2005.

Ayres, Robert. *Turning Point: The End of the Growth Paradigm*. London, England: Earthscan Publications, 1998.

Barnes, Peter. *Capitalism 3.0: A Guide to Reclaiming the Commons*. San Francisco: Berrett-Koehler, 2006.

Brown, Lester R. *Eco-Economy: Building an Economy for the Earth*. New York: W.W. Norton and Company, 2001.

Cahn, Edgar. *No More Throw-Away People: The Coproduction Imperative*. Washington, DC: Essential, 2000.

Cobb, John B., Jr. and Herman Daly. *For the Common Good: Redirecting the Economy Toward Community, the Environment, and a Sustainable Future*. Boston: Beacon Press, 1989.

Greider, William. *The Soul of Capitalism: Opening Paths to a Moral Economy*. New York: Simon & Schuster, 2003.

Hawken, Paul. *The Ecology of Commerce*. New York: HarperCollins, 1993.

McKibben, Bill. *Deep Economy: The Wealth of Communities and the Durable Future*. New York: Times Books, Henry Holt and Company, 2007.

Michalos, Alex. *Good Taxes: The Case for Taxing Foreign Currency Exchange and Other Financial Transactions*. Toronto: Dundurn Press, 1997.

Perkins, John. *Confessions of an Economic Hit Man*. San Francisco: Berrett-Koehler Publishers, Inc., 2004.

Fair Trade and Micro-Lending

DeCarlo, Jacqueline. *Fair Trade: A Beginner's Guide*. Oxford, England: OneWorld Publications, 2007.

Jaffee, Daniel. *Brewing Justice: Fair Trade Coffee, Sustainability, and Survival*. Berkeley: University of California Press, 2007.

Nicholls, Alex and Charlotte Opal. *Fair Trade: Market-Driven Ethical Consumption*. London: Sage Publications, 2004.

Wilkes, Susan Cornell and Jim Klobuchar. *The Miracles of Barefoot Capitalism: A Compelling Case for Microcredit*. Minneapolis, Minnesota: Kirk House Publishers, 2003.

Yunus, Muhammad. *Banker to the Poor: Micro-Lending and the Battle Against World Poverty*. New York: Public Affairs, 1999, 2003.

International Development and Perspectives

Anderson, Sarah, Ed. *Views from the South: The Effects of Globalization and the WTO on Third World Countries.* San Francisco: Institute for Food and Development Policy, 2000.

Aristide, Jean-Bertrand. *Eyes of the Heart: Seeking a Path for the Poor in the Age of Globalization.* Monroe, Maine: Common Courage Press, 2000.

Bello, Walden. *The Future in the Balance: Essays on Globalization and Resistance.* Oakland, California: Food First Books, 2000.

Easterly, William. *The Elusive Quest for Growth: Economists' Adventures and Misadventures in the Tropics.* Cambridge, Massachusetts: MIT Press, 2002.

Mander, Jerry, and Victoria Tauli-Corpuz. *Paradigm Wars: Indigenous Peoples' Resistance to Economic Globalization.* San Francisco: International Forum on Globalization, 2006.

Norberg-Hodge, Helena. *Ancient Futures: Learning from Ladakh.* San Francisco: Sierra Club Books, 1991.

Sachs, Jeffrey. *The End of Poverty: Economic Possibilities for Our Time.* New York: The Penguin Press, 2005.

Investments, Consumption and the Individual

Andrews, Cecile. *Slow is Beautiful: New Visions of Community, Leisure and* Joie de Vivre. Gabriola, British Columbia: New Society Publishers, 2006.

Barber. Benjamin. *Consumed: How Markets Corrupt Children, Infantilize Adults, and Swallow Citizens Whole.* New York: W.W. Norton and Company, 2007.

de Graaf, John, David Wann, and Thomas H. Naylor. *Affluenza: The All-Consuming Epidemic.* San Francisco: Berrett-Koehler Publishers, 2001.

Domini, Amy. *Socially Responsible Investing: Making a Difference and Making Money.* Chicago, Illinois: Dearborn Trade, 2001.

Harrison, Rob, Terry Newholm, Deirdre Shaw, Eds. *The Ethical Consumer.* London: Sage Publications, 2005.

Kasser, Tim. *The High Price of Materialism.* Cambridge, Massachusetts: MIT Press, 2002.

Kasser, Tim and Allen Kanner, Eds. *Psychology and Consumer Culture: The Struggle for a Good Life in a Materialistic Culture.* Washington, DC: American Psychological Association, 2004.

Robin, Vicki and Joe Dominguez. *Your Money or Your Life: Transforming Your Relationship with Money and Achieving Financial Independence.* New York: Penguin Books, 1992.

Rogers, Pam, Chuck Collins and Joan P. Garner. *Robin Hood Was Right: A Guide to Giving Your Money for Social Change.* New York: W.W. Norton and Company, 2000.

Ryan, John C. and Alan Thein Durning. *Stuff: The Secret Lives of Everyday Things.* Seattle: Northwest Environment Watch, 1997.

Philosophy and History of Money

Boyle, David. *The Little Money Book.* Great Britain: Alistair Sawday Publishing Company, 2003.

Davies, Glyn. *A History of Money: From Ancient Times to the Present Day.* Cardiff: University of Wales Press, 2002.

Hyde, Lewis. *The Gift: Imagination and the Erotic Life of Property.* New York: Vintage Books, 1979.

Lietaer, Bernard, and Stephen Belgin. *Of Human Wealth.* Boulder, Colorado: Galley Edition, Human Wealth Books and Talks, 2004.

Simmel, Georg. *The Philosophy of Money.* Third Enlarged Edition, edited by David Frisby. New York: Routledge, 2004.

Weatherford, Jack. *The History of Money: From Sandstone to Cyberspace.* New York: Crown Publishers, 1997.

Spirituality of Money

Buchan, James. *Frozen Desire: The Meaning of Money.* New York: Farrar, Straus, Giroux, 1997.

Castle, Victoria. *The Trance of Scarcity.* Clinton, Washington: Sagacious Press, 2006.

Needleman, Jacob. *Money and the Meaning of Life.* New York: Doubleday, 1991.

Nemeth, Maria. *The Energy of Money: A Spiritual Guide to Financial and Personal Fulfillment.* New York: The Ballantine Publishing Group, 1997.

Twist, Lynne. *The Soul of Money: Transforming Your Relationship with Life and Money.* New York: W.W. Norton, 2003.

Others

Barry, Dave. *Dave Barry's Money Secrets: Like Why Is There a Giant Eyeball on the Dollar?* New York: Crown Publishing, 2006.

Berry, Wendell. *Citizenship Papers.* Washington, DC: Shoemaker and Hoard, 2003.

Kingsolver, Barbara. *Small Wonder.* New York: HarperCollins, 2002.

Notes

Simpler Living
Compassionate Life

a christian perspective

with Henri Nouwen, Richard Foster
Cecile Andrews and others

foreword by Bill McKibben
edited & compiled by Michael Schut

includes study guide for groups and individuals

6" x 9", 296 pages, paperback, 978-1-8891-0862-9

BEST-SELLER!

Simpler Living
Compassionate Life
edited and compiled by Michael Schut

$14.95

In a rare collection of voices, Henri Nouwen, Cecile Andrews, Richard Foster and others examine how voluntary simplicity can enrich your path to wholeness and abundance. Contemplative readings blend with practical suggestions to encourage you on the journey. Includes a study guide for group experience or individual reflection.

"This wonderful anthology on money, time, environment, community and related topics offers a compelling alternative vision of a healthy, whole and balanced life."

— Jim Wallis
Editor-in-Chief, *Sojourners*

To order, contact your local bookstore or call 1-800-242-1918.

Food & Faith
justice, joy and daily bread

with Wendell Berry, Thomas Moore,
Elizabeth Johnson, John Robbins
and others

edited & compiled by Michael Schut

includes study guide for groups and individuals

6" x 9", 164 pages, paperback, 978-1-8891-0890-2

Food and Faith $14.95

edited and compiled by Michael Schut

Food is itself a joyful gift—recall how the gift of food so often mediates the sanctity and preciousness
of life. This new collection of reflections by Wendell Berry, Elizabeth Johnson and others helps you
start thinking about the moral, spiritual and economic implications of eating. Readings focus on
the enjoyment and spirituality of good food—ways in which eating connects us to the land and to
each other and on the economic, environmental and cultural impacts of daily food choices. *Food and
Faith* includes an eight-week study guide for groups or individuals, which leads to action: setting a
table that is healthy, joyful and just.

To order, contact your local bookstore or call 1-800-242-1918.